With _____ rse
to ror _____ opportuni-
ties while gaining valuable insight into yourself and others.
Offering a daily outlook for 18 full months, this fascinating
guide shows you:

- The important dates in your life
- What to expect from an astrological reading
- How the stars can help you stay healthy and fit
  And more!

Let this sound advice guide you through a year of heavenly
possibilities—for today and for every day of 2010!

SYDNEY OMARR'S® DAY-BY-DAY
ASTROLOGICAL GUIDE FOR

ARIES—March 21–April 19
TAURUS—April 20–May 20
GEMINI—May 21–June 20
CANCER—June 21–July 22
LEO—July 23–August 22
VIRGO—August 23–September 22
LIBRA—September 23–October 22
SCORPIO—October 23–November 21
SAGITTARIUS—November 22–December 21
CAPRICORN—December 22–January 19
AQUARIUS—January 20–February 18
PISCES—February 19–March 20

IN 2010

Sydney Omarr's®

DAY-BY-DAY ASTROLOGICAL GUIDE FOR

TAURUS

APRIL 20–MAY 20

2010

by Trish MacGregor
with Carol Tonsing

A SIGNET BOOK

SIGNET
Published by New American Library, a division of
Penguin Group (USA) Inc., 375 Hudson Street,
New York, New York 10014, USA
Penguin Group (Canada), 90 Eglinton Avenue East, Suite 700, Toronto,
Ontario M4P 2Y3, Canada (a division of Pearson Penguin Canada Inc.)
Penguin Books Ltd., 80 Strand, London WC2R 0RL, England
Penguin Ireland, 25 St. Stephen's Green, Dublin 2,
Ireland (a division of Penguin Books Ltd.)
Penguin Group (Australia), 250 Camberwell Road, Camberwell, Victoria 3124,
Australia (a division of Pearson Australia Group Pty. Ltd.)
Penguin Books India Pvt. Ltd., 11 Community Centre, Panchsheel Park,
New Delhi - 110 017, India
Penguin Group (NZ), 67 Apollo Drive, Rosedale, North Shore 0645
New Zealand (a division of Pearson New Zealand Ltd.)
Penguin Books (South Africa) (Pty.) Ltd., 24 Sturdee Avenue,
Rosebank, Johannesburg 2196, South Africa

Penguin Books Ltd., Registered Offices:
80 Strand, London WC2R 0RL, England

First Printing, June 2009
10 9 8 7 6 5 4 3 2 1

First published by Signet, an imprint of New American Library,
a division of Penguin Group (USA) Inc.

Copyright © The Estate of Sydney Omarr, 2009
All rights reserved

Sydney Omarr's is a registered trademark of Writers House, LLC.

Sydney Omarr® is syndicated worldwide by Los Angeles Times Syndicate.

 REGISTERED TRADEMARK—MARCA REGISTRADA

Printed in the United States of America

Without limiting the rights under copyright reserved above, no part of this publication may be reproduced, stored in or introduced into a retrieval system, or transmitted, in any form, or by any means (electronic, mechanical, photocopying, recording, or otherwise), without the prior written permission of both the copyright owner and the above publisher of this book.

PUBLISHER'S NOTE
While the author has made every effort to provide accurate telephone numbers and Internet addresses at the time of publication, neither the publisher nor the author assumes any responsibility for errors, or for changes that occur after publication. Further, publisher does not have any control over and does not assume any responsibility for author or third-party Web sites or their content.

If you purchased this book without a cover you should be aware that this book is stolen property. It was reported as "unsold and destroyed" to the publisher and neither the author nor the publisher has received any payment for this "stripped book."

The scanning, uploading and distribution of this book via the Internet or via any other means without the permission of the publisher is illegal and punishable by law. Please purchase only authorized electronic editions, and do not participate in or encourage electronic piracy of copyrighted materials. Your support of the author's rights is appreciated.

CONTENTS

Introduction: Seize the Moment ... 1
1. The Top Trends of 2010: Transition Times ... 3
2. How to Find Your Best Times This Year ... 9
3. Introduction to Astrology ... 22
4. The Moon: Your Inner Light ... 33
5. The Planets: The Power of Ten ... 39
6. Where It All Happens: Your Rising Sign ... 95
7. The Keys to Reading Your Horoscope: The Glyphs ... 104
8. Join the Astrology Community ... 116
9. The Best Astrology Software: Take Your Knowledge to the Next Level ... 124
10. Ask the Expert: A Personal Reading Could Help ... 130
11. Loving Every Sign in the Zodiac ... 136
12. Financial Tips from the Stars ... 145
13. Children of 2010 ... 152
14. Give the Perfect Gift to Every Sign ... 163
15. Your Pet-Scope for 2010: How to Choose Your Best Friend for Life ... 170
16. Your Taurus Personality and Potential: The Roles You Play in Life ... 177
17. Taurus Fashion and Decor Tips: Elevate Your Mood with Taurus Style! ... 185

18. The Taurus Way to Stay Healthy and Age Well	190
19. Add Taurus Star Power to Your Career: What It Takes to Succeed in 2010	193
20. Learn from Taurus Celebrities	196
21. Your Taurus Relationships with Every Other Sign: The Green Lights and Red Flags	200
22. The Big Picture for Taurus in 2010	208
23. Eighteen Months of Day-by-Day Predictions: July 2009 to December 2010	214

INTRODUCTION

Seize the Moment

"Timing is everything" is a saying worth repeating this year. Astrology is the art of interpreting moments in time, and astrology fans from the rich and famous to the readers of daily horoscope columns realize that some moments are more favorable for certain actions than others. Knowing that they can plan their actions in tune with the rhythm of the cosmic cycles gives them confidence that they are making wise choices. This could be a challenging year for many, so let this guide help you seize the moment and turn those challenges into opportunities by using the tools astrology provides.

In our toolbox for 2010, you'll find secrets of astrological timing—how to find the most auspicious dates this year. For those who are new to astrology or would like to know more about it, we offer easy techniques to start using astrology in your daily life. You'll learn all about your sun sign and how to interpret the mysterious symbols on a horoscope chart. You can use the convenient tables in this book to look up other planets in your horoscope, each of which sheds light on a different facet of your personality.

Many people turn to astrology to help them find love or figure out what went wrong with a relationship. At your service is the world's oldest dating and mating coach, ready to help you decide whether that new passion has potential or might burn out fast. We'll go through the pros and cons of all the possible sun-sign combinations, with celebrities to illustrate the romantic chemistry.

Contemplating a career change? Our sun-sign chapters can help you build your confidence and focus your job search in the most fulfilling direction by highlighting your natural talents and abilities.

Many readers have explored astrology on the Internet, where there are a mind-boggling variety of sites. Our suggestions are well worth your surfing time. We show you where to get free horoscopes, connect with other astrology fans, find the right astrology software for your ability, and even find an accredited college that specializes in astrological studies.

Whether it's money matters, fashion tips, or ideas for vacation getaways, we'll provide ways to use astrology in your life every day. Before giving yourself or your home a makeover, be sure to consult your sun sign, for the colors and styles that will complement your personality.

To make the most of each day, there are eighteen months of on-target daily horoscopes. So here's hoping this year's guide will help you use your star power wisely to make 2010 a happy, successful year!

CHAPTER 1

The Top Trends of 2010: Transition Times

Astrologers judge the trends of a year by following the slow-moving planets, from Jupiter through Pluto. A change in sign indicates a new cycle, with new emphasis. The farthest planets (Uranus, Neptune, and Pluto) which stay in a sign for at least seven years, cause a very significant change in the atmosphere when they change signs. Shifts in Jupiter, which changes every year, and Saturn, every two years, are more obvious in current events and daily lives. Jupiter generally brings a fortunate, expansive emphasis to its new sign, while Saturn's two-year cycle is a reality check, bringing tests of maturity, discipline, and responsibility. This year, Jupiter in Pisces and Saturn in Libra are in auspicious signs for most of the year, which should act as a balance to more volatile elements in the comos.

Little Pluto—The Mighty Mite

Though astronomers have demoted tiny Pluto from being a full-fledged planet to a dwarf planet, astrologers have been tracking its influence since Pluto was discovered in 1930 and have witnessed that this minuscule celestial body has a powerful effect on both a personal and global level. So Pluto, which moved into the sign of Capricorn in 2008, will still be called a "planet" by astrologers and will be given just as much importance as before.

3

Until 2024, Pluto will exert its influence in this practical, building, healing earth sign. Capricorn relates to structures, institutions, order, mountains and mountain countries, mineral rights, issues involving the elderly and growing older—all of which will be emphasized in the coming years. It is the sign of established order, corporations, big business—all of which will be accented. Possibly, it will fall to business structures to create a new sense of order in the world.

You should now feel the rumblings of change in the Capricorn area of your horoscope and in the world at large. The last time Pluto was in Capricorn was the years up to and during the Revolutionary War; therefore this should be an important time in the U.S. political scene, as well as a reflection of the aging and maturing of American society in general. Both the rise and the fall of the Ottoman Empire happened under Pluto in Capricorn.

The Pisces Factor

This year, Jupiter moves from experimental, humanitarian Aquarius to creative, imaginative Pisces. Jupiter is the coruler of Pisces, along with Neptune, so this is a particularly auspicious place for the planet of luck and expansion to be. During the year that Jupiter remains in a sign, the fields associated with that sign are the ones that currently arouse excitement and enthusiasm, usually providing excellent opportunities.

Jupiter in Pisces expands the influence of Neptune in Aquarius; there should be many artistic and scientific breakthroughs. International politics also comes under this influence, as Neptune in Aquarius raises issues of global boundaries and political structures not being as solid as they seem. This could continue to produce rebellion and chaos in the environment. However, with the generally benevolent force of Jupiter backing up the creative side of Neptune, it is possible that highly original and effective solutions to global problems will be found, which could transcend the current social and cultural barriers.

Another place we notice the Jupiter influence is in fashion, which should veer into a Pisces fantasy mood, with more theatrical, dramatic styles and a special emphasis on footwear. Look for exciting beachwear and seaside resorts that appeal to our desire to escape reality.

Those born under Pisces should have many opportunities during the year. However, the key is to keep your feet on the ground. The flip side of Jupiter is that there are no limits. You can expand off the planet under a Jupiter transit, which is why the planet is often called the "Gateway to Heaven." If something is going to burst (such as an artery) or overextend or go over the top in some way, it could happen under a supposedly lucky Jupiter transit, so be aware.

Those born under Virgo may find their best opportunities working with partners this year, as Jupiter will be transiting their seventh house of relationships.

During the summer months, Jupiter dips into Aries, which should give us a preview of happenings next year. In this headstrong fire sign, Jupiter promotes pioneering ventures, start-ups, all that is new and exciting. It can also promote impatience with more conservative forces, especially in early summer, which looks like the most volatile time this year. Jupiter returns to Pisces in September for the rest of the year.

Saturn in Libra

Saturn, the planet of limitation, testing, and restriction, will be moving through Libra, the sign of its exhaltation and one of its most auspicious signs, this year. In Libra, Saturn can steady the scales of justice and promote balanced, responsible judgment. There should be much deliberation over duty, honor, and fairness, which will be ongoing for the next two years, balancing the more impulsive energy of other planets. Far-reaching new legislation and diplomatic moves are possible, perhaps resolving difficult international standoffs. As this placement works well with the humanitarian Aquarius influence of Neptune, there should be new hope of resolving conflicts. Previously, Saturn was in Libra during the early 1920s, the early 1950s, and again in the early 1980s.

Continuing Trends

Uranus and Neptune continue to do a kind of astrological dance called a "mutual reception." This is a supportive relationship where Uranus is in Pisces, the sign ruled by Neptune, while Neptune is in Aquarius, the sign ruled by Uranus. When this dance is over in 2011, it is likely that we will be living under very different political and social circumstances.

Uranus in Pisces and Aries

Uranus, known as the Great Awakener, tends to cause both upheaval and innovation in the sign it transits. This year, it is accompanied by Jupiter, as it is preparing to leave Pisces and dip its toe into Aries from June to mid-August. However, the Pisces influence will predominate, since Jupiter will be in Pisces most of the year.

During previous episodes of Uranus in Pisces, great religions and spiritual movements have come into being, most recently Mormonism and Christian Fundamentalism. In its most positive mode, Pisces promotes imagination and creativity, the art of illusion in theater and film, and the inspiration of great artists.

A water sign, Pisces is naturally associated with all things liquid—such as oceans, oil, and alcohol—and with those creatures that live in the water—fish, the fishing industry, fish habitats, and fish farming. Currently there is a great debate going on about overfishing, contamination of fish, and fish farming. The underdogs, the enslaved, and the disenfranchised should also benefit from Uranus in Pisces. Since Uranus is a disruptive influence that aims to challenge the status quo, the forces of nature that manifest now will most likely be in the Pisces area—the oceans, seas, and rivers. We have so far seen unprecedented rainy seasons, floods, mud slides, and disastrous hurricanes. Note that 2005's devastating Hurricane Katrina hit an area known for both the oil and fishing industries.

Pisces is associated with the prenatal phase of life, which is related to regenerative medicine. The controversy over embryonic stem cell research will continue to be debated, but recent developments may make the arguments moot. Petroleum issues, both in the oil-producing countries and offshore oil drilling, will come to a head. Uranus in Pisces suggests that development of new hydroelectric sources may provide the power we need to continue our current power-thirsty lifestyle.

As in previous eras, there should continue to be a flourishing of the arts. We are seeing many new artistic forms developing now, such as computer-created actors and special effects. The sky's the limit on this influence.

Those who have problems with Uranus are those who resist change, so the key is to embrace the future.

As Uranus prepares to enter Aries, an active fire sign, we should have a preview of coming influences over the summer.

Neptune in Aquarius

Neptune is a planet of imagination and creativity, but also of deception and illusion. Neptune is associated with hospitals, which have been the subject of much controversy. On the positive side, hospitals are acquiring cutting-edge technology. The atmosphere of many hospitals is already changing from the intimidating and sterile environment of the past to that of a health-promoting spa. Alternative therapies, such as massage, diet counseling, and aromatherapy, are becoming commonplace, which expresses this Neptune trend. New procedures in plastic surgery, also a Neptune glamour field, and antiaging therapies are giving the illusion of youth.

However, issues involving the expense and quality of health care, medication, and the evolving relationship between doctors, drug companies, and HMOs reflect a darker side of this trend.

Neptune is finishing up its stay in Aquarius and will begin its transit of Pisces, which it rules, in 2011. So this should be a time of transition into a much more Neptunian era, when Pisces-related issues will be of paramount importance.

Lunar Eclipses Are Movers and Shakers

Eclipses could shake up the financial markets and rock your world in 2010. The eclipses in late June and July are the ones to watch as they coincide with a close contact of Jupiter and Uranus in Aries. This is a potentially volatile time, so it would be wise to be prepared. As several recent studies have shown the stock market to be linked to the lunar cycle, track investments more carefully during this time.

New Celestial Bodies

Our solar system is getting crowded, as astronomers continue to discover new objects circling the sun. In addition to the familiar planets, there are dwarf planets, comets, cometoids, asteroids, and strange icy bodies in the Kuiper Belt beyond Neptune. A dwarf planet christened Eris, discovered in 2005, is now being observed and analyzed by astrologers. Eris was named after a goddess of discord and strife. In mythology, she was a troublemaker who made men think their opinions were right and others wrong. What an appropriate name for a planet discovered during a time of discord in the Middle East and elsewhere! Eris has a companion moon named Dysnomia for her daughter, described as a demon spirit of lawlessness. With mythological associations like these, we wonder what the effect of this mother-daughter duo will be. Once Eris's orbit is established, astrologers will track the impact of this planet on our horoscopes. Eris takes about 560 years to orbit the sun, which means its emphasis in a given astrological sign will affect several generations.

CHAPTER 2

How to Find Your Best Times This Year

It's no secret that some of the most powerful and famous people, from Julius Caesar to Queen Elizabeth I, from financier J. P. Morgan to Ronald Reagan, have consulted astrologers before they made their moves. If astrology helps the rich and famous stay on course through life's ups and downs, why not put it to work for you? Anyone can follow the planetary movements, and once you know how to interpret them, you won't need an expert to grasp the overall trends and make use of them.

For instance, when mischievous Mercury creates havoc with communications, it's time to back up your vital computer files, read between the lines of contracts, and be very patient with coworkers. When Venus passes through your sign, you're more alluring, so it's time to try out a new outfit or hairstyle, and then ask someone you'd like to know better to dinner. Venus timing can also help you charm clients with a stunning sales pitch or make an offer they won't refuse.

In this chapter you will find the tricks of astrological time management. You can find your red-letter days as well as which times to avoid. You will also learn how to make the magic of the moon work for you. Use the information in this chapter and the planet tables in this book and also the moon sign listings in your daily forecasts.

Here are the happenings to note on your agenda:

- Dates of your sun sign (high-energy period)
- The month previous to your sun sign (low-energy time)

- Dates of planets in your sign this year
- Full and new moons (Pay special attention when these fall in your sun sign!)
- Eclipses
- Moon in your sun sign every month, as well as moon in the opposite sign (listed in daily forecast)
- Mercury retrogrades
- Other retrograde periods

Your Most Proactive Time

Every birthday starts off a new cycle of solar energy for you. You should feel a new surge of vitality as the powerful sun enters your sign. This is the time when predominant energies are most favorable to you. So go for it! Start new projects, and make your big moves (especially when the new moon is in your sign, doubling your charisma). You'll get the recognition you deserve now, when everyone is attuned to your sun sign. Look in the tables in this book to see if other planets will also be passing through your sun sign at this time. Venus (love, beauty), Mars (energy, drive), and Mercury (communication, mental sharpness) reinforce the sun and give an extra boost to your life in the areas they affect. Venus will rev up your social and love life, making you seem especially attractive. Mars amplifies your energy and drive. Mercury fuels your brainpower and helps you communicate. Jupiter signals an especially lucky period of expansion.

There are two downtimes related to the sun. During the month before your birthday period, when you are winding up your annual cycle, you could be feeling especially vulnerable and depleted. So at that time get extra rest, watch your diet, and take it easy. Don't overstress yourself. Use this time to gear up for a big push when the sun enters your sign.

Another downtime is when the sun is in the sign opposite your sun sign (six months from your birthday). This is a reactive time, when the prevailing energies are very different from yours. You may feel at odds with the world. You'll have to work harder for recognition because people are not on your wavelength. However, this could be a good time to work on a team, in cooperation with others, or behind the scenes.

Be a Moon Watcher

The moon is a powerful tool to divine the mood of the moment. You can work with the moon in two ways. Plan by the sign the moon is in; plan by the phase of the moon. The sign will tell you the kind of activities that suit the moon's mood. The phase will tell you the best time to start or finish a certain activity.

Working with the phases of the moon is as easy as looking up at the night sky. During the new moon, when both the sun and moon are in the same sign, begin new ventures—especially activities that are favored by that sign. Then you'll utilize the powerful energies pulling you in the same direction. You'll be focused outward, toward action, and in a doing mode. Postpone breaking off, terminating, deliberating, or reflecting—activities that require introspection and passive work. These are better suited to a later moon phase.

Get your project under way during the first quarter. Then go public at the full moon, a time of high intensity, when feelings come out into the open. This is your time to shine—to express yourself. Be aware, however, that because pressures are being released, other people will also be letting off steam. Since confrontations are possible, take advantage of this time either to air grievances or to avoid arguments.

About three days after the full moon comes the disseminating phase, a time when the energy of the cycle begins to wind down. From the last quarter of the moon to the next new moon, it's a time to cut off unproductive relationships, do serious thinking, and focus on inward-directed activities.

You'll feel some new and full moons more strongly than others, especially when they fall in your sun sign. That full moon happens at your low-energy time of year, and is likely to be an especially stressful time in a relationship, when any hidden problems or unexpressed emotions could surface.

Full and New Moons in 2010

All dates are calculated for eastern standard time and eastern daylight time.

New Moon—January 15 in Capricorn (solar eclipse)
Full Moon—January 30 in Leo

New Moon—February 13 in Aquarius
Full Moon—February 28 in Virgo

New Moon—March 15 in Pisces
Full Moon—March 29 in Libra

New Moon—April 14 in Aries
Full Moon—April 28 in Scorpio

New Moon—May 13 in Taurus
Full Moon—May 27 in Sagittarius

New Moon—June 12 in Gemini
Full Moon—June 26 in Capricorn (lunar eclipse)

New Moon—July 11 in Cancer (solar eclipse)
Full Moon—July 25 in Aquarius

New Moon—August 9 in Leo
Full Moon—August 24 in Pisces

New Moon—September 8 in Virgo
Full Moon—September 23 in Aries

New Moon—October 7 in Libra
Full Moon—October 22 in Aries

New Moon—November 5 in Scorpio
Full Moon—November 21 in Taurus

New Moon—December 5 in Sagittarius
Full Moon—December 21 in Gemini (lunar eclipse)

Timing by the Moon's Sign

To forecast the daily emotional "weather," to determine your monthly high and low days, or to synchronize your activities with the cycles of the moon, take note of the moon's sign under your daily forecast at the end of the book. Here are some of the activities favored and the moods you are likely to encounter under each moon sign.

Moon in Aries: Get Moving

The new moon in Aries is an ideal time to start new projects. Everyone is pushy, raring to go, rather impatient, and short-tempered. Leave details and follow-up for later. Competitive sports or martial arts are great ways to let off steam. Quiet types could use some assertiveness, but it's a great day for dynamos. Be careful not to step on too many toes.

Moon in Taurus: Lay the Foundations for Success

Do solid, methodical tasks like follow-through or backup work. Make investments, buy real estate, do appraisals, or do some hard bargaining. Attend to your property. Get out in the country or spend some time in your garden. Enjoy creature comforts, music, a good dinner, or sensual lovemaking. Forget starting a diet—this is a day when you'll feel self-indulgent.

Moon in Gemini: Communicate

Talk means action today. Telephone, write letters, and fax! Make new contacts; stay in touch with steady customers. You can juggle lots of tasks today. It's a great time for mental activity of any kind. Don't try to pin people down—they too are feeling restless. Keep it light. Flirtations and socializing are good. Watch gossip—and don't give away secrets.

Moon in Cancer: Pay Attention to Loved Ones

This is a moody, sensitive, emotional time. People respond to personal attention and mothering. Stay at home, have a family dinner, or call your mother. Nostalgia, memories, and psychic powers are heightened. You'll want to hang on to people and things (don't clean out your closets now). You could have shrewd insights into what others really need and want. Pay attention to dreams, intuition, and gut reactions.

Moon in Leo: Be Confident

Everybody is in a much more confident, warm, generous mood. It's a good day to ask for a raise, show what you can do, or dress like a star. People will respond to flattery and enjoy a bit of drama and theater. You may be extravagant, treat yourself royally, and show off a bit—but don't break the bank! Be careful not to promise more than you can deliver.

Moon in Virgo: Be Practical

Do practical, down-to-earth chores. Review your budget, make repairs, or be an efficiency expert. Not a day to ask for a raise. Tend to personal care and maintenance. Have a health checkup, go on a diet, or buy vitamins or health food. Make your home spotless. Take care of details and piled-up chores. Reorganize your work and life so they run more smoothly and efficiently. Save money. Be prepared for others to be in critical, fault-finding moods.

Moon in Libra: Be Diplomatic

Attend to legal matters. Negotiate contracts. Arbitrate. Do things with your favorite partner. Socialize. Be romantic. Buy a special gift or a beautiful object. Decorate yourself or your surroundings. Buy new clothes. Throw a party. Have an elegant, romantic evening. Smooth over any ruffled feathers. Avoid confrontations. Stick to civilized discussions.

Moon in Scorpio: Solve Problems

This is a day to do things with passion. You'll have excellent concentration and focus. Try not to get too intense emotionally. Avoid sharp exchanges with loved ones. Others may tend to go to extremes, get jealous, or overreact. Great for troubleshooting, problem solving, research, scientific work—and making love. Pay attention to those psychic vibes.

Moon in Sagittarius: Sell and Motivate

A great time for travel, philosophical discussions, or setting long-range career goals. Work out, do sports, or buy athletic equipment. Others will be feeling upbeat, exuberant, and adventurous. Taking risks is favored. You may feel like gambling, betting on the horses, visiting a local casino, or buying a lottery ticket. Teaching, writing, and spiritual activities also get the green light. Relax outdoors. Take care of animals.

Moon in Capricorn: Get Organized

You can accomplish a lot now, so get on the ball! Attend to business. Issues concerning your basic responsibilities, duties, family, and elderly parents could crop up. You'll be expected to deliver on promises. Weed out the deadwood from your life. Get a dental checkup. Not a good day for gambling or taking risks.

Moon in Aquarius: Join the Group

A great day for doing things with groups—clubs, meetings, outings, politics, or parties. Campaign for your candidate. Work for a worthy cause. Deal with larger issues that affect humanity—the environment and metaphysical questions. Buy a computer or electronic gadget. Watch TV. Wear something outrageous. Try something you've never done before. Present an original idea. Don't stick to a rigid schedule; go with the flow. Take a class in meditation, mind control, or yoga.

Moon in Pisces: Be Creative

This can be a very creative day, so let your imagination work overtime. Film, theater, music, and ballet could inspire you. Spend some time resting and reflecting, reading, or writing poetry. Daydreams can also be profitable. Help those less fortunate. Lend a listening ear to someone who may be feeling blue. Don't overindulge in self-pity or escapism. People are especially vulnerable to substance abuse. Turn your thoughts to romance and someone special.

Eclipses Clear the Air

Eclipses can bring on milestones in your life, if they aspect a key point in your horoscope. In general, they shake up the status quo, bringing hidden areas out into the open. During this time, problems you've been avoiding or have brushed aside can surface to demand your attention. A good coping strategy is to accept whatever comes up as a challenge that could make a positive difference in your life. And don't forget the power of your sense of humor. If you can laugh at something, you'll never be afraid of it.

When the natural rhythms of the sun and moon are disturbed, it's best to postpone important activities. Be sure to mark eclipse days on your calendar, especially if the eclipse falls in your birth sign. This year, those born under Capricorn, Cancer, and Gemini should take special note of the feelings that arise. If your moon is in one of these signs, you may be especially affected. With lunar eclipses, some possibilities could be a break from attachments, or the healing of an illness or substance abuse that was triggered by the subconscious. The temporary event could be a healing time, when you gain perspective. During solar eclipses, when you might be in a highly subjective state, pay attention to the hidden subconscious patterns that surface, the emotional truth that is revealed at this time.

The effect of the eclipse can reverberate for some time, often months after the event. But it is especially important to stay cool and make no major moves during the period known as the shadow of the eclipse, which begins about a week before and lasts until at least three days after the eclipse. After three days, the daily rhythms should return to normal, and you can proceed with business as usual.

This Year's Eclipse Dates

January 15: Solar Eclipse in Capricorn
June 26: Lunar Eclipse in Capricorn
July 11: Solar Eclipse in Cancer
December 21: Lunar Eclipse in Gemini

Retrogrades: When the Planets Seem to Backstep

All the planets, except for the sun and moon, have times when they appear to move backward—or retrograde—as it seems from our point of view on Earth. At these times, planets do not work as they normally do. So it's best to "take a break" from that planet's energies in our life and to do some work on an inner level.

Mercury Retrograde: The Key Is in "Re"

Mercury goes into retrograde most often, and its effects can be especially irritating. When it reaches a short distance ahead of the sun several times a year, it seems to move backward from our point of view. Astrologers often compare retrograde motion to the optical illusion that occurs when we ride on a train that passes another train traveling at a different speed—the second train appears to be moving in reverse.

What this means to you is that the Mercury-ruled areas of your life—analytical thought processes, communications, scheduling—are subject to all kinds of confusion. Be prepared. Communications equipment can break down. Schedules may be changed on short notice. People are late for appointments or don't show up at all. Traffic is terrible. Major purchases malfunction, don't work out, or get delivered in the wrong color. Letters don't arrive or are delivered to the wrong address. Employees will make errors that have to be corrected later. Contracts don't work out or must be renegotiated.

Since most of us can't put our lives on "hold" during Mercury retrogrades, we should learn to tame the trickster and make it work for us. The key is in the prefix re-. This is the time to go back over things in your life, reflect on what you've done during the previous months. Now you can get deeper insights, and spot errors you've missed. So take time to review and reevaluate what has happened. Rest and reward yourself—it's a good time to take a vacation, especially if you revisit a favorite place. Reorganize your work and finish up projects that are backed up. Clean out your desk and closets. Throw away what you can't recycle. If you must sign contracts or agreements, do so with a contingency clause that lets you reevaluate the terms later.

Postpone major purchases or commitments for the time being. Don't get married (unless you're remarrying the same person). Try not to rely on other people keeping appointments, contracts, or agreements to the letter; have several alternatives. Double-check and read between the lines. Don't buy anything connected with communications or transportation (if you must, be sure to cover yourself).

Mercury retrograding through your sun sign will intensify its effect on your life.

If Mercury was retrograde when you were born, you may be one of the lucky people who don't suffer the frustrations of this period. If so, your mind probably works in a very intuitive, insightful way.

The sign in which Mercury is retrograding can give you an idea of what's in store—as well as the sun signs that will be especially challenged.

Mercury Retrogrades in 2010

Mercury has four retrograde periods this year, since it will be retrograde as the year begins. During the retrograde periods, it will be especially important to watch all activities which involve mental processes and communication.

December 26, 2009, to January 15 in Capricorn
April 17 to May 11 in Taurus
August 20 to September 12 in Virgo
December 10 to December 30 from Capricorn to Sagittarius

Venus Retrograde: Relationships Are Affected

Retrograding Venus can cause your relationships to take a backward step, or you may feel that a key relationship is on hold. Singles may be especially lonely, yet find it difficult to connect with someone special. If you wish to make amends in an already troubled relationship, make peaceful overtures at this time. You may feel more extravagant or overindulge in shopping or sweet treats. Shopping till you drop and buying what you cannot afford are bad at this time. It's *not* a good time to redecorate—you'll hate the color of the walls later. Postpone getting a new hairstyle. It only lasts for a relatively short time this year; however, Scorpio and Libra should take special note.

Venus Retrogrades in 2010

Venus retrogrades from October 8 to November 18, from Scorpio to Libra.

Use the Power of Mars

Mars shows how and when to get where you want to go. Timing your moves with Mars on your side can give you a big push. On the other hand, pushing Mars the wrong way can guarantee that you'll run into frustrations around every corner. Your best times to forge ahead are during the weeks when Mars is traveling through your sun sign or your Mars sign (look these up in the planet tables in this book). Also consider times when Mars is in a compatible sign (fire signs with air signs, or earth signs with water signs). You'll be sure to have planetary power on your side.

Mars began a lengthy retrograde in extravagant Leo on December 20, 2009. Your patience may have been tested more than usual during last year's festivities. The Mars retrograde in Leo will last until March 10, during which time there are sure to be repercussions on the international level.

Mars Retrogrades in 2010

Mars turns retrograde in Leo on December 20, 2009, until March 10, 2010.

When Other Planets Retrograde

The slower-moving planets stay retrograde for many months at a time (Jupiter, Saturn, Neptune, Uranus, and Pluto).

When Saturn is retrograde, it's an uphill battle with self-discipline. You may not be in the mood for work. You may feel more like hanging out at the beach than getting things done.

Neptune retrograde promotes a dreamy escapism from reality, when you may feel you're in a fog (Pisces will feel this, especially).

Uranus retrograde may mean setbacks in areas where there have been sudden changes, when you may be forced to regroup or reevaluate the situation.

Pluto retrograde is a time to work on establishing proportion and balance in areas where there have been recent dramatic transformations.

When the planets move forward again, there's a shift in the atmosphere. Activities connected with each planet start moving ahead; plans that were stalled get rolling. Make a special note of those days on your calendar and proceed accordingly.

Other Retrogrades in 2010

The five slower-moving planets all go retrograde in 2010.

Jupiter retrogrades from July 23 in Aries to November 18 in Pisces.

Saturn retrogrades from January 13 in Libra to May 30 in Virgo.

Uranus retrogrades from July 5 in Aries to December 5 in Pisces.

Neptune retrogrades from May 31 to November 7 in Aquarius.

Pluto retrogrades from April 6 to September 13 in Capricorn.

CHAPTER 3

Introduction to Astrology

Astrology is a powerful tool that can help you discover and access your personal potential, understand others and interpret events in your life and the world at large. You don't have to be an expert in astrology to put it to work for you. It's easy to pick up enough basic knowledge to go beyond the realm of your sun sign into the deeper areas of this fascinating subject, which combines science, art, spirituality, and psychology. Perhaps from here you'll upgrade your knowledge with computer software that calculates charts for everyone you know in a nanosecond or join an astrology group in your city.

In this chapter, we'll introduce you to the basics of astrology. You'll be able to define a sign and figure out why astrologers say what they do about each sign. As you look at your astrological chart, you'll have a good idea of what's going on in each portion of the horoscope. Let's get started.

Know the Difference Between Signs and Constellations

Most readers know their signs, but many often confuse them with constellations. *Signs* are actually a type of celestial real estate, located on the *zodiac*, an imaginary 360-degree belt circling the earth. This belt is divided into twelve equal 30-degree portions, which are the *signs*. There's a lot of confusion about the difference between the *signs* and the *constellations* of the zodiac, patterns of stars which originally marked the twelve divisions, like signposts. Though a *sign* is named after the *constellation* that once marked the same area, the constellations are no longer in the same place relative to the earth that they were many centuries ago. Over hundreds of years, the earth's orbit has shifted, so that from our point of view here on earth, the constellations seem to have moved. However, the signs remain in place. (Most Western astrology uses the twelve-equal-part division of the zodiac, though there are some other methods of astrology that still use the constellations instead of the signs.)

Most people think of themselves in terms of their sun sign. A *sun sign* refers to the sign the sun is orbiting through at a given moment (from our point of view here on earth). For instance, if someone says, "I'm an Aries," the sun was passing through Aries when that person was born. However, there are nine other planets (plus asteroids, fixed stars, and sensitive points) that also form our total astrological personality, and some or many of these will be located in other signs. No one is completely "Aries," with all their astrological components in one sign! (Please note that, in astrology, the sun and moon are usually referred to as "planets," though of course they're not. Though there is some controversy over Pluto, it is still called a "planet" by astrologers.)

As we mentioned before, the sun signs are *places* on the zodiac. They do not *do* anything (the planets are the doers). However, they are associated with many things, depending on their location on the zodiac.

How Do We Define a Sign's Characteristics?

The definitions of the signs evolved systematically from four interrelated components: a sign's element, its quality, its polarity or sex, and its order in the progression of the zodiac. All these factors work together to tell us what the sign is like.

The system is magically mathematical: the number 12—as in the twelve signs of the zodiac—is divisible by 4, by 3, and by

2. There are four elements, three qualities, and two polarities, which follow one another in sequence around the zodiac.

The four elements (earth, air, fire, and water) are the building blocks of astrology. The use of an element to describe a sign probably dates from man's first attempts to categorize what he saw. Ancient sages believed that all things were composed of combinations of these basic elements—earth, air, fire, and water. This included the human character, which was fiery/choleric, earthy/melancholy, airy/sanguine, or watery/phlegmatic. The elements also correspond to our emotional (water), physical (earth), mental (air), and spiritual (fire) natures. The energies of each of the elements were then observed to relate to the time of year when the sun was passing through a certain segment of the zodiac.

Those born with the sun in fire signs—Aries, Leo, Sagittarius—embody the characteristics of that element. Optimism, warmth, hot tempers, enthusiasm, and "spirit" are typical of these signs. Taurus, Virgo, and Capricorn are "earthy"—more grounded, physical, materialistic, organized, and deliberate than fire sign people. Air sign people—Gemini, Libra, and Aquarius—are mentally oriented communicators. Water signs—Cancer, Scorpio, and Pisces—are emotional, sensitive, and creative.

Think of what each element does to the others: water puts out fire or evaporates under heat. Air fans the flames or blows them out. Earth smothers fire, drifts and erodes with too much wind, and becomes mud or fertile soil with water. Those are often perfect analogies for the relationships between people of different sun-sign elements. This astrochemistry was one of the first ways man described his relationships. Fortunately, no one is entirely "air" or "water." We all have a bit, or a lot, of each element in our horoscopes. It is this unique mix that defines each astrological personality.

Within each element, there are three qualities that describe types of behavior associated with the sign. Those of cardinal signs are activists, go-getters. These four signs—Aries, Cancer, Libra, and Capricorn—begin each season. Fixed signs, which happen in the middle of the season, are associated with builders and stabilizers. You'll find that Taurus, Leo, Scorpio, and Aquarius are usually gifted with concentration, stamina, and focus. Mutable signs—Gemini, Virgo, Sagittarius, and Pisces—fall at the end of each season and thus are considered catalysts for change. People born under mutable signs are flexible and adaptable.

The polarity of a sign is either its positive or negative "charge." It can be masculine, active, positive, and yang, like air or fire signs, or it can be feminine, reactive, negative, and yin, like the water and earth signs. The polarities alternate, moving energy around the zodiac like the poles of a battery.

Finally, we consider the sign's place in the order of the zodiac. This is vital to the balance of all the forces and the transmission of energy moving through the signs. You may have noticed that your sign is quite different from your neighboring sign on either side. Yet each seems to grow out of its predecessor like links in a chain and transmits a synthesis of energy gathered along the "chain" to the following sign, beginning with the fire-powered positive charge of Aries.

How the Signs Add Up

SIGN	ELEMENT	QUALITY	POLARITY	PLACE
Aries	fire	cardinal	masculine	first
Taurus	earth	fixed	feminine	second
Gemini	air	mutable	masculine	third
Cancer	water	cardinal	feminine	fourth
Leo	fire	fixed	masculine	fifth
Virgo	earth	mutable	feminine	sixth
Libra	air	cardinal	masculine	seventh
Scorpio	water	fixed	feminine	eighth
Sagittarius	fire	mutable	masculine	ninth
Capricorn	earth	cardinal	feminine	tenth
Aquarius	air	fixed	masculine	eleventh
Pisces	water	mutable	feminine	twelfth

Each Sign Has a Special Planet

Each sign has a "ruling" planet that is most compatible with its energies. Mars adds its fiery assertive characteristics to Aries. The sensual beauty and comfort-loving side of Venus rules Taurus, whereas the idealistic side of Venus rules Libra. Quick-moving Mercury rules two mutable signs, Gemini and Virgo. Its mental agility belongs to Gemini while its analytical side is best expressed in Virgo. The changeable emotional moon is associated with Cancer, while the outgoing Leo personality is ruled by the sun. Scorpio originally shared Mars, but when Pluto was discovered in the last century, its powerful magnetic energies were deemed more suitable to the intense vibrations of the fixed water sign Scorpio. Though Pluto has, as of this writing, been downgraded, it is still considered by astrologers to be a powerful force in the horoscope. Disciplined Capricorn is ruled by Saturn, and expansive Sagittarius by Jupiter. Unpredictable Aquarius is ruled by Uranus and creative, imaginative Pisces by Neptune. In a horoscope, if a planet is placed in the sign it rules, it is sure to be especially powerful.

The Layout of a Horoscope Chart

A horoscope chart is a map of the heavens at a given moment in time. It looks like a wheel with twelve spokes. In between each of the "spokes" is a section called a *house*.

Each house deals with a different area of life and is influenced by a special sign and a planet. Astrologers look at the houses to tell in what area of life an event is happening or about to happen.

The house is governed by the sign passing over the spoke (or cusp of the house) at that particular moment. Though the first house is naturally associated with Aries and Mars, it would also have an additional Capricorn influence if that sign was passing over the house cusp at the time the chart was cast. The sequence of the houses starts with the first house located at the left center spoke (or the number 9 position, if you were reading a clock). The houses are then read *counterclockwise* around the chart, with the fourth house at the bottom of the chart, the tenth house at the top or twelve o'clock position.

Where do the planets belong? Around the horoscope, planets are placed within the houses according to their location at the time of the chart. That is why it is so important to have an accurate time; with no specific time, the planets have no specific location in the houses and one cannot determine which area of life they will apply to. Since the signs move across the houses as the earth turns, planets in a house will naturally intensify the importance of that house. The house that contains the sun is naturally one of the most prominent.

The First House: Self

The sign passing over the first house at the time of your birth is known as your ascendant, or rising sign. The first house is the house of "firsts"—the first impression you make, how you initiate matters, the image you choose to project. This is where you advertise yourself, where you project your personality. Planets that fall here will intensify the way you come across to others. It is the home of Aries and the planet Mars.

The Second House: The Material You

This house is where you experience the material world, what you value. Here are your attitudes about money, possessions, and finances, as well as your earning and spending capacity. On a deeper level, this house reveals your sense of self-worth, the inner values that draw wealth in various forms. It is the natural home of Taurus and the planet Venus.

The Third House: Your Thinking Process

This house describes how you communicate with others, how you reach out to others nearby and interact with the immediate environment. It shows how your thinking process works and the way you express your thoughts. Are you articulate or tongue-tied? Can you think on your feet? This house also shows your first relationships, your experiences with brothers and sisters, as well as how you deal with people close to you, such as your neighbors or pals. It's where you take short trips, write letters, or use the telephone. It shows how your mind works in terms of left-brain logical and analytical functions. It is the home of Gemini and the planet Mercury.

The Fourth House: Your Home Life

The fourth house shows the foundation of life, the psychological underpinnings. Located at the bottom of the chart, this house shows how you are nurtured and made to feel secure—your roots! It shows your early home environment and the circumstances at the end of your life (your final "home"), as well as the place you call home now. Astrologers look here for information about the parental nurturers in your life. It is the home of Cancer and the moon.

The Fifth House: Your Self-Expression

The Leo house is where the creative potential develops. Here you express yourself and procreate, in the sense that children are outgrowths of your creative ability. But this house most represents your inner childlike self, who delights in play. If your inner security has been established by the time you reach this house, you are now free to have fun, romance, and love affairs and to give of yourself. This is also the place astrologers look for playful love affairs, flirtations, and brief romantic encounters (rather than long-term commitments). It is the home of Leo and the sun.

The Sixth House: Care and Maintenance

The sixth house has been called the "care and maintenance" department. This house shows how you take care of your body and organize yourself to perform efficiently in the world. Here is where you get things done, where you look after others and fulfill service duties, such as taking care of pets. Here is what you do to survive on a day-to-day basis. The sixth house demands order in your life; otherwise there would be chaos. The house is your "job" (as opposed to your career, which is the domain of the tenth house), your diet, and your health and fitness regimens. It is the home of Virgo and the planet Mercury.

The Seventh House: Your Relationships

This house shows your attitude toward your partners and those with whom you enter commitments, contracts, or agreements. Here is the way you relate to others, as well as your close, intimate, one-on-one relationships (including open enemies—those you "face off" with). Open hostilities, lawsuits, divorces, and marriages happen here. If the first house represents the "I," the seventh or opposite house is the "not I"—the complementary partner you attract by the way you come across. If you are having trouble with partnerships, consider what you are attracting by the energies of your first and seventh house. It is the home of Libra and the planet Venus.

The Eighth House: Your Power House

The eighth house refers to how you merge with something or someone, and how you handle power and control. This is one of the most mysterious and powerful houses, where your energy transforms itself from "I" to "we." As you give up power and control by uniting with something or someone, two kinds of energies merge and become something greater, leading to a regeneration of the self on a higher level. Here are your attitudes toward sex, shared resources, and taxes (what you share with the government). Because this house involves what belongs to others, you face issues of control and power struggles, or undergo a deep psychological transformation as you bond with another. Here you transcend yourself through dreams, drugs, and occult or psychic experiences that reflect the collective unconscious. It is the home of Scorpio and the planet Pluto.

The Ninth House: Your Worldview

The ninth house shows your search for wisdom and higher knowledge: your belief system. As the third house represents the "lower mind," its opposite on the wheel, the ninth house, is the "higher mind," the abstract, intuitive, spiritual mind that asks "big" questions, like "Why we are here?" After the third house has explored what was close at hand, the ninth stretches out to broaden you mentally with higher education and travel. Here you stretch spiritually with religious activity. Since you are concerned with how everything is related, you tend to push boundaries and take risks. Here is where you express your ideas in a book or thesis, where you pontificate, philosophize, or preach. It is the home of Sagittarius and the planet Jupiter.

The Tenth House: Your Public Life

The tenth house is associated with your public life and high-profile activities. Located directly overhead at the "high noon" position on the horoscope wheel, this is the most "visible" house in the chart, the one where the world sees you. It deals with your career (but not your routine "job") and your reputation. Here is where you go public, take on responsibilities (as opposed to the fourth house, where you stay home). This will affect the career you choose and your "public relations." This house is also associated with your father figure or the main authority figure in your life. It is the home of Capricorn and the planet Saturn.

The Eleventh House: Your Social Concerns

The eleventh house is where you extend yourself to a group, a goal, or a belief system. This house is where you define what you really want: the kinds of friends you have, your political affiliations, and the kind of groups you identify with as an equal. Here is where you become concerned with "what other people think" or where you rebel against social conventions. It's where you become a socially conscious humanitarian or a partying social butterfly. It's where you look to others to stimulate you and discover your kinship to the rest of humanity. The sign on this house can help you understand what you gain and lose from friendships. It is the home of Aquarius and the planet Uranus.

The Twelfth House: Where You Become Selfless

Old-fashioned astrologers used to put a rather negative spin on this house, calling it the "house of self-undoing." When we "undo ourselves," we surrender control, boundaries, limits, and rules. The twelfth house is where the boundaries between yourself and others become blurred and you become selfless. But instead of being self-undoing, the twelfth house can be a place of great creativity and talent. It is the place where you can tap into the collective unconscious, where your imagination is limitless.

In your trip around the zodiac, you've gone from the "I" of self-assertion in the first house to the final house, which symbolizes the dissolution that happens before rebirth. The twelfth house is where accumulated experiences are processed in the unconscious. Spiritually oriented astrologers look to this house for evidence of past lives and karma. Places where we go for solitude or to do spiritual or reparatory work belong here, such as retreats, religious institutions, or hospitals. Here is also where we withdraw from society voluntarily or involuntarily, and where we are put in prison because of antisocial activity. Selfless giving through charitable acts is part of this house, as is helpless receiving or dependence on charity.

In your daily life, the twelfth house reveals your deepest intimacies, your best-kept secrets, especially those you hide from yourself and repress deep in the unconscious. It is where we surrender a sense of a separate self to a deep feeling of wholeness, such as selfless service in religion or any activity that involves merging with the greater whole. Many sports stars have important planets in the twelfth house, which enable them to play in the zone, finding an inner, almost mystical, strength that transcends their limits. The twelfth house is the home of Pisces and the planet Neptune.

Which Are the Most Powerful Houses?

Houses are stronger or weaker depending on how many planets are inhabiting them. If there are many planets in a given house, it follows that the activities of that house will be especially important in your life. If the planet that rules the house is also located there, this too adds power to the house. The most powerful houses are the first, fourth, seventh, and tenth. These are the houses on "the angles" of a horoscope.

CHAPTER 4

The Moon: Your Inner Light

In some astrology-conscious lands, the moon is given as much importance in a horoscope as the sun. Astrologers often refer to these two bodies as the "lights," an appropriate description, since the sun and moon are not planets, but a star and a satellite. But it is also true that these two bodies shed the most "light" on a horoscope reading.

As the sun shines *out* in a horoscope, revealing the personality, the moon shines *in*. The sign the moon was transiting at the time of your birth reveals much about the inner you, secrets like what you really care about, what makes you feel comfortable and secure. It represents the receptive, reflective, female, nurturing self. It also reflects the one who nurtured you, the mother or mother figure in your chart. In a man's chart, the moon position describes his receptive, emotional, yin side, as well as the woman in his life who will have the deepest effect, usually his mother. (Venus reveals the kind of woman who will attract him physically.)

The moon is more at home in some signs than in others. It rules maternal Cancer and is exalted in Taurus—both comforting, home-loving signs where the natural emotional energies of the moon are easily and productively expressed. But when the moon is in the opposite signs—Capricorn and Scorpio—it leaves the comfortable nest and deals with emotional issues of power and achievement in the outside world. If you were born with the moon in one of these signs, you may find your emotional role in life more challenging.

To determine your moon sign, it is worthwhile to have an accurate horoscope cast, either by an astrologer, a computer program, or one of the online astrology sites that offer free charts. Since detailed moon tables are too extensive for this book, check through the following listing to find the moon sign that feels most familiar.

Moon in Aries

This placement makes you both independent and ardent. You are an idealist, and you tend to fall in and out of love easily. You love a challenge but could cool once your quarry is captured. Your emotional reactions are fast and fiery, quickly expressed and quickly forgotten. You may not think before expressing your feelings. It's not easy to hide how you feel. Channeling all your emotional energy could be one of your big challenges.

Celebrity example: Angelina Jolie

Moon in Taurus

You are a sentimental soul who is very fond of the good life and gravitates toward solid, secure relationships. You like displays of affection and creature comforts—all the tangible trappings of a cozy, safe, calm atmosphere. You are sensual and steady emotionally, but very stubborn, possessive, and determined. You can't be pushed and tend to dislike changes. You should make an effort to broaden your horizons and to take a risk sometimes. You may become very attached to your home turf, your garden, and your possessions. You may also be a collector of objects that are meaningful to you.

Celebrity example: Prince Charles

Moon in Gemini

You crave mental stimulation and variety in life, which you usually get via a varied social life, the excitement of flirtation, or multiple professional involvements. You may marry more than once and have a rather chaotic emotional life due to your difficulty with commitment and settling down, as well as your need to be constantly on the go. (Be sure to find a partner who is as outgoing as you are.) You will have to learn at some point to focus your energies because you tend to be somewhat fragmented—to do two things at once, to have two homes, or even to have two lovers. If you can find a creative way to express your many-faceted nature, you'll be ahead of the game.

Celebrity example: Jim Carrey

Moon in Cancer

This is the most powerful lunar position, which is sure to make a deep imprint on your character. Your needs are very much associated with your reaction to the needs of others. You are very sensitive, caring, and self-protective, though some of you may mask this with a hard shell, like the moon-sensitive crab. This placement also gives an excellent memory, keen intuition, and an uncanny ability to perceive the needs of others. All of the lunar phases will affect you, especially full moons and eclipses, so you would do well to mark them on your calendar. Because you're happiest at home, you may work at home or turn your office into a second home, where you can nurture and comfort people. (You may tend to mother the world.) With natural psychic, intuitive ability, you might be drawn to occult work in some way. Or you may get professionally involved with providing food and shelter to others.

Celebrity example: Tom Cruise

Moon in Leo

This warm, passionate moon takes everything to heart. You are attracted to all that is noble, generous, and aristocratic in life (and you may be a bit of a snob). You have an innate ability to take command emotionally, but you do need strong support, loyalty, and loud applause from those you love. You are possessive of your loved ones and your turf and will roar if anyone threatens to take over your territory.

Celebrity example: Paul McCartney

Moon in Virgo

You are rather cool until you decide if others measure up. But once someone or something meets your high standards, you hold up your end of the arrangement perfectly. You may, in fact, drive yourself too hard to attain some notion of perfection. Try to be a bit easier on yourself and others. Don't always act the censor! You love to be the teacher; you are drawn to situations where you can change others for the better, but sometimes you must learn to accept others for what they are—enjoy what you have!

Celebrity example: John F. Kennedy

Moon in Libra

Like other air-sign moons, you think before you feel. Therefore, you may not immediately recognize the emotional needs of others. However, you are relationship-oriented and may find it difficult to be alone or to do things alone. After you have learned emotional balance by leaning on yourself first, you can have excellent partnerships. It is best for you to avoid extremes, which set your scales swinging and can make your love life precarious. You thrive in a rather conservative, traditional, romantic relationship, where you receive attention and flattery—but not possessiveness—from your partner. You'll be your most charming in an elegant, harmonious atmosphere.

Celebrity example: Leonardo DiCaprio

Moon in Scorpio

This is a moon that enjoys and responds to intense, passionate feelings. You may go to extremes and have a very dramatic emotional life, full of ardor, suspicion, jealousy, and obsession. It would be much healthier to channel your need for power and control into meaningful work. This is a good position for anyone in the fields of medicine, police work, research, the occult, psychoanalysis, or intuitive work, because life-and-death situations don't faze you. However, you do take personal disappointments very hard.

Celebrity example: Elizabeth Taylor

Moon in Sagittarius

You take life's ups and downs with good humor and the proverbial grain of salt. You'll love 'em and leave 'em or take off on a great adventure at a moment's notice. "Born free" could be your slogan. Attracted by the exotic, you have mental and physical wanderlust. You may be too much in search of new mental and spiritual stimulation to ever settle down.
   Celebrity example: Donald Trump

Moon in Capricorn

Are you ever accused of being too cool and calculating? You have an earthy side, but you take prestige and position very seriously. Your strong drive to succeed extends to your romantic life, where you will be devoted to improving your lifestyle and rising to the top. A structured situation where you can advance methodically makes you feel wonderfully secure. You may be attracted to someone older or very much younger or from a different social world. It may be difficult to look at the lighter side of emotional relationships. Though this moon is placed in the sign to your detriment, the good news is that you tend to be very dutiful and responsible to those you care for.
   Celebrity example: Brad Pitt

Moon in Aquarius

You are a people collector with many friends of all backgrounds. You are happiest surrounded by people, and you may feel uneasy when left alone. Though you usually stay friends with lovers, intense emotions and demanding one-on-one relationships turn you off. You don't like anything to be too rigid or scheduled. Though tolerant and understanding, you can be emotionally unpredictable; you may opt for an unconventional love life. With plenty of space, you will be able to sustain relationships with liberal, freedom-loving types.
   Celebrity example: Princess Diana

Moon in Pisces

You are very responsive and empathetic to others, especially if they have problems or are the underdog. (Be on guard against attracting too many people with sob stories.) You'll be happiest if you can express your creative imagination in the arts or in the spiritual or healing professions. Because you may tend to escape in fantasies or overreact to the moods of others, you need an emotional anchor to help you keep a firm foothold in reality. Steer clear of too much escapism (especially in alcohol) or reclusiveness. Places near water soothe your moods. Working in a field that gives you emotional variety will also help you be productive.

Celebrity example: Elvis Presley

CHAPTER 5

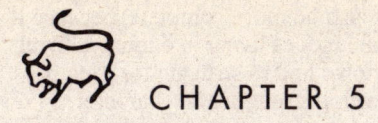

The Planets: The Power of Ten

If you know a person's sun sign, you can learn some very useful generic information, but when you know the placement of all ten planets (eight planets plus the sun and moon), you've got a much more accurate profile of the person's character. Then the subject of the horoscope becomes a unique individual, as well as a member of a certain sun sign. You'll discover what makes him angry (Mars), pleased (Venus), or fearful (Saturn).

The planets are the doers of the horoscope, each representing a basic force in life. The sign and house where the planet is located indicate how and where its force will operate. For a moment, think of the horoscope as real estate. Prime property is close to the rising sign or at the top of the chart. If two or more planets are grouped together in one sign, they usually operate like a team, playing off each other, rather than expressing their energy singularly. But a loner, a planet that stands far away from the others, is usually outstanding and often calls the shots.

The sign of a planet also has a powerful influence. In some signs, the planet's energies are very much at home and can easily express themselves. In others, the planet has to work harder and is slightly out of sorts. The sign that most corresponds to the planet's energies is said to be ruled by that planet and obviously is the best place for that planet to be. The next best place is a sign where it is exalted, or especially harmonious. On the other hand, there are places in the horoscope where a planet has to stretch itself to play its role, such as the sign opposite a planet's rulership, which embodies the opposite area of life, and the sign opposite its exaltation. However, a planet that must work harder can also be more complete, because it must grow to meet the challenges of living in a more difficult sign. Like world leaders who've had to struggle for greatness, this planet may actually develop strength and character.

Here's a list of the best places for each planet to be. Note that, as new planets were discovered in the last century, they replaced the traditional rulers of signs which best complemented their energies.

ARIES—Mars
TAURUS—Venus, in its most sensual form
GEMINI—Mercury, in its communicative role
CANCER—the moon
LEO—the sun
VIRGO—also Mercury, this time in its more critical capacity
LIBRA—also Venus, in its more aesthetic, judgmental form
SCORPIO—Pluto, co-ruled by Mars
SAGITTARIUS—Jupiter
CAPRICORN—Saturn
AQUARIUS—Uranus, replacing Saturn, its original ruler
PISCES—Neptune, replacing Jupiter, its original ruler

Those who have many planets in exalted signs are lucky indeed, for here is where the planet can accomplish the most and be its most influential and creative.

SUN—exalted in Aries, where its energy creates action
MOON—exalted in Taurus, where instincts and reactions operate on a highly creative level
MERCURY—exalted in Aquarius, where it can reach analytical heights
VENUS—exalted in Pisces, a sign whose sensitivity encourages love and creativity
MARS—exalted in Capricorn, a sign that puts energy to work productively
JUPITER—exalted in Cancer, where it encourages nurturing and growth
SATURN—at home in Libra, where it steadies the scales of justice and promotes balanced, responsible judgment

URANUS—powerful in Scorpio, where it promotes transformation

NEPTUNE—especially favored in Cancer, where it gains the security to transcend to a higher state

PLUTO—exalted in Pisces, where it dissolves the old cycle, to make way for transition to the new

The Personal Planets: Mercury, Venus, and Mars

These planets work in your immediate personal life.

Mercury affects how you communicate and how your mental processes work. Are you a quick study who grasps information rapidly, or do you learn more slowly and thoroughly? How is your concentration? Can you express yourself easily? Are you a good writer? All these questions can be answered by your Mercury placement.

Venus shows what you react to. What turns you on? What appeals to you aesthetically? Are you charming to others? Are you attractive to look at? Your taste, your refinement, your sense of balance and proportion are all Venus-ruled.

Mars is your outgoing energy, your drive and ambition. Do you reach out for new adventures? Are you assertive? Are you motivated? Self-confident? Hot-tempered? How you channel your energy and drive is revealed by your Mars placement.

Mercury Shows How Your Mind Works

Since Mercury never travels far from the sun, read Mercury in your sun sign, and then the signs preceding and following it. Then decide which reflects the way you think.

Mercury in Aries

Your mind is very active and assertive. It approaches a plan aggressively. You never hesitate to say what you think, never shy away from a battle. In fact, you may relish a verbal confrontation. Tact is not your strong point, so you may have to learn not to trip over your tongue.

Mercury in Taurus

This is a much more cautious Mercury. Though you may be a slow learner, you have good concentration and mental stamina. You want to make your ideas really happen. You'll attack a problem methodically and consider every angle thoroughly, never jumping to conclusions. You'll stick with a subject until you master it.

Mercury in Gemini

You are a wonderful communicator with great facility for expressing yourself both verbally and in writing. You love gathering all kinds of information. You probably finish other people's sentences and express yourself with eloquent hand gestures. You can talk to anybody anytime and probably have phone and E-mail bills to prove it. You read anything from sci-fi to Shakespeare and might need an extra room just for your book collection. Though you learn fast, you may lack focus and discipline. Watch a tendency to jump from subject to subject.

Mercury in Cancer

You rely on intuition more than logic. Your mental processes are usually colored by your emotions, so you may seem shy or hesitant to voice your opinions. However, this placement gives you the advantage of great imagination and empathy in the way you communicate with others.

Mercury in Leo

You are enthusiastic and very dramatic in the way you express yourself. You like to hold the attention of groups and could be a great public speaker. Your mind thinks big, so you'd prefer to deal with the overall picture rather than with the details.

Mercury in Virgo

This is one of the best places for Mercury. It should give you critical ability, attention to details, and thorough analysis. Your mind focuses on the practical side of things. This type of thinking is very well suited to being a teacher or editor.

Mercury in Libra

You're either a born diplomat who smoothes over ruffled feathers or a talented debater. Many lawyers have this placement. However, since you're forever weighing the pros and cons of a situation, you may vacillate when making decisions.

Mercury in Scorpio

This is an investigative mind that stops at nothing to get the answers. You may have a sarcastic, stinging wit, a gift for the cutting remark. There's always a grain of truth to your verbal sallies, thanks to your penetrating insight.

Mercury in Sagittarius

You are a super salesman with a tendency to expound. Though you are very broad-minded, you can be dogmatic when it comes to telling others what's good for them. You won't hesitate to tell the truth as you see it, so watch a tendency toward tactlessness. On the plus side, you have a great sense of humor. This position of Mercury is often considered by astrologers to be at a disadvantage because Sagittarius opposes Gemini, the sign Mercury rules, and squares off with Virgo, another Mercury-ruled sign. What often happens is that Mercury in Sagittarius oversteps its bounds and loses sight of the facts in a situation. Do a reality check before making promises that you may not be able to deliver.

Mercury in Capricorn

This placement endows good mental discipline. You have a love of learning and a very orderly approach to your subjects. You will patiently plod through the facts and figures until you have mastered the tasks. You grasp structured situations easily, but may be short on creativity.

Mercury in Aquarius

An independent, original thinker, you'll have more cutting-edge ideas than the average person. You'll be quick to check out any unusual opportunities. Your opinions are so well-researched and grounded that once your mind is made up, it is difficult to change.

Mercury in Pisces

You have the psychic intuitive mind of a natural poet. Learn to make use of your creative imagination. You may think in terms of helping others, but check a tendency to be vague and forgetful of details.

Venus Is the Popularity Planet

Venus tells how you relate to others and to your environment. It shows where you receive pleasure and what you love to do. Find your Venus placement on the chart in this book by looking for the year of your birth in the left-hand column. Then follow the line of that year across the page until you reach the time period of your birthday. The sign heading that column will be your Venus. If you were born on a day when Venus was changing signs, check the signs preceding or following that day to determine if that feels more like your Venus nature.

Venus in Aries

You can't stand to be bored, confined, or ordered around. But a good challenge, maybe even a rousing row, turns you on. Confess—don't you pick a fight now and then just to get someone stirred up? You're attracted by the chase, not the catch, which could cause some problems in your love life, if the object of your affection becomes too attainable. You like to wear red and can spot a trend before anyone else.

Venus in Taurus

All your senses work in high gear. You love to be surrounded by glorious tastes, smells, textures, sounds, and visuals—austerity is not for you. Neither is being rushed. You like time to enjoy your pleasures. Soothing surroundings with plenty of creature comforts are your cup of tea. You like to feel secure in your nest, with no sudden jolts or surprises. You like familiar objects—in fact, you may hate to let anything or anyone go.

Venus in Gemini

You are a lively, sparkling personality who thrives in a situation that affords a constant variety and a frequent change of scenery. A varied social life is important to you, with plenty of mental stimulation and a chance to engage in some light flirtation. Commitment may be difficult, because playing the field is so much fun.

Venus in Cancer

An atmosphere where you feel protected, coddled, and mothered is best for you. You love to be surrounded by children in a cozy, homelike situation. You are attracted to those who are tender and nurturing, who make you feel secure and well provided for. You may be quite secretive about your emotional life or attracted to clandestine relationships.

Venus in Leo

First-class attention in large doses turns you on, and so does the glitter of real gold and the flash of mirrors. You like to feel like a star at all times, surrounded by your admiring audience. The side effect is that you may be attracted to flatterers and tinsel, while the real gold requires some digging.

Venus in Virgo

Everything neatly in its place? On the surface, you are attracted to an atmosphere where everything is in perfect order, but underneath are some basic, earthy urges. You are attracted to those who appeal to your need to teach, be of service, or play out a Pygmalion fantasy. You are at your best when you are busy doing something useful.

Venus in Libra

Elegance and harmony are your key words. You can't abide an atmosphere of contention. Your taste tends toward the classic, with light harmonies of color—nothing clashing, trendy, or outrageous. You love doing things with a partner and should be careful to pick one who is decisive, but patient enough to let you weigh the pros and cons. And steer clear of argumentative types.

Venus in Scorpio

Mysteries intrigue you—in fact, anything that is too open and aboveboard is a bit of a bore. You surely have a stack of whodunits by the bed, along with an erotic magazine or two. You like to solve puzzles. You may also be fascinated with the occult, crime, or scientific research. Intense, all-or-nothing situations add spice to your life, and you love to ferret out the secrets of others. But you could get burned by your flair for living dangerously. The color black, spicy food, dark wood furniture, and heady perfume put you in the right mood.

Venus in Sagittarius

If you are not actually a world traveler, your surroundings are sure to reflect your love of faraway places. You like a casual outdoor atmosphere and a dog or two to pet. There should be plenty of room for athletic equipment and suitcases. You're attracted to kindred souls who love to travel and who share your freedom-loving philosophy of life. Athletics and spiritual or New Age pursuits could be other interests.

Venus in Capricorn

No fly-by-night relationships for you! You want substance in life, and you are attracted to whatever will help you get where you are going. Status objects turn you on. And so do those who have a serious, responsible, businesslike approach, or who remind you of a beloved parent. It is characteristic of this placement to be attracted to someone of a different generation. Antiques, traditional clothing, and dignified behavior are becoming to you.

Venus in Aquarius

This Venus wants to make friends, to be "cool." You like to be in a group, particularly one pushing a worthy cause. You feel quite at home surrounded by people, and could even court fame, yet all the while, you tend to remain detached from intense commitment. Original ideas and unpredictable people fascinate you. You prefer spontaneity and delightful surprises, rather than a well-planned schedule of events.

Venus in Pisces

This Venus loves to give of yourself, and you find plenty of takers. Stray animals and people appeal to your heart and your pocketbook, but be careful to look at their motives realistically once in a while. You are extremely vulnerable to sob stories of all kinds. Fantasy, the arts (especially film, dance, and theater), and psychic or spiritual activities also speak to you.

Mars: The Action Hero

Mars is the mover and shaker in your life. It shows how you pursue your goals, whether you have energy to burn or proceed in a slow, steady pace. It will also show how you get angry. Do you explode, or do a slow burn, or hold everything inside and then get revenge later?

To find your Mars, turn to the chart on pages 82–94. Then find your birth year in the left-hand column and find the line headed by the month of your birth. There you will find an abbreviation of your Mars sign. If the description of your Mars sign doesn't ring true, read the description of the signs preceding and following it. You might have been born on a day when Mars was changing signs, in which case your Mars might fall into the adjacent sign.

Mars in Aries

In the sign it rules, Mars shows its brilliant fiery nature. You have an explosive temper and can be quite impatient. On the other hand, you have tremendous courage, energy, and drive. You'll let nothing stand in your way as you race to be first! Obstacles are met head-on and broken through by force. However, problems that require patience and persistence to solve can have you exploding in rage. You're a great starter, but not necessarily around for the finish.

Mars in Taurus

Slow, steady, concentrated energy gives you the power to last until the finish line. You've great stamina, and you never give up. Your tactic is to wear away obstacles with your persistence. Often you come out a winner because you've had the patience to hang in there. When angered, you do a slow burn.

Mars in Gemini

You can't sit still for long. This Mars craves variety. You often have two or more things going on at once—it's all an amusing game to you. Your life can get very complicated, but that only adds spice and stimulation. What drives you into a nervous, hyper state? Boredom, sameness, routine, and confinement. You can do wonderful things with your hands, and you have a way with words.

Mars in Cancer

You rarely attack head-on. Instead, you'll keep things to yourself, make plans in secret, and always cover your actions. This might be interpreted by some as manipulative, but you are only being self-protective. You get furious when anyone knows too much about you. But you do like to know all about others. Your mothering and feeding instincts can be put to good use, if you work in the food, hotel, or child-care-related businesses. You may have to overcome your fragile sense of security, which prompts you not to take risks and to get physically upset when criticized. Don't take things so personally!

Mars in Leo

You have a very dominant personality that takes center stage—modesty is not one of your traits, nor is taking a back seat. You prefer giving the orders and have been known to make a dramatic scene if they are not obeyed. Properly used, this Mars confers leadership ability, endurance, and courage.

Mars in Virgo

You are the fault-finder of the zodiac, who notices every detail. Mistakes of any kind make you very nervous. You may worry, even if everything is going smoothly. You may not express your anger directly, but you sure can nag. You have definite likes and dislikes, and you are sure you can do the job better than anyone else. You are certainly more industrious and detail-oriented than other signs. Your Mars energy is often most positively expressed in some kind of teaching role.

Mars in Libra

This Mars will have a passion for beauty, justice, and art. Generally, you will avoid confrontations at all costs. You prefer to spend your energy finding diplomatic solutions or weighing pros and cons. Your other techniques are passive aggression or exercising your well-known charm to get people to do what you want.

Mars in Scorpio

This is a powerful placement, so intense that it demands careful channeling into worthwhile activities. Otherwise, you could become obsessed with your sexuality or might use your need for power and control to manipulate others. You are strong-willed, shrewd, and very private about your affairs, and you'll usually have a secret agenda behind your actions. Your great stamina, focus, and discipline would be excellent assets for careers in the military or medical fields, especially research or surgery. When angry, you don't get mad—you get even!

Mars in Sagittarius

This expansive Mars often propels people into sales, travel, athletics or philosophy. Your energies function well when you are on the move. You have a hot temper and are inclined to say what you think before you consider the consequences. You shoot for high goals—and talk endlessly about them—but you may be weak on groundwork. This Mars needs a solid foundation. Watch a tendency to take unnecessary risks.

Mars in Capricorn

This is an ambitious Mars with an excellent sense of timing. You have an eye for those who can be of use to you, and you may dismiss people ruthlessly when you're angry. But you drive yourself hard and deliver full value. This is a good placement for an executive. You'll aim for status and a high material position in life, and keep climbing despite the odds. A great Mars to have!

Mars in Aquarius

This is the most rebellious Mars. You seem to have a drive to assert yourself against the status quo. You may enjoy provoking people, shocking them out of traditional views. Or this placement could express itself in an offbeat sex life. Somehow you often find yourself in unconventional situations. You enjoy being a leader of an active group, which pursues forward-looking studies, politics, or goals.

Mars in Pisces

This Mars is a good actor who knows just how to appeal to the sympathies of others. You create and project wonderful fantasies or use your sensitive antennae to crusade for those less fortunate. You get what you want through creating a veil of illusion and glamour. This is a good Mars for someone in the creative and imaginative fields—a dancer, a performer, a photographer, or an actor. Many famous film stars have this placement. Watch a tendency to manipulate by making others feel sorry for you.

Jupiter Is the Optimist

This big, bright, swirling mass of gases is associated with abundance, prosperity, and the kind of windfall you get without too much hard work. You're optimistic under Jupiter's influence, when anything seems possible. You'll travel, expand your mind with higher education, and publish to share your knowledge widely. On the other hand, Jupiter's influence is neither discriminating nor disciplined. It represents the principle of growth without judgment. Therefore, if not kept in check, it could result in extravagance, weight gain, laziness, and carelessness.

Be sure to look up your Jupiter in the tables in this book. When the current position of Jupiter is favorable, you may get that lucky break. This is a great time to try new things, take risks, travel, or get more education. Opportunities seem to open up easily, so take advantage of them.

Once a year, Jupiter changes signs. That means you are due for an expansive time every twelve years, when Jupiter travels through your sun sign. You'll also have periods every four years when Jupiter is in the same element as your sun sign.

Jupiter in Aries

You are the soul of enthusiasm and optimism. Your luckiest times are when you are getting started on an exciting project or selling an ideal that you really believe in. You may have to watch a tendency to be arrogant with those who do not share your enthusiasm. You follow your impulses, often ignoring budget or other commonsense limitations. To produce real, solid benefits, you'll need patience and the will to follow through wherever this Jupiter falls in your horoscope.

Jupiter in Taurus

You'll spend money on beautiful material things, especially those that come from nature—items made of rare woods, natural fabrics, or precious gems, for instance. You can't have too much comfort or too many sensual pleasures. Watch a tendency to overindulge in good food, or to overpamper yourself with nothing but the best. Spartan living is not for you! You may be especially lucky in matters of real estate.

Jupiter in Gemini

You are the great talker of the zodiac, and you may be a great writer too. But restlessness could be your weak point. You jump around and talk too much; you could be a jack-of-all-trades. Keeping a secret is especially difficult, so you'll also have to watch a tendency to spill the beans. Since you love to be at the center of a beehive of activity, you'll have a vibrant social life. Your best opportunities will come through your talent for language: speaking, writing, communicating, and selling.

Jupiter in Cancer

You are luckiest in situations where you can find emotional closeness or deal with basic security needs, such as food, nurturing, or shelter. You may be a great collector, and you may simply love to accumulate things—you are the one who stashes things away for a rainy day. You probably have a very good memory and love children—in fact, you may have many children to care for. The food, hotel, child-care, and shipping businesses hold good opportunities for you.

Jupiter in Leo

You are a natural showman who loves to live in a larger-than-life way. Yours is a personality full of color that always finds its way into the limelight. You can't have too much attention. Showbiz is a natural place for you, and so is any area where you can play to a crowd. Exercising your flair for drama, your natural playfulness, and your romantic nature brings you good fortune. But watch a tendency to be overextravagant or to monopolize center stage.

Jupiter in Virgo

You actually love those minute details others find boring. To you, they make all the difference between the perfect and the ordinary. You are the fine craftsman who spots every flaw. You expand your awareness by finding the most efficient methods and by being of service to others. Many will be drawn to medical or teaching fields. You'll also have luck in publishing, crafts, nutrition, and service professions. Watch out for a tendency to overwork.

Jupiter in Libra

This is an other-directed Jupiter that develops best with a partner, for the stimulation of others helps you grow. You are also most comfortable in harmonious, beautiful situations, and you work well with artistic people. You have a great sense of fair play and an ability to evaluate the pros and cons of a situation. You usually prefer to play the role of diplomat rather than that of adversary.

Jupiter in Scorpio

You love the feeling of power and control, of taking things to their limit. You can't resist a mystery, and your shrewd, penetrating mind sees right through to the heart of most situations and people. You have luck in work that provides for solutions to matters of life and death. You may be drawn to undercover work, behind-the-scenes intrigue, psychotherapy, the occult, and sex-related ventures. Your challenge will be to develop a sense of moderation and tolerance for other beliefs. You may have luck in handling other people's money—insurance, taxes, and inheritance can bring you a windfall.

Jupiter in Sagittarius

Independent, outgoing, and idealistic, you'll shoot for the stars. This Jupiter compels you to travel far and wide, both physically and mentally, via higher education. You may have luck while traveling in an exotic place. You also have luck with outdoor ventures, exercise, and animals, particularly horses. Since you tend to be very open about your opinions, watch a tendency to be tactless and to exaggerate. Instead, use your wonderful sense of humor to make your point.

Jupiter in Capricorn

Jupiter is much more restrained in Capricorn, the sign of rules and authority. Here, Jupiter can make you overwork and heighten any ambition or sense of duty you may have. You'll expand in areas that advance your position, putting you higher up the social or corporate ladder. You are lucky working within the establishment in a very structured situation, where you can show off your ability to organize and reap rewards for your hard work.

Jupiter in Aquarius

This is another freedom-loving Jupiter, with great tolerance and originality. You are at your best when you are working for a humanitarian cause and in the company of many supporters. This is a good Jupiter for a political career. You'll relate to all kinds of people on all social levels. You have an abundance of original ideas, but you are best off away from routine and any situation that imposes rigid rules. You need mental stimulation!

Jupiter in Pisces

You are a giver whose feelings and pocketbook are easily touched by others, so choose your companions with care. You could be the original sucker for a hard-luck story. Better find a worthy hospital or charity to appreciate your selfless support. You have a great creative imagination and may attract good fortune in fields related to oil, perfume, pharmaceuticals, petroleum, dance, footwear, and alcohol. But beware not to overindulge in alcohol—focus on a creative outlet instead.

Saturn Puts on the Brakes

Jupiter speeds you up with lucky breaks, and then along comes Saturn to slow you down with the disciplinary brakes. It is the planet that can help you achieve lasting goals. Saturn has unfairly been called a malefic planet, one of the bad guys of the zodiac. On the contrary, Saturn is one of our best friends—the kind who tells you what you need to hear, even if it's not good news. Under a Saturn transit, we grow up, take responsibility for our lives, and emerge from whatever test this planet has in store as far wiser, more capable, and mature human beings. After all, it is when we are under pressure that we grow stronger.

When Saturn hits a critical point in your horoscope, you can count on an experience that will make you slow up, pull back, and reexamine your life. It is a call to eliminate what is not working and to shape up. By the end of its twenty-eight-year trip around the zodiac, Saturn will have tested you in all areas of your life. The major tests happen in seven-year cycles, when Saturn passes over the angles of your chart—your rising sign, the top of your chart or midheaven, your descendant, and the nadir or bottom of your chart. This is when the real life-changing experiences happen. But you are also in for a testing period whenever Saturn passes a planet in your chart or stresses that planet from a distance. Therefore, it is useful to check your planetary positions with the timetable of Saturn to prepare in advance, or at least to brace yourself.

When Saturn returns to its location at the time of your birth, at approximately age twenty-eight, you'll have your first Saturn return. At this time, a person usually takes stock or settles down to find his mission in life and assumes full adult duties and responsibilities.

Another way Saturn helps us is to reveal the karmic lessons from previous lives and give us the chance to overcome them. So look at Saturn's challenges as much-needed opportunities for self-improvement. Under a Jupiter influence, you'll have more fun, but Saturn gives you solid, long-lasting results.

Look up your natal Saturn in the tables in this book for clues on where you need work.

Saturn in Aries

Saturn here puts the brakes on Aries's natural drive and enthusiasm. There is often an angry side to this placement. You don't let anyone push you around and you know what's best for yourself. Following orders is not your strong point, nor is diplomacy. You tend to be quick to go on the offensive in relationships, attacking first, before anyone attacks you. Because no one quite lives up to your standards, you often wind up doing everything yourself. You'll have to learn to cooperate and tone down any self-centeredness. Pat Buchanan has this Saturn.

Saturn in Taurus

A big issue is getting control of the cash flow. There will be lean periods that can be frightening, but you have the patience and endurance to stick them out and the methodical drive to prosper in the end. Learn to take a philosophical attitude like Ben Franklin, who also had this placement, and who said, "A penny saved is a penny earned."

Saturn in Gemini

You are a serious student of life, who may have difficulty communicating or sharing your knowledge. You may be shy, speak slowly, or have fears about communicating, like Eleanor Roosevelt. You dwell in the realms of science, theory, or abstract analysis, even when you are dealing with the emotions, like Sigmund Freud, who also had this placement.

Saturn in Cancer

Your tests come with establishing a secure emotional base. In doing so, you may have to deal with some very basic fears centering on your early home environment. Most of your Saturn tests will have emotional roots in those early-childhood experiences. You may have difficulty remaining objective in terms of what you try to achieve, so it will be especially important for you to deal with negative feelings such as guilt, paranoia, jealousy, resentment, and suspicion. Galileo and Michelangelo also navigated these murky waters.

Saturn in Leo

This is an authoritarian Saturn—a strict, demanding parent who may deny the pleasure principle in your zeal to see that rules are followed. Though you may feel guilty about taking the spotlight, you are very ambitious and loyal. You have to watch a tendency toward rigidity, also toward overwork and holding back affection. Joseph Kennedy and Billy Graham share this placement.

Saturn in Virgo

This is a cautious, exacting Saturn, intensely hard on yourself. Most of all, you give yourself the roughest time with your constant worries about every little detail, often making yourself sick. You may have difficulties setting priorities and getting the job done. Your tests will come in learning tolerance and understanding of others. Charles de Gaulle, Mae West, and Nathaniel Hawthorne had this meticulous Saturn.

Saturn in Libra

Saturn is exalted here, which makes this planet an ally. You may choose very serious, older partners in life, perhaps stemming from a fear of dependency. You need to learn to stand solidly on your own before you commit to another. Since you are extremely cautious, you deliberate every involvement—with good reason. It is best that you find an occupation that makes good use of your sense of duty and honor. Steer clear of fly-by-night situations. Both Khrushchev and Mao Tse-tung had this placement.

Saturn in Scorpio

You have great staying power. This Saturn tests you in situations involving the control of others. You may feel drawn to some kind of intrigue or undercover work, like J. Edgar Hoover. Or there may be an air of mystery surrounding your life and death, like Marilyn Monroe and Robert Kennedy, who both had this placement. There are lessons to be learned from your sexual involvements. Often sex is used for manipulation or is somehow out of the ordinary. The Roman emperor Caligula and the transsexual Christine Jorgensen are extreme cases.

Saturn in Sagittarius

Your challenges and lessons will come from tests of your spiritual and philosophical values, as happened to Martin Luther King Jr. and Gandhi. You are high-minded and sincere with this reflective, moral placement. Uncompromising in your ethical standards, you could become a benevolent despot.

Saturn in Capricorn

With the help of Saturn at maximum strength, your judgment will improve with age. And, like Spencer Tracy's screen image, you'll be the gray-haired hero with a strong sense of responsibility. You advance in life slowly but steadily, always with a strong hand at the helm and an eye for the advantageous situation. Like Pat Robertson, you're likely to stand for conservative values. Negatively, you may be a loner, prone to periods of melancholy.

Saturn in Aquarius

Your tests come from relationships with groups. Do you care too much about what others think? Do you feel like an outsider, like Greta Garbo? You may fear being different from others and therefore slight your own unique, forward-looking gifts. Or like Lord Byron and Howard Hughes, you may take the opposite tack and rebel in the extreme. You can apply discipline to accomplish great humanitarian goals, as Albert Schweitzer did.

Saturn in Pisces

Your fear of the unknown and the irrational may lead you to the safety and protection of an institution. You may go on the run like Jesse James to avoid looking too deeply inside. Or you might go in the opposite, more positive direction and develop a disciplined psychoanalytic approach, which puts you more in control of your feelings. Some of you will take refuge in work with hospitals, charities, or religious institutions. Queen Victoria, who had this placement, symbolized an era when institutions of all kinds were sustained. Discipline applied to artistic work, especially poetry and dance, or spiritual work, such as yoga or meditation, might be helpful.

How Uranus, Neptune, and Pluto Influence Your Generation

These three planets remain in signs such a long time that a whole generation bears the imprint of the sign. Mass movements, great sweeping changes, fads that characterize a generation, and even the issues of the conflicts and wars of the time are influenced by these outer three planets. When one of these distant planets changes signs, there is a definite shift in the atmosphere, the feeling of the end of an era.

Since these planets are so far away from the sun—too distant to be seen by the naked eye—they pick up signals from the universe at large. These planetary receivers literally link the sun with distant energies, and then perform a similar function in your horoscope by linking your central character with intuitive, spiritual, transformative forces from the cosmos. Each planet has a special domain and will reflect this in the area of your chart where it falls.

Uranus Is the Surprise Ingredient

Uranus is the surprise ingredient that sets you and your generation apart. There is nothing ordinary about this quirky green planet that seems to be traveling on its side, surrounded by a swarm of moons. Is it any wonder that astrologers assigned it to Aquarius, the most eccentric and gregarious sign? Uranus seems to wend its way around the sun, marching to its own tune.

Significantly, Uranus follows Saturn, the planet of limitations and structures. Often we get caught up in the structures we have created to give ourselves a sense of security. However, if we lose contact with our spiritual roots in the process, Uranus is likely to jolt us out of our comfortable rut and wake us up.

Uranus energy is electrical, happening in sudden flashes. It is not influenced by karma or past events, nor does it regard tradition, sex, or sentiment. Uranus's key words are surprise and awakening. Suddenly, there's that flash of inspiration, that bright idea, or that totally new approach that revolutionizes whatever scheme you were undertaking. A Uranus event takes you by surprise, for better or for worse. The Uranus place in your life is where you awaken and become your own person, leaving the structures of Saturn behind. And it is probably the most unconventional place in your chart.

Look up the sign of Uranus at the time of your birth and see where you follow your own tune.

Uranus in Aries

Birth Dates:
March 31, 1927–November 4, 1927
January 13, 1928–June 6, 1934
October 10, 1934–March 28, 1935

Your generation is original, creative, and pioneering. It developed the computer, the airplane, and the cyclotron. You let nothing hold you back from exploring the unknown, and you have a powerful mixture of fire and electricity behind you. Women of your generation were among the first to be liberated. You were the unforgettable style setters. You have a surprise in store for everyone. As with Yoko Ono, Grace Kelly, and Jacqueline Onassis, your life may be jolted by sudden and violent changes.

Uranus in Taurus

Birth Dates:
June 6, 1934–October 10, 1934
March 28, 1935–August 7, 1941
October 5, 1941–May 15, 1942

The great territorial shakeups of World War II began during your generation. You're independent; you're probably self-employed or you would like to be. You have original ideas about making money, and you brace yourself for sudden changes of fortune. This Uranus can cause shake-ups, particularly in finances, but it can also make you a born entrepreneur, like Martha Stewart.

Uranus in Gemini

Birth Dates:
 August 7, 1941–October 5, 1941
 May 15, 1942–August 30, 1948
 November 12, 1948–June 10, 1949

You were the first children to be influenced by television, and in your adult years, your generation stocks up on answering machines, cell phones, computers, and fax machines—any new way you can communicate. You have an inquiring mind, but your interests may be rather short-lived. This Uranus can be easily fragmented if there is no structure and focus.

Uranus in Cancer

Birth Dates:
 August 30–November 12, 1948
 June 10, 1949–August 24, 1955
 January 28, 1956–June 10, 1956

This generation came at a time when divorce was becoming commonplace, so your home image is unconventional. You may have an unusual relationship with your parents, or come from a broken home or an unconventional one. You'll have unorthodox ideas about parenting, intimacy, food, and shelter. You may also be interested in dreams, psychic phenomena, and memory work.

Uranus in Leo

Birth Dates:
 August 24, 1955–January 28, 1956
 June 10, 1956–November 1, 1961
 January 10, 1962–August 10, 1962

This generation understood how to use electronic media. Many of your group are now leaders in the high-tech industries, and you also understand how to use the new media to promote yourself. Like Isadora Duncan, you may have a very eccentric kind of charisma and a life that is sparked by unusual love affairs. Your children may have traits that are out of the ordinary. Where this planet falls in your chart, you'll have a love of freedom, be a bit of an egomaniac, and show the full force of your personality in a unique way, like tennis great Martina Navratilova.

Uranus in Virgo

Birth Dates:
November 1, 1961–January 10, 1962
August 10, 1962–September 28, 1968
May 20, 1969–June 24, 1969

You'll have highly individual work methods, and many will be finding newer, more practical ways to use computers. Like Einstein, who had this placement, you'll break the rules brilliantly. Your generation came at a time of student rebellions, the civil rights movement, and the general acceptance of health foods. Chances are, you're concerned about pollution and cleaning up the environment. You may also be involved with nontraditional healing methods.

Uranus in Libra

Birth Dates:
September 28, 1968–May 20, 1969
June 24, 1969–November 21, 1974
May 1, 1975–September 8, 1975

Your generation will be always changing partners. Born during the era of women's liberation, you may have come from a broken home and may have no clear image of what a marriage entails. There will be many sudden splits and experiments before you settle down. Your generation will be much involved in legal and political reforms and in changing artistic and fashion looks.

Uranus in Scorpio

Birth Dates:
November 21, 1974–May 1, 1975
September 8, 1975–February 17, 1981
March 20, 1981–November 16, 1981

Interest in transformation, meditation, and life after death signaled the beginning of New Age consciousness. Your generation recognizes no boundaries, no limits, and no external controls. You'll have new attitudes toward death and dying, psychic phenomena, and the occult. Like Mae West and Casanova, you'll shock 'em sexually.

Uranus in Sagittarius

Birth Dates:
February 17, 1981–March 20, 1981
November 16, 1981–February 15, 1988
May 27, 1988–December 2, 1988

Could this generation be the first to travel in outer space? The new generation with this placement included Charles Lindbergh and a time when the first zeppelins and the Wright Brothers were conquering the skies. Uranus here forecasts great discoveries, mind expansion, and long-distance travel. Like Galileo and Martin Luther, those born in these years will generate new theories about the cosmos and man's relation to it.

Uranus in Capricorn

Birth Dates:
December 20, 1904–January 30, 1912
September 4, 1912–November 12, 1912
February 15, 1988–May 27, 1988
December 2, 1988–April 1, 1995
June 9, 1995–January 12, 1996

This generation, now reaching adulthood, will challenge traditions. In these years, we got organized with the help of technology put to practical use. The Internet was born after the great economic boom of the 1990s. Great leaders who were movers and shakers of history, like Julius Caesar and Henry VIII, were born under this placement.

Uranus in Aquarius

Birth Dates:
January 30, 1912–September 4, 1912
November 12, 1912–April 1, 1919

August 16, 1919–January 22, 1920
April 1, 1995–June 9, 1995
January 12, 1996–March 10, 2003
September 15, 2003–December 30, 2003

Uranus in Aquarius is the strongest placement for this planet. Recently, we've had the opportunity to witness the full force of its power of innovation, as well as its sudden wake-up calls and insistence on humanitarian values. This was a time of high-tech development, when home computers became as ubiquitous as television. It was a time of globalization, surprise attacks (9/11), and underdeveloped countries demanding attention. The last generation with this placement produced great innovative minds, such as Leonard Bernstein and Orson Welles. The next will become another radical breakthrough generation, much concerned with global issues that involve all humanity.

Uranus in Pisces

Birth Dates:
April 1, 1919–August 16, 1919
January 22, 1920–March 31, 1927
November 4, 1927–January 12, 1928
March 10, 2003–September 15, 2003
December 30, 2003–May 28, 2010

Uranus is now in Pisces, ushering in a new generation. In the past century, Uranus in Pisces focused attention on the rise of electronic entertainment—radio and the cinema—and the secretiveness of Prohibition. This produced a generation of idealists exemplified by Judy Garland's theme, "Somewhere over the Rainbow." Uranus in Pisces also hints at stealth activities, at hospital and prison reform, at high-tech drugs and medical experiments, at shake-ups in the petroleum industry and new locations for Pisces-ruled off-shore drilling. Issues regarding the water and oil supply, water-related storm damage (Hurricane Katrina), sudden hurricanes, droughts, and floods demand our attention.

Neptune Is the Magic Solvent

Neptune is often maligned as the planet of illusions that dissolves reality, enabling you to escape the material world. Under Neptune's influence, you see what you want to see. But Neptune also encourages you to create. It embodies glamour, subtlety, mystery, and mysticism, and governs anything that takes you beyond the mundane world, including out-of-body experiences.

Neptune breaks through and transcends your ordinary perceptions to take you to another level, where you experience either confusion or ecstasy. Its force can pull you off course only if you allow this to happen. Those who use Neptune wisely can translate their daydreams into poetry, theater, design, or inspired moves in the business world, avoiding the tricky con artist side of this planet.

Find your Neptune listed below:

Neptune in Cancer

Birth Dates:
July 19, 1901–December 25, 1901
May 21, 1902–September 23, 1914
December 14, 1914–July 19, 1915
March 19, 1916–May 2, 1916

Dreams of the homeland, idealistic patriotism, and glamorization of the nurturing assets of women characterized this time. You who were born here have unusual psychic ability and deep insights into basic needs of others.

Neptune in Leo

Birth Dates:
September 23, 1914–December 14, 1914
July 19, 1915–March 19, 1916
May 2, 1916–September 21, 1928
February 19, 1929–July 24, 1929

Neptune in Leo brought us the glamour and high living of the 1920s and the big spenders of that time. Neptune temptations of gambling, seduction, theater, and lavish entertaining distracted from the realities of the age. Those born in that generation also made great advances in the arts.

Neptune in Virgo

Birth Dates:
September 21, 1928–February 19, 1929
July 24, 1929–October 3, 1942
April 17, 1943–August 2, 1943

Neptune in Virgo encompassed the 1930s, the Great Depression, and the beginning of World War II, when a new order was born. This was a time of facing what didn't work. Many were unemployed and found solace at the movies, watching the great Virgo star Greta Garbo or the escapist dance films of Busby Berkeley. New public services were born. Those with Neptune in Virgo later spread the gospel of health and fitness. This generation's devotion to spending hours at the office inspired the word *workaholic*.

Neptune in Libra

Birth Dates:
October 3, 1942–April 17, 1943
August 2, 1943–December 24, 1955
March 12, 1956–October 19, 1956
June 15, 1957–August 6, 1957

This was the time of World War II, and the immediate postwar period, when the world regained balance and returned to relative stability. Neptune in Libra was the romantic generation who would later be concerned with relating. As this generation matured, there was a new trend toward marriage and commitment. Racial and sexual equality became important issues, as they redesigned traditional roles to suit modern times.

Neptune in Scorpio

Birth Dates:
December 24, 1955–March 12, 1956
October 19, 1956–June 15, 1957
August 6, 1957–January 4, 1970

May 3, 1970–November 6, 1970

Neptune in Scorpio brought in a generation that would become interested in transformative power. Born in an era that glamorized sex, drugs, rock and roll, and Eastern religion, they matured in a more sobering time of AIDS, cocaine abuse, and New Age spirituality. As they evolve, they will become active in healing the planet from the results of the abuse of power.

Neptune in Sagittarius

Birth Dates:
January 4, 1970–May 3, 1970
November 6, 1970–January 19, 1984
June 23, 1984–November 21, 1984

Neptune in Sagittarius was the time when space travel became a reality. The Neptune influence glamorized new approaches to mysticism, religion, and mind expansion. This generation will take a new approach to spiritual life, with emphasis on visions, mysticism, and clairvoyance.

Neptune in Capricorn

Birth Dates:
January 19, 1984–June 23, 1984
November 21, 1984–January 29, 1998

Neptune in Capricorn brought a time when delusions about material power were glamorized in the mideighties and nineties. There was a boom in the stock market, and the Internet era spawned young tycoons who later lost all their wealth. It was also a time when the psychic and occult worlds spawned a new category of business enterprise, and sold services on television.

Neptune in Aquarius

Birth Dates:
January 29, 1998–April 4, 2011

This should continue to be a time of breakthroughs. Here the creative influence of Neptune reaches a universal audience. This is a time of dissolving barriers and globalization—when we truly become one world. During this transit of high-tech Aquarius, new kinds of entertainment media reach across cultural differences. However, the transit of Neptune has also raised boundary issues between cultures, especially in Middle Eastern countries with Neptune-ruled oil fields. As Neptune raises issues of social and political structures not being as solid as they seem, this could continue to produce rebellion and chaos in the environment. However, by using imagination (Neptune) in partnership with a global view (Aquarius), we could reach creative solutions.

Those born with this placement should be true citizens of the world, with a remarkable creative ability to transcend social and cultural barriers.

Pluto Can Transform You

Though Pluto is a tiny, mysterious body in space, its influence is great. When Pluto zaps a strategic point in your horoscope, your life changes dramatically.

Little Pluto is the power behind the scenes; it affects you at deep levels of consciousness, causing events to come to the surface that will transform you and your generation. Nothing escapes, or is sacred, with this probing planet. Its purpose is to wipe out the past so something new can happen.

The Pluto place in your horoscope is where you have invisible power (Mars governs the visible power), where you can transform, heal, and affect the unconscious needs of the masses. Pluto tells lots about how your generation projects power and what makes it seem cool to others. And when Pluto changes signs, there is a whole new concept of what's cool. Pluto's strange elliptical orbit occasionally runs inside the orbit of neighboring Neptune. Because of its eccentric path, the length of time Pluto stays in any given sign can vary from thirteen to thirty-two years. It covered only seven signs in the last century.

Pluto in Gemini

Late 1800s–May 26, 1914

This was a time of mass suggestion and breakthroughs in communications, when many brilliant writers, such as Ernest Hemingway and F. Scott Fitzgerald, were born. Henry Miller, D. H. Lawrence, and James Joyce scandalized society by using explicit sexual images and language in their literature. "Muckraking" journalists exposed corruption. Pluto-ruled Scorpio president Theodore Roosevelt said, "Speak softly, but carry a big stick." This generation had an intense need to communicate and made major breakthroughs in knowledge. A compulsive restlessness and a thirst for a variety of experiences characterize many of this generation.

Pluto in Cancer

Birth Dates:
May 26, 1914–June 14, 1939

Dictators and mass media arose to wield emotional power over the masses. Women's rights were a popular issue. Deep sentimental feelings, acquisitiveness, and possessiveness characterized these times and people. Most of the great stars of the Hollywood era who embodied the American image were born during this period: Grace Kelly, Esther Williams, Frank Sinatra, and Lana Turner, to name a few.

Pluto in Leo

Birth Dates:
June 14, 1939–August 19, 1957

The performing arts played on the emotions of the masses. Mick Jagger, John Lennon, and rock and roll were born at this time. So were baby boomers like Bill and Hillary Clinton. Those born here tend to be self-centered, powerful, and boisterous. This generation does its own thing, for better or for worse. They are quick to embrace self-transformation in the form of antiaging and plastic surgery techniques, to stay forever young and stay relevant in society.

Pluto in Virgo

Birth Dates:
   August 19, 1957–October 5, 1971
   April 17, 1972–July 30, 1972

This is the yuppie generation that sparked a mass movement toward fitness, health, and career. It is a much more sober, serious, and driven generation than the fun-loving Pluto in Leo. During this time, machines were invented to process detail work efficiently. Inventions took a practical turn with answering machines, fax machines, car phones, and home-office equipment—all making the workplace far more efficient.

Pluto in Libra

Birth Dates:
   October 5, 1971–April 17, 1972
   July 30, 1972–November 5, 1983
   May 18, 1984–August 27, 1984

A mellower generation, people born at this time are concerned with partnerships, working together, and finding diplomatic solutions to problems. Marriage is important to this generation, and they will define it by combining traditional values with equal partnership. This was a time of women's liberation, gay rights, the ERA, and legal battles over abortion—all of which transformed our ideas about relationships.

Pluto in Scorpio

Birth Dates:
   November 5, 1983–May 18, 1984
   August 27, 1984–January 17, 1995

Pluto was in its ruling sign for a comparatively short period of time. However, this was a time of record achievements, destructive sexually transmitted diseases, nuclear power controversies, and explosive political issues. Pluto destroys in order to create new understanding—the phoenix rising from the ashes—which should be some consolation for those of you who felt Pluto's force before 1995. Sexual shockers were par for the course during these intense years, when black clothing, transvestites, body piercing, tattoos, and sexually explicit advertising pushed the boundaries of good taste.

Pluto in Sagittarius

Birth Dates:
January 17, 1995–April 20, 1995
November 10, 1995–January 27, 2008
June 13, 2008–November 26, 2008

During the most recent Pluto transit, we were pushed to expand our horizons and find deeper spiritual meaning in life.

Pluto's opposition with Saturn in 2001 brought an enormous conflict between traditional societies and the forces of change. It signaled a time when religious convictions exerted power in our political life as well.

Since Sagittarius is associated with travel, Pluto, the planet of extremes, made space travel a reality for wealthy adventurers, who paid for the privilege of travel on space shuttles. Globalization transformed business and traditional societies as outsourcing became the norm.

New dimensions in electronic publishing, concern with animal rights and the environment, and an increasing emphasis on extreme forms of religion were other signs of Pluto in Sagittarius. Charismatic religious leaders asserted themselves and questions of the boundaries between church and state arose. There were also sexual scandals associated with the church, which transformed the religious power structure.

Pluto in Capricorn

Birth Dates:
January 25, 2008–June 13, 2008
November 26, 2008–January 20, 2024

As Pluto in Jupiter-ruled Sagittarius signaled a time of expansion and globalization, Pluto's entry into Saturn-ruled Capricorn in 2008 signaled a time of adjustment, of facing reality and limitations, then finding pragmatic solutions. It will be a time when a new structure is imposed, when we become concerned with what actually works.

As Capricorn is associated with corporations and also with

responsibility and duty, look for dramatic changes in business practices, hopefully with more attention paid to ethical and social responsibility as well as the bottom line. Big business will have enormous power during this transit, perhaps handling what governments have been unable to accomplish. There will be an emphasis on trimming down, perhaps a new belt-tightening regime. And, since Capricorn is the sign of Father Time, there will be a new emphasis on the aging of the population. The generation born now is sure to be a more practical and realistic one than that of their older Pluto in Sagittarius siblings.

VENUS SIGNS 1901–2010

	Aries	Taurus	Gemini	Cancer	Leo	Virgo
1901	3/29–4/22	4/22–5/17	5/17–6/10	6/10–7/5	7/5–7/29	7/29–8/23
1902	5/7–6/3	6/3–6/30	6/30–7/25	7/25–8/19	8/19–9/13	9/13–10/7
1903	2/28–3/24	3/24–4/18	4/18–5/13	5/13–6/9	6/9–7/7	7/7–8/17 9/6–11/8
1904	3/13–5/7	5/7–6/1	6/1–6/25	6/25–7/19	7/19–8/13	8/13–9/6
1905	2/3–3/6 4/9–5/28	3/6–4/9 5/28–7/8	7/8–8/6	8/6–9/1	9/1–9/27	9/27–10/21
1906	3/1–4/7	4/7–5/2	5/2–5/26	5/26–6/20	6/20–7/16	7/16–8/11
1907	4/27–5/22	5/22–6/16	6/16–7/11	7/11–8/4	8/4–8/29	8/29–9/22
1908	2/14–3/10	3/10–4/5	4/5–5/5	5/5–9/8	9/8–10/8	10/8–11/3
1909	3/29–4/22	4/22–5/16	5/16–6/10	6/10–7/4	7/4–7/29	7/29–8/23
1910	5/7–6/3	6/4–6/29	6/30–7/24	7/25–8/18	8/19–9/12	9/13–10/6
1911	2/28–3/23	3/24–4/17	4/18–5/12	5/13–6/8	6/9–7/7	7/8–11/18
1912	4/13–5/6	5/7–5/31	6/1–6/24	6/24–7/18	7/19–8/12	8/13–9/5
1913	2/3–3/6 5/2–5/30	3/7–5/1 5/31–7/7	7/8–8/5	8/6–8/31	9/1–9/26	9/27–10/20
1914	3/14–4/6	4/7–5/1	5/2–5/25	5/26–6/19	6/20–7/15	7/16–8/10
1915	4/27–5/21	5/22–6/15	6/16–7/10	7/11–8/3	8/4–8/28	8/29–9/21
1916	2/14–3/9	3/10–4/5	4/6–5/5	5/6–9/8	9/9–10/7	10/8–11/2
1917	3/29–4/21	4/22–5/15	5/16–6/9	6/10–7/3	7/4–7/28	7/29–8/21
1918	5/7–6/2	6/3–6/28	6/29–7/24	7/25–8/18	8/19–9/11	9/12–10/5
1919	2/27–3/22	3/23–4/16	4/17–5/12	5/13–6/7	6/8–7/7	7/8–11/8
1920	4/12–5/6	5/7–5/30	5/31–6/23	6/24–7/18	7/19–8/11	8/12–9/4
1921	2/3–3/6 4/26–6/1	3/7–4/25 6/2–7/7	7/8–8/5	8/6–8/31	9/1–9/25	9/26–10/20
1922	3/13–4/6	4/7–4/30	5/1–5/25	5/26–6/19	6/20–7/14	7/15–8/9
1923	4/27–5/21	5/22–6/14	6/15–7/9	7/10–8/3	8/4–8/27	8/28–9/20
1924	2/13–3/8	3/9–4/4	4/5–5/5	5/6–9/8	9/9–10/7	10/8–11/12
1925	3/28–4/20	4/21–5/15	5/16–6/8	6/9–7/3	7/4–7/27	7/28–8/21
1926	5/7–6/2	6/3–6/28	6/29–7/23	7/24–8/17	8/18–9/11	9/12–10/5
1927	2/27–3/22	3/23–4/16	4/17–5/11	5/12–6/7	6/8–7/7	7/8–11/9

74

Libra	Scorpio	Sagittarius	Capricorn	Aquarius	Pisces
8/23–9/17	9/17–10/12	10/12–1/16	1/16–2/9 11/7–12/5	2/9–3/5 12/5–1/11	3/5–3/29
10/7–10/31	10/31–11/24	11/24–12/18	12/18–1/11	2/6–4/4	1/11–2/6 4/4–5/7
8/17–9/6 11/8–12/9	12/9–1/5			1/11–2/4	2/4–2/28
9/6–9/30	9/30–10/25	1/5–1/30 10/25–11/18	1/30–2/24 11/18–12/13	2/24–3/19 12/13–1/7	3/19–4/13
10/21–11/14	11/14–12/8	12/8–1/1/06			1/7–2/3
8/11–9/7	9/7–10/9 12/15–12/25	10/9–12/15 12/25–2/6	1/1–1/25	1/25–2/18	2/18–3/14
9/22–10/16	10/16–11/9	11/9–12/3	2/6–3/6 12/3–12/27	3/6–4/2 12/27–1/20	4/2–4/27
11/3–11/28	11/28–12/22	12/22–1/15			1/20–2/4
8/23–9/17	9/17–10/12	10/12–11/17	1/15–2/9 11/17–12/5	2/9–3/5 12/5–1/15	3/5–3/29
10/7–10/30	10/31–11/23	11/24–12/17	12/18–12/31	1/1–1/15 1/29–4/4	1/16–1/28 4/5–5/6
11/19–12/8	12/9–12/31		1/1–1/10	1/11–2/2	2/3–2/27
9/6–9/30	1/1–1/4 10/1–10/24	1/5–1/29 10/25–11/17	1/30–2/23 11/18–12/12	2/24–3/18 12/13–12/31	3/19–4/12
10/21–11/13	11/14–12/7	12/8–12/31		1/1–1/6	1/7–2/2
8/11–9/6	9/7–10/9 12/6–12/30	10/10–12/5 12/31	1/1–1/24	1/25–2/17	2/18–3/13
9/22–10/15	10/16–11/8	1/1–2/6 11/9–12/2	2/7–3/6 12/3–12/26	3/7–4/1 12/27–12/31	4/2–4/26
11/3–11/27	11/28–12/21	12/22–12/31		1/1–1/19	1/20–2/13
8/22–9/16	9/17–10/11	1/1–1/14 10/12–11/6	1/15–2/7 11/7–12/5	2/8–3/4 12/6–12/31	3/5–3/28
10/6–10/29	10/30–11/22	11/23–12/16	12/17–12/31	1/1–4/5	4/6–5/6
11/9–12/8	12/9–12/31		1/1–1/9	1/10–2/2	2/3–2/26
9/5–9/30	1/1–1/3 9/31–10/23	1/4–1/28 10/24–11/17	1/29–2/22 11/18–12/11	2/23–3/18 12/12–12/31	3/19–4/11
10/21–11/13	11/14–12/7	12/8–12/31		1/1–1/6	1/7–2/2
8/10–9/6	9/7–10/10 11/29–12/31	10/11–11/28	1/1–1/24	1/25–2/16	2/17–3/12
9/21–10/14	1/1 10/15–11/7	1/2–2/6 11/8–12/1	2/7–3/5 12/2–12/25	3/6–3/31 12/26–12/31	4/1–4/26
11/13–11/26	11/27–12/21	12/22–12/31		1/1–1/19	1/20–2/12
8/22–9/15	9/16–10/11	1/1–1/14 10/12–11/6	1/15–2/7 11/7–12/5	2/8–3/3 12/6–12/31	3/4–3/27
10/6–10/29	10/30–11/22	11/23–12/16	12/17–12/31	1/1–4/5	4/6–5/6
11/10–12/8	12/9–12/31	1/1–1/7	1/8	1/9–2/1	2/2–2/26

75

VENUS SIGNS 1901–2010

	Aries	Taurus	Gemini	Cancer	Leo	Virgo
1928	4/12–5/5	5/6–5/29	5/30–6/23	6/24–7/17	7/18–8/11	8/12–9/4
1929	2/3–3/7 4/20–6/2	3/8–4/19 6/3–7/7	7/8–8/4	8/5–8/30	8/31–9/25	9/26–10/19
1930	3/13–4/5	4/6–4/30	5/1–5/24	5/25–6/18	6/19–7/14	7/15–8/9
1931	4/26–5/20	5/21–6/13	6/14–7/8	7/9–8/2	8/3–8/26	8/27–9/19
1932	2/12–3/8	3/9–4/3	4/4–5/5 7/13–7/27	5/6–7/12 7/28–9/8	9/9–10/6	10/7–11/1
1933	3/27–4/19	4/20–5/28	5/29–6/8	6/9–7/2	7/3–7/26	7/27–8/20
1934	5/6–6/1	6/2–6/27	6/28–7/22	7/23–8/16	8/17–9/10	9/11–10/4
1935	2/26–3/21	3/22–4/15	4/16–5/10	5/11–6/6	6/7–7/6	7/7–11/8
1936	4/11–5/4	5/5–5/28	5/29–6/22	6/23–7/16	7/17–8/10	8/11–9/4
1937	2/2–3/8 4/14–6/3	3/9–4/13 6/4–7/6	7/7–8/3	8/4–8/29	8/30–9/24	9/25–10/18
1938	3/12–4/4	4/5–4/28	4/29–5/23	5/24–6/18	6/19–7/13	7/14–8/8
1939	4/25–5/19	5/20–6/13	6/14–7/8	7/9–8/1	8/2–8/25	8/26–9/19
1940	2/12–3/7	3/8–4/3	4/4–5/5 7/5–7/31	5/6–7/4 8/1–9/8	9/9–10/5	10/6–10/31
1941	3/27–4/19	4/20–5/13	5/14–6/6	6/7–7/1	7/2–7/26	7/27–8/20
1942	5/6–6/1	6/2–6/26	6/27–7/22	7/23–8/16	8/17–9/9	9/10–10/3
1943	2/25–3/20	3/21–4/14	4/15–5/10	5/11–6/6	6/7–7/6	7/7–11/8
1944	4/10–5/3	5/4–5/28	5/29–6/21	6/22–7/16	7/17–8/9	8/10–9/2
1945	2/2–3/10 4/7–6/3	3/11–4/6 6/4–7/6	7/7–8/3	8/4–8/29	8/30–9/23	9/24–10/18
1946	3/11–4/4	4/5–4/28	4/29–5/23	5/24–6/17	6/18–7/12	7/13–8/8
1947	4/25–5/19	5/20–6/12	6/13–7/7	7/8–8/1	8/2–8/25	8/26–9/18
1948	2/11–3/7	3/8–4/3	4/4–5/6 6/29–8/2	5/7–6/28 8/3–9/7	9/8–10/5	10/6–10/31
1949	3/26–4/19	4/20–5/13	5/14–6/6	6/7–6/30	7/1–7/25	7/26–8/19
1950	5/5–5/31	6/1–6/26	6/27–7/21	7/22–8/15	8/16–9/9	9/10–10/3
1951	2/25–3/21	3/22–4/15	4/16–5/10	5/11–6/6	6/7–7/7	7/8–11/9
1952	4/10–5/4	5/5–5/28	5/29–6/21	6/22–7/16	7/17–8/9	8/10–9/3
1953	2/2–3/3 4/1–6/5	3/4–3/31 6/6–7/7	7/8–8/3	8/4–8/29	8/30–9/24	9/25–10/18

Libra	Scorpio	Sagittarius	Capricorn	Aquarius	Pisces
9/5–9/28	1/1–1/3	1/4–1/28	1/29–2/22	2/23–3/17	3/18–4/11
	9/29–10/23	10/24–11/16	11/17–12/11	12/12–12/31	
10/20–11/12	11/13–12/6	12/7–12/30	12/31	1/1–1/5	1/6–2/2
8/10–9/6	9/7–10/11	10/12–11/21	1/1–1/23	1/24–2/16	2/17–3/12
	11/22–12/31				
9/20–10/13	1/1–1/3	1/4–2/6	2/7–3/4	3/5–3/31	4/1–4/25
	10/14–11/6	11/7–11/30	12/1–12/24	12/25–12/31	
11/2–11/25	11/26–12/20	12/21–12/31		1/1–1/18	1/19–2/11
8/21–9/14	9/15–10/10	1/1–1/13	1/14–2/6	2/7–3/2	3/3–3/26
		10/11–11/5	11/6–12/4	12/5–12/31	
10/5–10/28	10/29–11/21	11/22–12/15	12/16–12/31	1/1–4/5	4/6–5/5
11/9–12/7	12/8–12/31		1/1–1/7	1/8–1/31	2/1–2/25
9/5–9/27	1/1–1/2	1/3–1/27	1/28–2/21	2/22–3/16	3/17–4/10
	9/28–10/22	10/23–11/15	11/16–12/10	12/11–12/31	
10/19–11/11	11/12–12/5	12/6–12/29	12/30–12/31	1/1–1/5	1/6–2/1
8/9–9/6	9/7–10/13	10/14–11/14	1/1–1/22	1/23–2/15	2/16–3/11
	11/15–12/31				
9/20–10/13	1/1–1/3	1/4–2/5	2/6–3/4	3/5–3/30	3/31–4/24
	10/14–11/6	11/7–11/30	12/1–12/24	12/25–12/31	
11/1–11/25	11/26–12/19	12/20–12/31		1/1–1/18	1/19–2/11
8/21–9/14	9/15–10/9	1/1–1/12	1/13–2/5	2/6–3/1	3/2–3/26
		10/10–11/5	11/6–12/4	12/5–12/31	
10/4–10/27	10/28–11/20	11/21–12/14	12/15–12/31	1/1–4/5	4/6–5/5
11/9–12/7	12/8–12/31		1/1–1/7	1/8–1/31	2/1–2/24
9/3–9/27	1/1–1/2	1/3–1/27	1/28–2/20	2/21–3/16	3/17–4/9
	9/28–10/21	10/22–11/15	11/16–12/10	12/11–12/31	
10/19–11/11	11/12–12/5	12/6–12/29	12/30–12/31	1/1–1/4	1/5–2/1
8/9–9/6	9/7–10/15	10/16–11/7	1/1–1/21	1/22–2/14	2/15–3/10
	11/8–12/31				
9/19–10/12	1/1–1/4	1/5–2/5	2/6–3/4	3/5–3/29	3/30–4/24
	10/13–11/5	11/6–11/29	11/30–12/23	12/24–12/31	
11/1–11/25	11/26–12/19	12/20–12/31		1/1–1/17	1/18–2/10
8/20–9/14	9/15–10/9	1/1–1/12	1/13–2/5	2/6–3/1	3/2–3/25
		10/10–11/5	11/6–12/5	12/6–12/31	
10/4–10/27	10/28–11/20	11/21–12/13	12/14–12/31	1/1–4/5	4/6–5/4
11/10–12/7	12/8–12/31		1/1–1/7	1/8–1/31	2/1–2/24
9/4–9/27	1/1–1/2	1/3–1/27	1/28–2/20	2/21–3/16	3/17–4/9
	9/28–10/21	10/22–11/15	11/16–12/10	12/11–12/31	
10/19–11/11	11/12–12/5	12/6–12/29	12/30–12/31	1/1–1/5	1/6–2/1

VENUS SIGNS 1901–2010

	Aries	Taurus	Gemini	Cancer	Leo	Virgo
1954	3/12–4/4	4/5–4/28	4/29–5/23	5/24–6/17	6/18–7/13	7/14–8/8
1955	4/25–5/19	5/20–6/13	6/14–7/7	7/8–8/1	8/2–8/25	8/26–9/18
1956	2/12–3/7	3/8–4/4	4/5–5/7 6/24–8/4	5/8–6/23 8/5–9/8	9/9–10/5	10/6–10/31
1957	3/26–4/19	4/20–5/13	5/14–6/6	6/7–7/1	7/2–7/26	7/27–8/19
1958	5/6–5/31	6/1–6/26	6/27–7/22	7/23–8/15	8/16–9/9	9/10–10/3
1959	2/25–3/20	3/21–4/14	4/15–5/10	5/11–6/6	6/7–7/8 9/21–9/24	7/9–9/20 9/25–11/9
1960	4/10–5/3	5/4–5/28	5/29–6/21	6/22–7/15	7/16–8/9	8/10–9/2
1961	2/3–6/5	6/6–7/7	7/8–8/3	8/4–8/29	8/30–9/23	9/24–10/17
1962	3/11–4/3	4/4–4/28	4/29–5/22	5/23–6/17	6/18–7/12	7/13–8/8
1963	4/24–5/18	5/19–6/12	6/13–7/7	7/8–7/31	8/1–8/25	8/26–9/18
1964	2/11–3/7	3/8–4/4	4/5–5/9 6/18–8/5	5/10–6/17 8/6–9/8	9/9–10/5	10/6–10/31
1965	3/26–4/18	4/19–5/12	5/13–6/6	6/7–6/30	7/1–7/25	7/26–8/19
1966	5/6–5/31	6/1–6/26	6/27–7/21	7/22–8/15	8/16–9/8	9/9–10/2
1967	2/24–3/20	3/21–4/14	4/15–5/10	5/11–6/6	6/7–7/8 9/10–10/1	7/9–9/9 10/2–11/9
1968	4/9–5/3	5/4–5/27	5/28–6/20	6/21–7/15	7/16–8/8	8/9–9/2
1969	2/3–6/6	6/7–7/6	7/7–8/3	8/4–8/28	8/29–9/22	9/23–10/17
1970	3/11–4/3	4/4–4/27	4/28–5/22	5/23–6/16	6/17–7/12	7/13–8/8
1971	4/24–5/18	5/19–6/12	6/13–7/6	7/7–7/31	8/1–8/24	8/25–9/17
1972	2/11–3/7	3/8–4/3	4/4–5/10 6/12–8/6	5/11–6/11 8/7–9/8	9/9–10/5	10/6–10/30
1973	3/25–4/18	4/18–5/12	5/13–6/5	6/6–6/29	7/1–7/25	7/26–8/19
1974	5/5–5/31	6/1–6/25	6/26–7/21	7/22–8/14	8/15–9/8	9/9–10/2
1975	2/24–3/20	3/21–4/13	4/14–5/9	5/10–6/6	6/7–7/9 9/3–10/4	7/10–9/2 10/5–11/9
1976	4/8–5/2	5/2–5/27	5/27–6/20	6/20–7/14	7/14–8/8	8/8–9/1
1977	2/2–6/6	6/6–7/6	7/6–8/2	8/2–8/28	8/28–9/22	9/22–10/17
1978	3/9–4/2	4/2–4/27	4/27–5/22	5/22–6/16	6/16–7/12	7/12–8/6
1979	4/23–5/18	5/18–6/11	6/11–7/6	7/6–7/30	7/30–8/24	8/24–9/17
1980	2/9–3/6	3/6–4/3	4/3–5/12 6/5–8/6	5/12–6/5 8/6–9/7	9/7–10/4	10/4–10/30
1981	3/24–4/17	4/17–5/11	5/11–6/5	6/5–6/29	6/29–7/24	7/24–8/18

Libra	Scorpio	Sagittarius	Capricorn	Aquarius	Pisces
8/9–9/6	9/7–10/22	10/23–10/27	1/1–1/22	1/23–2/15	2/16–3/11
	10/28–12/31				
9/19–10/13	1/1–1/6	1/7–2/5	2/6–3/4	3/5–3/30	3/31–4/24
	10/14–11/5	11/6–11/30	12/1–12/24	12/25–12/31	
11/1–11/25	11/26–12/19	12/20–12/31		1/1–1/17	1/18–2/11
8/20–9/14	9/15–10/9	1/1–1/12	1/13–2/5	2/6–3/1	3/2–3/25
		10/10–11/5	11/6–12/6	12/7–12/31	
10/4–10/27	10/28–11/20	11/21–12/14	12/15–12/31	1/1–4/6	4/7–5/5
11/10–12/7	12/8–12/31		1/1–1/7	1/8–1/31	2/1–2/24
9/3–9/26	1/1–1/2	1/3–1/27	1/28–2/20	2/21–3/15	3/16–4/9
	9/27–10/21	10/22–11/15	11/16–12/10	12/11–12/31	
10/18–11/11	11/12–12/4	12/5–12/28	12/29–12/31	1/1–1/5	1/6–2/2
8/9–9/6	9/7–12/31		1/1–1/21	1/22–2/14	2/15–3/10
9/19–10/12	1/1–1/6	1/7–2/5	2/6–3/4	3/5–3/29	3/30–4/23
	10/13–11/5	11/6–11/29	11/30–12/23	12/24–12/31	
11/1–11/24	11/25–12/19	12/20–12/31		1/1–1/16	1/17–2/10
8/20–9/13	9/14–10/9	1/1–1/12	1/13–2/5	2/6–3/1	3/2–3/25
		10/10–11/5	11/6–12/7	12/8–12/31	
10/3–10/26	10/27–11/19	11/20–12/13	2/7–2/25	1/1–2/6	4/7–5/5
			12/14–12/31	2/26–4/6	
11/10–12/7	12/8–12/31		1/1–1/6	1/7–1/30	1/31–2/23
9/3–9/26	1/1	1/2–1/26	1/27–2/20	2/21–3/15	3/16–4/8
	9/27–10/21	10/22–11/14	11/15–12/9	12/10–12/31	
10/18–11/10	11/11–12/4	12/5–12/28	12/29–12/31	1/1–1/4	1/5–2/2
8/9–9/7	9/8–12/31		1/1–1/21	1/22–2/14	2/15–3/10
9/18–10/11	1/1–1/7	1/8–2/5	2/6–3/4	3/5–3/29	3/30–4/23
	10/12–11/5	11/6–11/29	11/30–12/23	12/24–12/31	
10/31–11/24	11/25–12/18	12/19–12/31		1/1–1/16	1/17–2/10
8/20–9/13	9/14–10/8	1/1–1/12	1/13–2/4	2/5–2/28	3/1–3/24
		10/9–11/5	11/6–12/7	12/8–12/31	
10/3–10/26	10/27–11/19	11/20–12/13	12/14–12/31	3/1–4/6	4/7–5/4
			1/30–2/28	1/1–1/29	
11/10–12/7	12/8–12/31		1/1–1/6	1/7–1/30	1/31–2/23
9/1–9/26	9/26–10/20	1/1–1/26	1/26–2/19	2/19–3/15	3/15–4/8
10/17–11/10	11/10–12/4	12/4–12/27	12/27–1/20/78		1/4–2/2
8/6–9/7	9/7–1/7			1/20–2/13	2/13–3/9
9/17–10/11	10/11–11/4	1/7–2/5	2/5–3/3	3/3–3/29	3/29–4/23
		11/4–11/28	11/28–12/22	12/22–1/16/80	
10/30–11/24	11/24–12/18	12/18–1/11/81			1/16–2/9
8/18–9/12	9/12–10/9	10/9–11/5	1/11–2/4	2/4–2/28	2/28–3/24
			11/5–12/8	12/8–1/23/82	

VENUS SIGNS 1901–2010

	Aries	Taurus	Gemini	Cancer	Leo	Virgo
1982	5/4–5/30	5/30–6/25	6/25–7/20	7/20–8/14	8/14–9/7	9/7–10/2
1983	2/22–3/19	3/19–4/13	4/13–5/9	5/9–6/6	6/6–7/10 8/27–10/5	7/10–8/27 10/5–11/9
1984	4/7–5/2	5/2–5/26	5/26–6/20	6/20–7/14	7/14–8/7	8/7–9/1
1985	2/2–6/6	6/7–7/6	7/6–8/2	8/2–8/28	8/28–9/22	9/22–10/16
1986	3/9–4/2	4/2–4/26	4/26–5/21	5/21–6/15	6/15–7/11	7/11–8/7
1987	4/22–5/17	5/17–6/11	6/11–7/5	7/5–7/30	7/30–8/23	8/23–9/16
1988	2/9–3/6	3/6–4/3	4/3–5/17 5/27–8/6	5/17–5/27 8/28–9/22	9/7–10/4 9/22–10/16	10/4–10/29
1989	3/23–4/16	4/16–5/11	5/11–6/4	6/4–6/29	6/29–7/24	7/24–8/18
1990	5/4–5/30	5/30–6/25	6/25–7/20	7/20–8/13	8/13–9/7	9/7–10/1
1991	2/22–3/18	3/18–4/13	4/13–5/9	5/9–6/6	6/6–7/11 8/21–10/6	7/11–8/21 10/6–11/9
1992	4/7–5/1	5/1–5/26	5/26–6/19	6/19–7/13	7/13–8/7	8/7–8/31
1993	2/2–6/6	6/6–7/6	7/6–8/1	8/1–8/27	8/27–9/21	9/21–10/16
1994	3/8–4/1	4/1–4/26	4/26–5/21	5/21–6/15	6/15–7/11	7/11–8/7
1995	4/22–5/16	5/16–6/10	6/10–7/5	7/5–7/29	7/29–8/23	8/23–9/16
1996	2/9–3/6	3/6–4/3	4/3–8/7	8/7–9/7	9/7–10/4	10/4–10/29
1997	3/23–4/16	4/16–5/10	5/10–6/4	6/4–6/28	6/28–7/23	7/23–8/17
1998	5/3–5/29	5/29–6/24	6/24–7/19	7/19–8/13	8/13–9/6	9/6–9/30
1999	2/21–3/18	3/18–4/12	4/12–5/8	5/8–6/5	6/5–7/12 8/15–10/7	7/12–8/15 10/7–11/9
2000	4/6–5/1	5/1–5/26	5/25–6/13	6/13–7/13	7/13–8/6	8/6–8/31
2001	2/2–6/6	6/6–7/5	7/5–8/1	8/1–8/26	8/26–9/20	9/20–10/15
2002	3/7–4/1	4/1–4/25	4/25–5/20	5/20–6/14	6/14–7/10	7/10–8/7
2003	4/21–5/16	5/16–6/9	6/9–7/4	7/4–7/29	7/29–8/22	8/22–9/15
2004	2/8–3/5	3/5–4/3	4/3–8/7	8/7–9/6	9/6–10/3	10/3–10/28
2005	3/22–4/15	4/15–5/10	5/10–6/3	6/3–6/28	6/28–7/23	7/23–8/17
2006	5/3–5/29	5/29–6/24	6/24–7/19	7/19–8/12	8/12–9/6	9/6–9/30
2007	2/21–3/16	3/17–4/10	4/11–5/7	5/8–6/4	6/5–7/13 8/8–10/6	7/14–8/7 10/7–11/7
2008	4/6–4/30	5/1–5/24	5/25–6/17	6/18–7/11	7/12–8/4	8/5–8/29
2009	2/2–4/11 4/24–6/6	6/6–7/5	7/5–7/31	731/–8/26	8/26–9/20	9/20–10/14
2010	3/7–3/31	3/31–4/25	4/25–5/20	5/20–6/14	6/14–7/10	7/10–8/7

Libra	Scorpio	Sagittarius	Capricorn	Aquarius	Pisces
10/2–10/26	10/26–11/18	11/18–12/12	1/23–3/2	3/2–4/6	4/6–5/4
			12/12–1/5/83		
11/9–12/6	12/6–1/1/84			1/5–1/29	1/29–2/22
9/1–9/25	9/25–10/20	1/1–1/25	1/25–2/19	2/19–3/14	3/14–4/7
		10/20–11/13	11/13–12/9	12/10–1/4	
10/16–11/9	11/9–12/3	12/3–12/27	12/28–1/19		1/4–2/2
8/7–9/7	9/7–1/7			1/20–2/13	2/13–3/9
9/16–10/10	10/10–11/3	1/7–2/5	2/5–3/3	3/3–3/28	3/28–4/22
		11/3–11/28	11/28–12/22	12/22–1/15	
10/29–11/23	11/23–12/17	12/17–1/10			1/15–2/9
8/18–9/12	9/12–10/8	10/8–11/5	1/10–2/3	2/3–2/27	2/27–3/23
			11/5–12/10	12/10–1/16/90	
10/1–10/25	10/25–11/18	11/18–12/12	1/16–3/3	3/3–4/6	4/6–5/4
			12/12–1/5		
11/9–12/6	12/6–12/31	12/31–1/25/92		1/5–1/29	1/29–2/22
8/31–9/25	9/25–10/19	10/19–11/13	1/25–2/18	2/18–3/13	3/13–4/7
			11/13–12/8	12/8–1/3/93	
10/16–11/9	11/9–12/2	12/2–12/26	12/26–1/19		1/3–2/2
8/7–9/7	9/7–1/7			1/19–2/12	2/12–3/8
9/16–10/10	10/10–11/13	1/7–2/4	2/4–3/2	3/2–3/28	3/28–4/22
		11/3–11/27	11/27–12/21	12/21–1/15	
10/29–11/23	11/23–12/17	12/17–1/10/97			1/15–2/9
8/17–9/12	9/12–10/8	10/8–11/5	1/10–2/3	2/3–2/27	2/27–3/23
			11/5–12/12	12/12–1/9	
9/30–10/24	10/24–11/17	11/17–12/11	1/9–3/4	3/4–4/6	4/6–5/3
11/9–12/5	12/5–12/31	12/31–1/24		1/4–1/28	1/28–2/21
8/31–9/24	9/24–10/19	10/19–11/13	1/24–2/18	2/18–3/12	3/13–4/6
			11/13–12/8	12/8	
10/15–11/8	11/8–12/2	12/2–12/26	12/26/01–1/18/02	12/8/00–1/3/01	1/3–2/2
8/7–9/7	9/7–1/7/03		12/26/01–1/18	1/18–2/11	2/11–3/7
9/15–10/9	10/9–11/2	1/7–2/4	2/4–3/2	3/2–3/27	3/27–4/21
		11/2–11/26	11/26–12/21	12/21–1/14/04	
10/28–11/22	11/22–12/16	12/16–1/9/05		1/1–1/14	1/14–2/8
8/17–9/11	9/11–10/8	10/8–11/15	1/9–2/2	2/2–2/26	2/26–3/22
			11/5–12/15	12/15–1/1/06	
9/30–10/24	10/24–11/17	11/17–12/11	1/1–3/5	3/5–4/6	4/6–5/3
11/8–12/4	12/5–12/29	12/30–1/24/08		1/3–1/26	1/27–2/20
8/6–9/7	9/7–1/7			1/20–2/13	2/13–3/9
8/30–9/22	9/23–10/17	10/18–11/11	1/24–2/16	2/17–3/11	3/12–4/5
			11/12–12/6	12/7–1/2/09	
10/14–11/7	11/7–12/1	12/1–12/25	12/25–1/18/10	12/7/08–1/31/09	1/3–2/2 4/11–4/24
8/7–9/8	9/8–11/8			1/18/10–2/11/10	2/11–3/7
11/8–11/30	11/30–1/7/11				

81

How to Use the Mars, Jupiter, and Saturn Tables

Find the year of your birth on the left side of each column. The dates when the planet entered each sign are listed on the right side of each column. (Signs are abbreviated to three letters.) Your birthday should fall on or between each date listed, and your planetary placement should correspond to the earlier sign of that period.

All planet changes are calculated for the Greenwich Mean Time zone.

MARS SIGNS 1901–2010

1901	MAR 1	Leo
	MAY 11	Vir
	JUL 13	Lib
	AUG 31	Scp
	OCT 14	Sag
	NOV 24	Cap
1902	JAN 1	Aqu
	FEB 8	Pic
	MAR 19	Ari
	APR 27	Tau
	JUN 7	Gem
	JUL 20	Can
	SEP 4	Leo
	OCT 23	Vir
	DEC 20	Lib
1903	APR 19	Vir
	MAY 30	Lib
	AUG 6	Scp
	SEP 22	Sag
	NOV 3	Cap
	DEC 12	Aqu
1904	JAN 19	Pic
	FEB 27	Ari
	APR 6	Tau
	MAY 18	Gem
	JUN 30	Can
	AUG 15	Leo

	OCT 1	Vir
	NOV 20	Lib
1905	JAN 13	Scp
	AUG 21	Sag
	OCT 8	Cap
	NOV 18	Aqu
	DEC 27	Pic
1906	FEB 4	Ari
	MAR 17	Tau
	APR 28	Gem
	JUN 11	Can
	JUL 27	Leo
	SEP 12	Vir
	OCT 30	Lib
	DEC 17	Scp
1907	FEB 5	Sag
	APR 1	Cap
	OCT 13	Aqu
	NOV 29	Pic
1908	JAN 11	Ari
	FEB 23	Tau
	APR 7	Gem
	MAY 22	Can
	JUL 8	Leo
	AUG 24	Vir
	OCT 10	Lib
	NOV 25	Scp

1909	JAN	10	Sag		MAR	9	Pic
	FEB	24	Cap		APR	16	Ari
	APR	9	Aqu		MAY	26	Tau
	MAY	25	Pic		JUL	6	Gem
	JUL	21	Ari		AUG	19	Can
	SEP	26	Pic		OCT	7	Leo
	NOV	20	Ari	1916	MAY	28	Vir
1910	JAN	23	Tau		JUL	23	Lib
	MAR	14	Gem		SEP	8	Scp
	MAY	1	Can		OCT	22	Sag
	JUN	19	Leo		DEC	1	Cap
	AUG	6	Vir	1917	JAN	9	Aqu
	SEP	22	Lib		FEB	16	Pic
	NOV	6	Scp		MAR	26	Ari
	DEC	20	Sag		MAY	4	Tau
1911	JAN	31	Cap		JUN	14	Gem
	MAR	14	Aqu		JUL	28	Can
	APR	23	Pic		SEP	12	Leo
	JUN	2	Ari		NOV	2	Vir
	JUL	15	Tau	1918	JAN	11	Lib
	SEP	5	Gem		FEB	25	Vir
	NOV	30	Tau		JUN	23	Lib
1912	JAN	30	Gem		AUG	17	Scp
	APR	5	Can		OCT	1	Sag
	MAY	28	Leo		NOV	11	Cap
	JUL	17	Vir		DEC	20	Aqu
	SEP	2	Lib	1919	JAN	27	Pic
	OCT	18	Scp		MAR	6	Ari
	NOV	30	Sag		APR	15	Tau
1913	JAN	10	Cap		MAY	26	Gem
	FEB	19	Aqu		JUL	8	Can
	MAR	30	Pic		AUG	23	Leo
	MAY	8	Ari		OCT	10	Vir
	JUN	17	Tau		NOV	30	Lib
	JUL	29	Gem	1920	JAN	31	Scp
	SEP	15	Can		APR	23	Lib
1914	MAY	1	Leo		JUL	10	Scp
	JUN	26	Vir		SEP	4	Sag
	AUG	14	Lib		OCT	18	Cap
	SEP	29	Scp		NOV	27	Aqu
	NOV	11	Sag	1921	JAN	5	Pic
	DEC	22	Cap		FEB	13	Ari
1915	JAN	30	Aqu		MAR	25	Tau

	MAY	6	Gem		OCT	26	Scp
	JUN	18	Can		DEC	8	Sag
	AUG	3	Leo	1928	JAN	19	Cap
	SEP	19	Vir		FEB	28	Aqu
	NOV	6	Lib		APR	7	Pic
	DEC	26	Scp		MAY	16	Ari
1922	FEB	18	Sag		JUN	26	Tau
	SEP	13	Cap		AUG	9	Gem
	OCT	30	Aqu		OCT	3	Can
	DEC	11	Pic		DEC	20	Gem
1923	JAN	21	Ari	1929	MAR	10	Can
	MAR	4	Tau		MAY	13	Leo
	APR	16	Gem		JUL	4	Vir
	MAY	30	Can		AUG	21	Lib
	JUL	16	Leo		OCT	6	Scp
	SEP	1	Vir		NOV	18	Sag
	OCT	18	Lib		DEC	29	Cap
	DEC	4	Scp	1930	FEB	6	Aqu
1924	JAN	19	Sag		MAR	17	Pic
	MAR	6	Cap		APR	24	Ari
	APR	24	Aqu		JUN	3	Tau
	JUN	24	Pic		JUL	14	Gem
	AUG	24	Aqu		AUG	28	Can
	OCT	19	Pic		OCT	20	Leo
	DEC	19	Ari	1931	FEB	16	Can
1925	FEB	5	Tau		MAR	30	Leo
	MAR	24	Gem		JUN	10	Vir
	MAY	9	Can		AUG	1	Lib
	JUN	26	Leo		SEP	17	Scp
	AUG	12	Vir		OCT	30	Sag
	SEP	28	Lib		DEC	10	Cap
	NOV	13	Scp	1932	JAN	18	Aqu
	DEC	28	Sag		FEB	25	Pic
1926	FEB	9	Cap		APR	3	Ari
	MAR	23	Aqu		MAY	12	Tau
	MAY	3	Pic		JUN	22	Gem
	JUN	15	Ari		AUG	4	Can
	AUG	1	Tau		SEP	20	Leo
1927	FEB	22	Gem		NOV	13	Vir
	APR	17	Can	1933	JUL	6	Lib
	JUN	6	Leo		AUG	26	Scp
	JUL	25	Vir		OCT	9	Sag
	SEP	10	Lib		NOV	19	Cap

	DEC	28	Aqu		FEB	17	Tau
1934	FEB	4	Pic		APR	1	Gem
	MAR	14	Ari		MAY	17	Can
	APR	22	Tau		JUL	3	Leo
	JUN	2	Gem		AUG	19	Vir
	JUL	15	Can		OCT	5	Lib
	AUG	30	Leo		NOV	20	Scp
	OCT	18	Vir	1941	JAN	4	Sag
	DEC	11	Lib		FEB	17	Cap
1935	JUL	29	Scp		APR	2	Aqu
	SEP	16	Sag		MAY	16	Pic
	OCT	28	Cap		JUL	2	Ari
	DEC	7	Aqu	1942	JAN	11	Tau
1936	JAN	14	Pic		MAR	7	Gem
	FEB	22	Ari		APR	26	Can
	APR	1	Tau		JUN	14	Leo
	MAY	13	Gem		AUG	1	Vir
	JUN	25	Can		SEP	17	Lib
	AUG	10	Leo		NOV	1	Scp
	SEP	26	Vir		DEC	15	Sag
	NOV	14	Lib	1943	JAN	26	Cap
1937	JAN	5	Scp		MAR	8	Aqu
	MAR	13	Sag		APR	17	Pic
	MAY	14	Scp		MAY	27	Ari
	AUG	8	Sag		JUL	7	Tau
	SEP	30	Cap		AUG	23	Gem
	NOV	11	Aqu	1944	MAR	28	Can
	DEC	21	Pic		MAY	22	Leo
1938	JAN	30	Ari		JUL	12	Vir
	MAR	12	Tau		AUG	29	Lib
	APR	23	Gem		OCT	13	Scp
	JUN	7	Can		NOV	25	Sag
	JUL	22	Leo	1945	JAN	5	Cap
	SEP	7	Vir		FEB	14	Aqu
	OCT	25	Lib		MAR	25	Pic
	DEC	11	Scp		MAY	2	Ari
1939	JAN	29	Sag		JUN	11	Tau
	MAR	21	Cap		JUL	23	Gem
	MAY	25	Aqu		SEP	7	Can
	JUL	21	Cap		NOV	11	Leo
	SEP	24	Aqu		DEC	26	Can
	NOV	19	Pic	1946	APR	22	Leo
1940	JAN	4	Ari		JUN	20	Vir

	AUG	9	Lib		OCT	12	Cap
	SEP	24	Scp		NOV	21	Aqu
	NOV	6	Sag		DEC	30	Pic
	DEC	17	Cap	1953	FEB	8	Ari
1947	JAN	25	Aqu		MAR	20	Tau
	MAR	4	Pic		MAY	1	Gem
	APR	11	Ari		JUN	14	Can
	MAY	21	Tau		JUL	29	Leo
	JUL	1	Gem		SEP	14	Vir
	AUG	13	Can		NOV	1	Lib
	OCT	1	Leo		DEC	20	Scp
	DEC	1	Vir	1954	FEB	9	Sag
1948	FEB	12	Leo		APR	12	Cap
	MAY	18	Vir		JUL	3	Sag
	JUL	17	Lib		AUG	24	Cap
	SEP	3	Scp		OCT	21	Aqu
	OCT	17	Sag		DEC	4	Pic
	NOV	26	Cap	1955	JAN	15	Ari
1949	JAN	4	Aqu		FEB	26	Tau
	FEB	11	Pic		APR	10	Gem
	MAR	21	Ari		MAY	26	Can
	APR	30	Tau		JUL	11	Leo
	JUN	10	Gem		AUG	27	Vir
	JUL	23	Can		OCT	13	Lib
	SEP	7	Leo		NOV	29	Scp
	OCT	27	Vir	1956	JAN	14	Sag
	DEC	26	Lib		FEB	28	Cap
1950	MAR	28	Vir		APR	14	Aqu
	JUN	11	Lib		JUN	3	Pic
	AUG	10	Scp		DEC	6	Ari
	SEP	25	Sag	1957	JAN	28	Tau
	NOV	6	Cap		MAR	17	Gem
	DEC	15	Aqu		MAY	4	Can
1951	JAN	22	Pic		JUN	21	Leo
	MAR	1	Ari		AUG	8	Vir
	APR	10	Tau		SEP	24	Lib
	MAY	21	Gem		NOV	8	Scp
	JUL	3	Can		DEC	23	Sag
	AUG	18	Leo	1958	FEB	3	Cap
	OCT	5	Vir		MAR	17	Aqu
	NOV	24	Lib		APR	27	Pic
1952	JAN	20	Scp		JUN	7	Ari
	AUG	27	Sag		JUL	21	Tau

	SEP	21	Gom		NOV	6	Vir
	OCT	29	Tau	1965	JUN	29	Lib
1959	FEB	10	Gem		AUG	20	Scp
	APR	10	Can		OCT	4	Sag
	JUN	1	Leo		NOV	14	Cap
	JUL	20	Vir		DEC	23	Aqu
	SEP	5	Lib	1966	JAN	30	Pic
	OCT	21	Scp		MAR	9	Ari
	DEC	3	Sag		APR	17	Tau
1960	JAN	14	Cap		MAY	28	Gem
	FEB	23	Aqu		JUL	11	Can
	APR	2	Pic		AUG	25	Leo
	MAY	11	Ari		OCT	12	Vir
	JUN	20	Tau		DEC	4	Lib
	AUG	2	Gem	1967	FEB	12	Scp
	SEP	21	Can		MAR	31	Lib
1961	FEB	5	Gem		JUL	19	Scp
	FEB	7	Can		SEP	10	Sag
	MAY	6	Leo		OCT	23	Cap
	JUN	28	Vir		DEC	1	Aqu
	AUG	17	Lib	1968	JAN	9	Pic
	OCT	1	Scp		FEB	17	Ari
	NOV	13	Sag		MAR	27	Tau
	DEC	24	Cap		MAY	8	Gem
1962	FEB	1	Aqu		JUN	21	Can
	MAR	12	Pic		AUG	5	Leo
	APR	19	Ari		SEP	21	Vir
	MAY	28	Tau		NOV	9	Lib
	JUL	9	Gem		DEC	29	Scp
	AUG	22	Can	1969	FEB	25	Sag
	OCT	11	Leo		SEP	21	Cap
1963	JUN	3	Vir		NOV	4	Aqu
	JUL	27	Lib		DEC	15	Pic
	SEP	12	Scp	1970	JAN	24	Ari
	OCT	25	Sag		MAR	7	Tau
	DEC	5	Cap		APR	18	Gem
1964	JAN	13	Aqu		JUN	2	Can
	FEB	20	Pic		JUL	18	Leo
	MAR	29	Ari		SEP	3	Vir
	MAY	7	Tau		OCT	20	Lib
	JUN	17	Gem		DEC	6	Scp
	JUL	30	Can	1971	JAN	23	Sag
	SEP	15	Leo		MAR	12	Cap

	MAY 3	Aqu		JUN 6	Tau
	NOV 6	Pic		JUL 17	Gem
	DEC 26	Ari		SEP 1	Can
1972	FEB 10	Tau		OCT 26	Leo
	MAR 27	Gem	1978	JAN 26	Can
	MAY 12	Can		APR 10	Leo
	JUN 28	Leo		JUN 14	Vir
	AUG 15	Vir		AUG 4	Lib
	SEP 30	Lib		SEP 19	Scp
	NOV 15	Scp		NOV 2	Sag
	DEC 30	Sag		DEC 12	Cap
1973	FEB 12	Cap	1979	JAN 20	Aqu
	MAR 26	Aqu		FEB 27	Pic
	MAY 8	Pic		APR 7	Ari
	JUN 20	Ari		MAY 16	Tau
	AUG 12	Tau		JUN 26	Gem
	OCT 29	Ari		AUG 8	Can
	DEC 24	Tau		SEP 24	Leo
1974	FEB 27	Gem		NOV 19	Vir
	APR 20	Can	1980	MAR 11	Leo
	JUN 9	Leo		MAY 4	Vir
	JUL 27	Vir		JUL 10	Lib
	SEP 12	Lib		AUG 29	Scp
	OCT 28	Scp		OCT 12	Sag
	DEC 10	Sag		NOV 22	Cap
1975	JAN 21	Cap		DEC 30	Aqu
	MAR 3	Aqu	1981	FEB 6	Pic
	APR 11	Pic		MAR 17	Ari
	MAY 21	Ari		APR 25	Tau
	JUL 1	Tau		JUN 5	Gem
	AUG 14	Gem		JUL 18	Can
	OCT 17	Can		SEP 2	Leo
	NOV 25	Gem		OCT 21	Vir
1976	MAR 18	Can		DEC 16	Lib
	MAY 16	Leo	1982	AUG 3	Scp
	JUL 6	Vir		SEP 20	Sag
	AUG 24	Lib		OCT 31	Cap
	OCT 8	Scp		DEC 10	Aqu
	NOV 20	Sag	1983	JAN 17	Pic
1977	JAN 1	Cap		FEB 25	Ari
	FEB 9	Aqu		APR 5	Tau
	MAR 20	Pic		MAY 16	Gem
	APR 27	Ari		JUN 29	Can

	AUG	13	Leo	1990	JAN	29	Cap
	SEP	30	Vir		MAR	11	Aqu
	NOV	18	Lib		APR	20	Pic
1984	JAN	11	Scp		MAY	31	Ari
	AUG	17	Sag		JUL	12	Tau
	OCT	5	Cap		AUG	31	Gem
	NOV	15	Aqu		DEC	14	Tau
	DEC	25	Pic	1991	JAN	21	Gem
1985	FEB	2	Ari		APR	3	Can
	MAR	15	Tau		MAY	26	Leo
	APR	26	Gem		JUL	15	Vir
	JUN	9	Can		SEP	1	Lib
	JUL	25	Leo		OCT	16	Scp
	SEP	10	Vir		NOV	29	Sag
	OCT	27	Lib	1992	JAN	9	Cap
	DEC	14	Scp		FEB	18	Aqu
1986	FEB	2	Sag		MAR	28	Pic
	MAR	28	Cap		MAY	5	Ari
	OCT	9	Aqu		JUN	14	Tau
	NOV	26	Pic		JUL	26	Gem
1987	JAN	8	Ari		SEP	12	Can
	FEB	20	Tau	1993	APR	27	Leo
	APR	5	Gem		JUN	23	Vir
	MAY	21	Can		AUG	12	Lib
	JUL	6	Leo		SEP	27	Scp
	AUG	22	Vir		NOV	9	Sag
	OCT	8	Lib		DEC	20	Cap
	NOV	24	Scp	1994	JAN	28	Aqu
1988	JAN	8	Sag		MAR	7	Pic
	FEB	22	Cap		APR	14	Ari
	APR	6	Aqu		MAY	23	Tau
	MAY	22	Pic		JUL	3	Gem
	JUL	13	Ari		AUG	16	Can
	OCT	23	Pic		OCT	4	Leo
	NOV	1	Ari		DEC	12	Vir
1989	JAN	19	Tau	1995	JAN	22	Leo
	MAR	11	Gem		MAY	25	Vir
	APR	29	Can		JUL	21	Lib
	JUN	16	Leo		SEP	7	Scp
	AUG	3	Vir		OCT	20	Sag
	SEP	19	Lib		NOV	30	Cap
	NOV	4	Scp	1996	JAN	8	Aqu
	DEC	18	Sag		FEB	15	Pic

	MAR	24	Ari		MAY	28	Can
	MAY	2	Tau		JUL	13	Leo
	JUN	12	Gem		AUG	29	Vir
	JUL	25	Can		OCT	15	Lib
	SEP	9	Leo		DEC	1	Scp
	OCT	30	Vir	2003	JAN	17	Sag
1997	JAN	3	Lib		MAR	4	Cap
	MAR	8	Vir		APR	21	Aqu
	JUN	19	Lib		JUN	17	Pic
	AUG	14	Scp		DEC	16	Ari
	SEP	28	Sag	2004	FEB	3	Tau
	NOV	9	Cap		MAR	21	Gem
	DEC	18	Aqu		MAY	7	Can
1998	JAN	25	Pic		JUN	23	Leo
	MAR	4	Ari		AUG	10	Vir
	APR	13	Tau		SEP	26	Lib
	MAY	24	Gem		NOV	11	Sep
	JUL	6	Can		DEC	25	Sag
	AUG	20	Leo	2005	FEB	6	Cap
	OCT	7	Vir		MAR	20	Aqu
	NOV	27	Lib		MAY	1	Pic
1999	JAN	26	Scp		JUN	12	Ari
	MAY	5	Lib		JUL	28	Tau
	JUL	5	Scp	2006	FEB	17	Gem
	SEP	2	Sag		APR	14	Can
	OCT	17	Cap		JUN	3	Leo
	NOV	26	Aqu		JUL	22	Vir
2000	JAN	4	Pic		SEP	8	Lib
	FEB	12	Ari		OCT	23	Scp
	MAR	23	Tau		DEC	6	Sag
	MAY	3	Gem	2007	JAN	16	Cap
	JUN	16	Can		FEB	25	Aqu
	AUG	1	Leo		APR	6	Pic
	SEP	17	Vir		MAY	15	Ari
	NOV	4	Lib		JUNE	24	Tau
	DEC	23	Scp		AUG	7	Gem
2001	FEB	14	Sag		SEP	28	Can
	SEP	8	Cap		DEC	31	Gem*
	OCT	27	Aqu	2008	MAR	4	Can
	DEC	8	Pic		MAY	9	Leo
2002	JAN	18	Ari		JUL	1	Vir
	MAR	1	Tau		AUG	19	Lib
	APR	13	Gem		OCT	3	Scp

	NOV	16	Sag		AUG	25	Can
	DEC	27	Cap		OCT	16	Leo
2009	FEB	4	Aqu	2010	JUN	7	Vir
	MAR	14	Pic		JUL	29	Lib
	APR	22	Ari		SEP	14	Scp
	MAY	31	Tau		OCT	28	Sag
	JUL	11	Gem		DEC	7	Cap

JUPITER SIGNS 1901–2010

1901	JAN	19	Cap	1927	JAN	18	Pic
1902	FEB	6	Aqu		JUN	6	Ari
1903	FEB	20	Pic		SEP	11	Pic
1904	MAR	1	Ari	1928	JAN	23	Ari
	AUG	8	Tau		JUN	4	Tau
	AUG	31	Ari	1929	JUN	12	Gem
1905	MAR	7	Tau	1930	JUN	26	Can
	JUL	21	Gem	1931	JUL	17	Leo
	DEC	4	Tau	1932	AUG	11	Vir
1906	MAR	9	Gem	1933	SEP	10	Lib
	JUL	30	Can	1934	OCT	11	Scp
1907	AUG	18	Leo	1935	NOV	9	Sag
1908	SEP	12	Vir	1936	DEC	2	Cap
1909	OCT	11	Lib	1937	DEC	20	Aqu
1910	NOV	11	Scp	1938	MAY	14	Pic
1911	DEC	10	Sag		JUL	30	Aqu
1913	JAN	2	Cap		DEC	29	Pic
1914	JAN	21	Aqu	1939	MAY	11	Ari
1915	FEB	4	Pic		OCT	30	Pic
1916	FEB	12	Ari		DEC	20	Ari
	JUN	26	Tau	1940	MAY	16	Tau
	OCT	26	Ari	1941	MAY	26	Gem
1917	FEB	12	Tau	1942	JUN	10	Can
	JUN	29	Gem	1943	JUN	30	Leo
1918	JUL	13	Can	1944	JUL	26	Vir
1919	AUG	2	Leo	1945	AUG	25	Lib
1920	AUG	27	Vir	1946	SEP	25	Scp
1921	SEP	25	Lib	1947	OCT	24	Sag
1922	OCT	26	Scp	1948	NOV	15	Cap
1923	NOV	24	Sag	1949	APR	12	Aqu
1924	DEC	18	Cap		JUN	27	Cap
1926	JAN	6	Aqu		NOV	30	Aqu

1950	APR	15	Pic	1970	APR	30	Lib
	SEP	15	Aqu		AUG	15	Scp
	DEC	1	Pic	1971	JAN	14	Sag
1951	APR	21	Ari		JUN	5	Scp
1952	APR	28	Tau		SEP	11	Sag
1953	MAY	9	Gem	1972	FEB	6	Cap
1954	MAY	24	Can		JUL	24	Sag
1955	JUN	13	Leo		SEP	25	Cap
	NOV	17	Vir	1973	FEB	23	Aqu
1956	JAN	18	Leo	1974	MAR	8	Pic
	JUL	7	Vir	1975	MAR	18	Ari
	DEC	13	Lib	1976	MAR	26	Tau
1957	FEB	19	Vir		AUG	23	Gem
	AUG	7	Lib		OCT	16	Tau
1958	JAN	13	Scp	1977	APR	3	Gem
	MAR	20	Lib		AUG	20	Can
	SEP	7	Scp		DEC	30	Gem
1959	FEB	10	Sag	1978	APR	12	Can
	APR	24	Scp		SEP	5	Leo
	OCT	5	Sag	1979	FEB	28	Can
1960	MAR	1	Cap		APR	20	Leo
	JUN	10	Sag		SEP	29	Vir
	OCT	26	Cap	1980	OCT	27	Lib
1961	MAR	15	Aqu	1981	NOV	27	Scp
	AUG	12	Cap	1982	DEC	26	Sag
	NOV	4	Aqu	1984	JAN	19	Cap
1962	MAR	25	Pic	1985	FEB	6	Aqu
1963	APR	4	Ari	1986	FEB	20	Pic
1964	APR	12	Tau	1987	MAR	2	Ari
1965	APR	22	Gem	1988	MAR	8	Tau
	SEP	21	Can		JUL	22	Gem
	NOV	17	Gem		NOV	30	Tau
1966	MAY	5	Can	1989	MAR	11	Gem
	SEP	27	Leo		JUL	30	Can
1967	JAN	16	Can	1990	AUG	18	Leo
	MAY	23	Leo	1991	SEP	12	Vir
	OCT	19	Vir	1992	OCT	10	Lib
1968	FEB	27	Leo	1993	NOV	10	Scp
	JUN	15	Vir	1994	DEC	9	Sag
	NOV	15	Lib	1996	JAN	3	Cap
1969	MAR	30	Vir	1997	JAN	21	Aqu
	JUL	15	Lib	1998	FEB	4	Pic
	DEC	16	Scp	1999	FEB	13	Ari

	JUN	28	Tau	2005	OCT	26	Scp
	OCT	23	Ari	2006	NOV	24	Sag
2000	FEB	14	Tau	2007	DEC	17	Cap
	JUN	30	Gem	2009	JAN	5	Aqu
2001	JUL	14	Can	2010	JAN	18	Pis
2002	AUG	1	Leo		JUN	6	Ari
2003	AUG	27	Vir		SEP	9	Pis
2004	SEP	24	Lib				

SATURN SIGNS 1903–2010

1903	JAN	19	Aqu		OCT	18	Pic
1905	APR	13	Pic	1938	JAN	14	Ari
	AUG	17	Aqu	1939	JUL	6	Tau
1906	JAN	8	Pic		SEP	22	Ari
1908	MAR	19	Ari	1940	MAR	20	Tau
1910	MAY	17	Tau	1942	MAY	8	Gem
	DEC	14	Ari	1944	JUN	20	Can
1911	JAN	20	Tau	1946	AUG	2	Leo
1912	JUL	7	Gem	1948	SEP	19	Vir
	NOV	30	Tau	1949	APR	3	Leo
1913	MAR	26	Gem		MAY	29	Vir
1914	AUG	24	Can	1950	NOV	20	Lib
	DEC	7	Gem	1951	MAR	7	Vir
1915	MAY	11	Can		AUG	13	Lib
1916	OCT	17	Leo	1953	OCT	22	Scp
	DEC	7	Can	1956	JAN	12	Sag
1917	JUN	24	Leo		MAY	14	Scp
1919	AUG	12	Vir		OCT	10	Sag
1921	OCT	7	Lib	1959	JAN	5	Cap
1923	DEC	20	Scp	1962	JAN	3	Aqu
1924	APR	6	Lib	1964	MAR	24	Pic
	SEP	13	Scp		SEP	16	Aqu
1926	DEC	2	Sag		DEC	16	Pic
1929	MAR	15	Cap	1967	MAR	3	Ari
	MAY	5	Sag	1969	APR	29	Tau
	NOV	30	Cap	1971	JUN	18	Gem
1932	FEB	24	Aqu	1972	JAN	10	Tau
	AUG	13	Cap		FEB	21	Gem
	NOV	20	Aqu	1973	AUG	1	Can
1935	FEB	14	Pic	1974	JAN	7	Gem
1937	APR	25	Ari		APR	18	Can

1975	SEP	17	Leo		JUN	30	Aqu
1976	JAN	14	Can	1994	JAN	28	Pic
	JUN	5	Leo	1996	APR	7	Ari
1977	NOV	17	Vir	1998	JUN	9	Tau
1978	JAN	5	Leo		OCT	25	Ari
	JUL	26	Vir	1999	MAR	1	Tau
1980	SEP	21	Lib	2000	AUG	10	Gem
1982	NOV	29	Scp		OCT	16	Tau
1983	MAY	6	Lib	2001	APR	21	Gem
	AUG	24	Scp	2003	JUN	3	Can
1985	NOV	17	Sag	2005	JUL	16	Leo
1988	FEB	13	Cap	2007	SEP	2	Vir
	JUN	10	Sag	2009	OCT	29	Lib
	NOV	12	Cap	2010	APR	7	Vir
1991	FEB	6	Aqu		JUL	21	Lib
1993	MAY	21	Pic				

CHAPTER 6

Where It All Happens: Your Rising Sign

To find out what's happening in a horoscope, you first have to look east. The degree of the zodiac ascending over the eastern horizon at the time you were born, which is called the rising sign or ascendant, marks the beginning of the first house, one of twelve divisions of the horoscope, each of which represents a different area of life. These "houses" contain the planets, the doers in a chart. After the rising sign, the other houses parade around the chart in sequence, with the following sign on the next house cusp. Therefore, the setup of the chart—*what* happens *where*—depends on the rising sign.

Though you can learn much about a person by the signs and interactions of the sun, moon, and planets in the horoscope, without a valid rising sign, the collection of planets has no "homes." One would have no idea which area of life could be influenced by a particular planet. For example, you might know that a person has Mars in Aries, which will describe that person's dynamic fiery energy. But if you also know that the person has a Capricorn rising sign, this Mars will fall in the fourth house of home and family, so you know where that energy will operate.

Due to the earth's rotation, the rising sign changes every two hours, which means that babies born later or earlier on the same day in the same hospital will have most planets in the same signs, but may not have the same rising sign. Therefore, their planets may fall in different houses in the chart. For instance, if Mars is in Gemini and your rising sign is Taurus,

Mars will most likely be active in the second or financial house of your chart. Someone born later in the same day when the rising sign is Virgo would have Mars positioned at the top of the chart, energizing the tenth house of career.

Most astrologers insist on knowing the exact time of a client's birth before they analyze a chart. The more accurate your birth time, the more accurately an astrologer can position the planets in your chart by determining the correct rising sign.

How Your Rising Sign Can Influence Your Sun Sign

Your rising sign has an important relationship with your sun sign. Some will complement the sun sign; others hide it under a totally different mask, as if playing an entirely different role, making it difficult to guess the person's sun sign from outer appearances. This may be the reason why you might not look or act like your sun sign's archetype. For example, a Leo with a conservative Capricorn ascendant would come across as much more serious than a Leo with a fiery Aries or Sagittarius ascendant.

Though the rising sign usually creates the first impression you make, there are exceptions. When the sun sign is reinforced by other planets in the same sign, this might overpower the impression of the rising sign. For instance, a Leo sun plus a Leo Venus and Leo Jupiter would counteract the more conservative image that would otherwise be conveyed by the person's Capricorn ascendant.

Those born early in the morning when the sun was on the horizon will be most likely to project the image of their sun sign. These people are often called a "double Aries" or a "double Virgo" because the same sun sign and ascendant reinforce each other.

Find Your Rising Sign

Look up your rising sign on the chart at the end of this chapter. Since rising signs change every two hours, it is important to know your birth time as close to the minute as possible. Even a few minutes' difference could change the rising sign and therefore the setup of your chart. If you are unsure about the exact time, but know within a few hours, check the following descriptions to see which is most like the personality you project.

Aries Rising: Alpha Energy

You are the most aggressive version of your sun sign, with boundless energy that can be used productively if it's channeled in the right direction. Watch a tendency to overreact emotionally and blow your top. You come across as openly competitive, a positive asset in business or sports. Be on guard against impatience, which could lead to head injuries. Your walk and bearing could have the telltale head-forward Aries posture. You may wear more bright colors, especially red, than others of your sign, or be a redhead. You may also have a tendency to drive your car faster.

Can you see the alpha Aries tendency in Barbra Streisand (a sun sign Taurus) and Bette Midler (a sun sign Sagittarius)?

Taurus Rising: Down-to-Earth

You're slow-moving, with a beautiful (or distinctive) speaking or singing voice. You probably surround yourself with comfort, good food, luxurious surroundings, and other sensual pleasures. You prefer welcoming others into your home to gadding about. You may have a talent for business, especially in trading, appraising, and real estate. A Taurus ascendant gives a well-padded physique that gains weight easily, like Liza Minnelli. This ascendant can also endow females with a curvaceous beauty.

Gemini Rising: A Way with Words

You're naturally sociable, with lighter, more ethereal mannerisms than others of your sign, especially if you're female. You love to communicate with people, and express your ideas easily, like former British prime minister Tony Blair. You may have a talent for writing or public speaking. You thrive on variety, a constantly changing scene, and a lively social life. However, you may relate to others at a deeper level than might be suspected. And you will be far more sympathetic and caring than you project. You will probably travel widely, changing partners and jobs several times (or juggle two at once). Physically, your nerves are quite sensitive. Occasionally, you would benefit from a calm, tranquil atmosphere away from your usual social scene.

Cancer Rising: Nurturing Instincts

You are naturally acquisitive, possessive, private, a moneymaker like Bill Gates or Michael Bloomberg. You easily pick up others' needs and feelings—a great gift in business, the arts, and personal relationships. But you must guard against overreacting or taking things too personally, especially during full-moon periods. Find creative outlets for your natural nurturing gifts, such as helping the less fortunate, particularly children. Your insights would be helpful in psychology. Your desire to feed and care for others would be useful in the restaurant, hotel, or child-care industries. You may be especially fond of wearing romantic old clothes, collecting antiques, and dining on exquisite food. Since your body may retain fluids, pay attention to your diet. To relax, escape to places near water.

Leo Rising: Diva Dazzle

You may come across as more poised than you really feel. However, you play it to the hilt, projecting a proud royal presence. A Leo ascendant gives you a natural flair for drama, like Marilyn Monroe, and you might be accused of stealing the spotlight. You'll also project a much more outgoing, optimistic, and sunny personality than others of your sign. You take care to please your public by always projecting star quality, probably tossing a luxuriant mane of hair, sporting a striking hairstyle, or dressing to impress. Females often dazzle with colorful clothing or spectacular jewelry. Since you may have a strong parental nature, you could well become a family matriarch or patriarch, like George H. W. Bush.

Virgo Rising: High Standards

Virgo rising endows you with a practical, analytical outer image. You seem neat, orderly, and more particular than others of your sign. Others in your life may feel they must live up to your high standards. Though at times you may be openly critical, this masks a well-meaning desire to have only the best for loved ones. Your sharp eye for details could be used in the financial world, or your literary skills could draw you to teaching or publishing. The healing arts, health care, and service-oriented professions attract many with a Virgo ascendant. You're likely to take good care of yourself, with great attention to health, diet, and exercise, like Madonna. You might even show some hypochondriac tendencies, like Woody Allen. Physically, you may have a very sensitive digestive system.

Libra Rising: The Charmer

Libra rising gives you a charming, social, and public persona, like John F. Kennedy and Bill Clinton. You tend to avoid confrontations in relationships, preferring to smooth the way or negotiate diplomatically rather than give in to an emotional reaction. Because you are interested in all aspects of a situation, you may be slow to reach decisions. Physically, you'll have good proportions and physical symmetry. You will move with natural grace and balance. You're likely to have pleasing, if not beautiful, facial features, with a winning smile, like Cary Grant. You'll show natural good taste and harmony in your clothes and home decor. Legal, diplomatic, or public relations professions could draw your interest.

Scorpio Rising: Air of Mystery

You project an intriguing air of mystery with this ascendant, as the Scorpio secretiveness and sense of underlying power combine with your sun sign. Like Jacqueline Kennedy Onassis, you convey that there's more to you than meets the eye. You seem like someone who is always in control and who can move comfortably in the world of power. Your physical look comes across as intense. Many of you have remarkable eyes, with a direct, penetrating gaze. But you'll never reveal your private agenda, and you tend to keep your true feelings under wraps (watch a tendency toward paranoia). You may have an interesting romantic history with secret love affairs, like Grace Kelly. Many of you heighten your air of mystery by wearing black. You're happiest near water; you should provide yourself with a seaside retreat.

Sagittarius Rising: The Explorer

You travel with this ascendant. You may also be a more outdoor, sportive type, with an athletic, casual, and outgoing air. Your moods are camouflaged with cheerful optimism or a philosophical attitude. Though you don't hesitate to speak your mind—like Ted Turner, who was called the Mouth of the South—you can also laugh at your troubles or crack a joke more easily than others of your sign. A Sagittarius ascendant can also draw you to the field of higher education or to spiritual life. You'll seem to have less attachment to things and people, and you may explore the globe. Your strong, fast legs are a physical bonus.

Capricorn Rising: Serious Business

This rising sign makes you come across as serious, goal-oriented, disciplined, and careful with cash. You are not one of the zodiac's big spenders, though you might splurge occasionally on items with good investment value. You're the conservative type in dress and environment, and you might come across as quite formal and businesslike, like Rupert Murdoch. You'll function well in a structured or corporate environment where you can climb to the top. (You are always aware of who's the boss.) In your personal life, you could be a loner or a single parent who is father and mother to your children.

Aquarius Rising: One of a Kind

You come across as less concerned about what others think and could even be a bit eccentric. Your appearance is sure to be unique and memorable. You're more at ease with groups of people than others in your sign, and you may be attracted to public life, like Jay Leno. Your appearance may be unique, either unconventional or unimportant to you. Those of you whose sun is in a water sign (Cancer, Scorpio, or Pisces) may exercise your nurturing qualities with a large group, an extended family, or a day-care or community center.

Pisces Rising: Romantic Roles

Your creative, nurturing talents are heightened and so is your ability to project emotional drama. And, like Antonio Banderas, your dreamy eyes and poetic air bring out the protective instinct in others. You could be attracted to the arts, especially theater, dance, film, and photography, or to psychology, spiritual practice, and charity work. You are happiest when you are using your creative ability to help others. Since you are vulnerable to mood swings, it is important for you to find interesting, creative work where you can express your talents and heighten your self-esteem. Accentuate the positive. Be wary of escapist tendencies, particularly involving alcohol or drugs to which you are supersensitive, like Whitney Houston.

RISING SIGNS—A.M. BIRTHS

	1 AM	2 AM	3 AM	4 AM	5 AM	6 AM	7 AM	8 AM	9 AM	10 AM	11 AM	12 NOON
Jan 1	Lib	Sc	Sc	Sc	Sag	Sag	Cap	Cap	Aq	Aq	Pis	Ar
Jan 9	Lib	Sc	Sc	Sag	Sag	Sag	Cap	Cap	Aq	Pis	Ar	Tau
Jan 17	Sc	Sc	Sc	Sag	Sag	Cap	Cap	Aq	Aq	Pis	Ar	Tau
Jan 25	Sc	Sc	Sag	Sag	Sag	Cap	Cap	Aq	Pis	Ar	Tau	Tau
Feb 2	Sc	Sc	Sag	Sag	Cap	Cap	Aq	Pis	Pis	Ar	Tau	Gem
Feb 10	Sc	Sag	Sag	Sag	Cap	Cap	Aq	Pis	Ar	Tau	Tau	Gem
Feb 18	Sc	Sag	Sag	Cap	Cap	Aq	Pis	Pis	Ar	Tau	Gem	Gem
Feb 26	Sag	Sag	Sag	Cap	Aq	Aq	Pis	Ar	Tau	Tau	Gem	Gem
Mar 6	Sag	Sag	Cap	Cap	Aq	Pis	Pis	Ar	Tau	Gem	Gem	Can
Mar 14	Sag	Cap	Cap	Aq	Aq	Pis	Ar	Tau	Tau	Gem	Gem	Can
Mar 22	Sag	Cap	Cap	Aq	Pis	Ar	Ar	Tau	Gem	Gem	Can	Can
Mar 30	Cap	Cap	Aq	Pis	Pis	Ar	Tau	Tau	Gem	Can	Can	Can
Apr 7	Cap	Cap	Aq	Pis	Ar	Ar	Tau	Gem	Gem	Can	Can	Leo
Apr 14	Cap	Aq	Aq	Pis	Ar	Tau	Tau	Gem	Gem	Can	Can	Leo
Apr 22	Cap	Aq	Pis	Ar	Ar	Tau	Gem	Gem	Gem	Can	Leo	Leo
Apr 30	Aq	Aq	Pis	Ar	Tau	Tau	Gem	Can	Can	Can	Leo	Leo
May 8	Aq	Pis	Ar	Ar	Tau	Gem	Gem	Can	Can	Leo	Leo	Leo
May 16	Aq	Pis	Ar	Tau	Gem	Gem	Can	Can	Can	Leo	Leo	Vir
May 24	Pis	Ar	Ar	Tau	Gem	Gem	Can	Can	Leo	Leo	Leo	Vir
June 1	Pis	Ar	Tau	Gem	Gem	Can	Can	Can	Leo	Leo	Vir	Vir
June 9	Ar	Ar	Tau	Gem	Gem	Can	Can	Leo	Leo	Leo	Vir	Vir
June 17	Ar	Tau	Gem	Gem	Can	Can	Can	Leo	Leo	Vir	Vir	Vir
June 25	Tau	Tau	Gem	Can	Can	Can	Leo	Leo	Leo	Vir	Vir	Lib
July 3	Tau	Gem	Gem	Can	Can	Can	Leo	Leo	Vir	Vir	Vir	Lib
July 11	Tau	Gem	Gem	Can	Can	Leo	Leo	Leo	Vir	Vir	Lib	Lib
July 18	Gem	Gem	Can	Can	Can	Leo	Leo	Vir	Vir	Vir	Lib	Lib
July 26	Gem	Gem	Can	Can	Leo	Leo	Vir	Vir	Vir	Lib	Lib	Lib
Aug 3	Gem	Can	Can	Can	Leo	Leo	Vir	Vir	Vir	Lib	Lib	Sc
Aug 11	Gem	Can	Can	Leo	Leo	Leo	Vir	Vir	Lib	Lib	Lib	Sc
Aug 18	Can	Can	Can	Leo	Leo	Vir	Vir	Vir	Lib	Lib	Sc	Sc
Aug 27	Can	Can	Leo	Leo	Leo	Vir	Vir	Lib	Lib	Lib	Sc	Sc
Sept 4	Can	Can	Leo	Leo	Leo	Vir	Vir	Vir	Lib	Lib	Sc	Sc
Sept 12	Can	Leo	Leo	Leo	Vir	Vir	Lib	Lib	Lib	Sc	Sc	Sag
Sept 20	Leo	Leo	Leo	Vir	Vir	Vir	Lib	Lib	Sc	Sc	Sc	Sag
Sept 28	Leo	Leo	Leo	Vir	Vir	Lib	Lib	Lib	Sc	Sc	Sag	Sag
Oct 6	Leo	Leo	Vir	Vir	Vir	Lib	Lib	Sc	Sc	Sc	Sag	Sag
Oct 14	Leo	Vir	Vir	Vir	Lib	Lib	Lib	Sc	Sc	Sag	Sag	Cap
Oct 22	Leo	Vir	Vir	Lib	Lib	Lib	Sc	Sc	Sc	Sag	Sag	Cap
Oct 30	Vir	Vir	Vir	Lib	Lib	Sc	Sc	Sc	Sag	Sag	Cap	Cap
Nov 7	Vir	Vir	Lib	Lib	Lib	Sc	Sc	Sc	Sag	Sag	Cap	Cap
Nov 15	Vir	Vir	Lib	Lib	Sc	Sc	Sc	Sag	Sag	Cap	Cap	Aq
Nov 23	Vir	Lib	Lib	Lib	Sc	Sc	Sag	Sag	Sag	Cap	Cap	Aq
Dec 1	Vir	Lib	Lib	Sc	Sc	Sc	Sag	Sag	Cap	Cap	Aq	Aq
Dec 9	Lib	Lib	Lib	Sc	Sc	Sag	Sag	Sag	Cap	Cap	Aq	Pis
Dec 18	Lib	Lib	Sc	Sc	Sc	Sag	Sag	Cap	Cap	Aq	Aq	Pis
Dec 28	Lib	Lib	Sc	Sc	Sag	Sag	Sag	Cap	Aq	Aq	Pis	Ar

RISING SIGNS—P.M. BIRTHS

	1 PM	2 PM	3 PM	4 PM	5 PM	6 PM	7 PM	8 PM	9 PM	10 PM	11 PM	12 MID-NIGHT
Jan 1	Tau	Gem	Gem	Can	Can	Can	Leo	Leo	Vir	Vir	Vir	Lib
Jan 9	Tau	Gem	Gem	Can	Can	Leo	Leo	Leo	Vir	Vir	Vir	Lib
Jan 17	Gem	Gem	Can	Can	Can	Leo	Leo	Vir	Vir	Vir	Lib	Lib
Jan 25	Gem	Gem	Can	Can	Leo	Leo	Leo	Vir	Vir	Lib	Lib	Lib
Feb 2	Gem	Can	Can	Can	Leo	Leo	Vir	Vir	Vir	Lib	Lib	Sc
Feb 10	Gem	Can	Can	Leo	Leo	Leo	Vir	Vir	Lib	Lib	Lib	Sc
Feb 18	Can	Can	Can	Leo	Leo	Vir	Vir	Vir	Lib	Lib	Sc	Sc
Feb 26	Can	Can	Leo	Leo	Leo	Vir	Vir	Lib	Lib	Lib	Sc	Sc
Mar 6	Can	Leo	Leo	Leo	Vir	Vir	Vir	Lib	Lib	Sc	Sc	Sc
Mar 14	Can	Leo	Leo	Vir	Vir	Vir	Lib	Lib	Lib	Sc	Sc	Sc
Mar 22	Leo	Leo	Leo	Vir	Vir	Lib	Lib	Lib	Sc	Sc	Sc	Sag
Mar 30	Leo	Leo	Vir	Vir	Vir	Lib	Lib	Sc	Sc	Sc	Sag	Sag
Apr 7	Leo	Leo	Vir	Vir	Lib	Lib	Lib	Sc	Sc	Sc	Sag	Sag
Apr 14	Leo	Vir	Vir	Vir	Lib	Lib	Sc	Sc	Sc	Sag	Sag	Cap
Apr 22	Leo	Vir	Vir	Lib	Lib	Lib	Sc	Sc	Sc	Sag	Sag	Cap
Apr 30	Vir	Vir	Vir	Lib	Lib	Sc	Sc	Sc	Sag	Sag	Cap	Cap
May 8	Vir	Vir	Lib	Lib	Lib	Sc	Sc	Sag	Sag	Sag	Cap	Cap
May 16	Vir	Vir	Lib	Lib	Sc	Sc	Sc	Sag	Sag	Cap	Cap	Aq
May 24	Vir	Lib	Lib	Lib	Sc	Sc	Sag	Sag	Sag	Cap	Cap	Aq
June 1	Vir	Lib	Lib	Sc	Sc	Sc	Sag	Sag	Cap	Cap	Aq	Aq
June 9	Lib	Lib	Lib	Sc	Sc	Sag	Sag	Sag	Cap	Cap	Aq	Pis
June 17	Lib	Lib	Sc	Sc	Sc	Sag	Sag	Cap	Cap	Aq	Aq	Pis
June 25	Lib	Lib	Sc	Sc	Sag	Sag	Sag	Cap	Cap	Aq	Pis	Ar
July 3	Lib	Sc	Sc	Sc	Sag	Sag	Cap	Cap	Aq	Aq	Pis	Ar
July 11	Lib	Sc	Sc	Sag	Sag	Sag	Cap	Cap	Aq	Pis	Ar	Tau
July 18	Sc	Sc	Sc	Sag	Sag	Cap	Cap	Aq	Aq	Pis	Ar	Tau
July 26	Sc	Sc	Sag	Sag	Sag	Cap	Cap	Aq	Pis	Pis	Ar	Tau
Aug 3	Sc	Sc	Sag	Sag	Cap	Cap	Aq	Aq	Pis	Ar	Tau	Gem
Aug 11	Sc	Sag	Sag	Sag	Cap	Cap	Aq	Pis	Ar	Tau	Tau	Gem
Aug 18	Sc	Sag	Sag	Cap	Cap	Aq	Pis	Pis	Ar	Tau	Gem	Gem
Aug 27	Sag	Sag	Sag	Cap	Cap	Aq	Pis	Ar	Tau	Tau	Gem	Gem
Sept 4	Sag	Sag	Cap	Cap	Aq	Pis	Pis	Ar	Tau	Gem	Gem	Can
Sept 12	Sag	Sag	Cap	Aq	Aq	Pis	Ar	Tau	Tau	Gem	Gem	Can
Sept 20	Sag	Cap	Cap	Aq	Aq	Pis	Pis	Ar	Tau	Gem	Gem	Can
Sept 28	Cap	Cap	Aq	Aq	Pis	Ar	Tau	Tau	Gem	Gem	Can	Can
Oct 6	Cap	Cap	Aq	Pis	Ar	Ar	Tau	Gem	Gem	Can	Can	Leo
Oct 14	Cap	Aq	Aq	Pis	Ar	Tau	Tau	Gem	Gem	Can	Can	Leo
Oct 22	Cap	Aq	Pis	Ar	Ar	Tau	Gem	Gem	Can	Can	Leo	Leo
Oct 30	Aq	Aq	Pis	Ar	Tau	Tau	Gem	Can	Can	Can	Leo	Leo
Nov 7	Aq	Aq	Pis	Ar	Tau	Tau	Gem	Can	Can	Leo	Leo	Leo
Nov 15	Aq	Pis	Ar	Tau	Tau	Gem	Can	Can	Can	Leo	Leo	Vir
Nov 23	Pis	Ar	Ar	Tau	Gem	Gem	Can	Can	Leo	Leo	Leo	Vir
Dec 1	Pis	Ar	Tau	Gem	Gem	Can	Can	Leo	Leo	Leo	Vir	Vir
Dec 9	Ar	Tau	Tau	Gem	Gem	Can	Can	Leo	Leo	Vir	Vir	Vir
Dec 18	Ar	Tau	Gem	Gem	Can	Can	Leo	Leo	Vir	Vir	Vir	Vir
Dec 28	Tau	Tau	Gem	Gem	Can	Can	Leo	Leo	Vir	Vir	Vir	Lib

CHAPTER 7

The Keys to Reading Your Horoscope: The Glyphs

Are you ready to take your astrology knowledge to the next level and read your first horoscope chart? If so, you'll encounter a new language of symbols, because horoscope charts are written in glyphs, a centuries-old pictographic language. These little "pictures" are a type of shorthand used by astrologers around the world to indicate the planets and the signs.

There's no way to avoid learning the glyphs, if you want to get deeper into astrology. Whether you download your chart from one of the many Internet sites that offer free charts or you buy one of the many interesting astrology programs, you'll find charts are always written in glyph language. Some software makes it easier for beginners by listing the planets and their signs in English alongside the chart and other programs will pop up an English interpretation as your roll your mouse over the glyph. However, in the long run, it's much easier—and more fun—to learn the glyphs yourself.

There's an extra bonus to learning the glyphs: They contain a kind of visual code, with built-in clues that will tell you not only which sign or planet each represents, but what the symbol means in a deeper, more esoteric sense. Actually the physical act of writing the symbol is a mystical experience in itself, a way to invoke the deeper meaning of the sign or planet through age-old visual elements that have been with us since time began.

Since there are only twelve signs and ten planets (not counting a few asteroids and other space objects some astrologers use), it's a lot easier than learning to read a foreign language. Here's a code cracker for the glyphs, beginning with the glyphs for the planets. To those who already know their glyphs, don't just skim over the chapter. These familiar graphics have hidden meanings you will discover!

The Glyphs for the Planets

The glyphs for the planets are easy to learn. They're simple combinations of the most basic visual elements: the circle, the semicircle or arc, and the cross. However, each component of a glyph has a special meaning in relation to the other parts of the symbol.

The circle, which has no beginning or end, is one of the oldest symbols of spirit or spiritual forces. Early diagrams of the heavens—spiritual territory—are shown in circular form. The never-ending line of the circle is the perfect symbol for eternity. The semicircle or arc is an incomplete circle, symbolizing the receptive, finite soul, which contains spiritual potential in the curving line.

The vertical line of the cross symbolizes movement from heaven to earth. The horizontal line describes temporal movement, here and now, in time and space. Combined in a cross, the vertical and horizontal planes symbolize manifestation in the material world.

The Sun Glyph ☉

The sun is always shown by this powerful solar symbol, a circle with a point in the center. The center point is you, your spiritual center, and the symbol represents your infinite personality incarnating (the point) into the finite cycles of birth and death.

The sun has been represented by a circle or disk since ancient Egyptian times when the solar disk represented the sun god, Ra. Some archaeologists believe the great stone circles found in England were centers of sun worship. This particular version of the symbol was brought into common use in the sixteenth century after German occultist and scholar Cornelius Agrippa (1486–1535) wrote a book called *Die Occulta Philosophia*, which became accepted as the authority in the field. Agrippa collected many of the medieval astrological and magical symbols in this book, which have been used by astrologers since then.

The Moon Glyph ☽

The moon glyph is the most recognizable symbol on a chart, a left-facing arc stylized into the crescent moon. As part of a circle, the arc symbolizes the potential fulfillment of the entire circle, the life force that is still incomplete. Therefore, it is the ideal representation of the reactive, receptive, emotional nature of the moon.

The Mercury Glyph ☿

Mercury contains all three elemental symbols: the crescent, the circle, and the cross in vertical order. This is the "Venus with a hat" glyph (compare with the symbol of Venus). With another stretch of the imagination, can't you see the winged cap of Mercury the messenger? Think of the upturned crescent as antennae that tune in and transmit messages from the sun, reminding you that Mercury is the way you communicate, the way your mind works. The upturned arc is receiving energy into the spirit or solar circle, which will later be translated into action on the material plane, symbolized by the cross. All the elements are equally sized because Mercury is neutral; it doesn't play favorites! This planet symbolizes objective, detached, unemotional thinking.

The Venus Glyph ♀

Here the relationship is between two components: the circle of spirit and the cross of matter. Spirit is elevated over matter, pulling it upward. Venus asks, "What is beautiful? What do you like best? What do you love to have done to you?" Consequently, Venus determines both your ideal of beauty and what feels good sensually. It governs your own allure and power to attract, as well as what attracts and pleases you.

The Mars Glyph ♂

In this glyph, the cross of matter is stylized into an arrowhead pointed up and outward, propelled by the circle of spirit. With a little imagination, you can visualize it as the shield and spear of Mars, the ancient god of war. You can deduce that Mars embodies your spiritual energy projected into the outer world. It's your assertiveness, your initiative, your aggressive drive, what you like to do to others, your temper. If you know someone's Mars, you know whether they'll blow up when angry or do a slow burn. Your task is to use your outgoing Mars energy wisely and well.

The Jupiter Glyph ♃

Jupiter is the basic cross of matter, with a large stylized crescent perched on the left side of the horizontal, temporal plane. You might think of the crescent as an open hand, because one meaning of Jupiter is "luck," what's handed to you. You don't have to work for what you get from Jupiter; it comes to you, if you're open to it.

The Jupiter glyph might also remind you of a jumbo jet plane, with a huge tail fin, about to take off. This is the planet of travel, mental and spiritual, of expanding your horizons via new ideas, new spiritual dimensions, and new places. Jupiter embodies the optimism and enthusiasm of the traveler about to embark on an exciting adventure.

The Saturn Glyph ♄

Flip Jupiter over, and you've got Saturn. This might not be immediately apparent because Saturn is usually stylized into an "h" form like the one shown here. The principle it expresses is the opposite of Jupiter's expansive tendencies. Saturn pulls you back to earth: the receptive arc is pushed down underneath the cross of matter. Before there are any rewards or expansion, the duties and obligations of the material world must be considered. Saturn says, "Stop, wait, finish your chores before you take off!"

Saturn's glyph also resembles the sickle of old "Father Time."

Saturn was first known as Chronos, the Greek god of time, for time brings all matter to an end. When it was the most distant planet (before the discovery of Uranus), Saturn was believed to be the place where time stopped. After the soul departed from earth, it journeyed back to the outer reaches of the universe and finally stopped at Saturn, or at "the end of time."

The Uranus Glyph ♅

The glyph for Uranus is often stylized to form a capital *H* after Sir William Herschel, who discovered the planet. But the more esoteric version curves the two pillars of the H into crescent antennae, or "ears," like satellite disks receiving signals from space. These are perched on the horizontal material line of the cross of matter and pushed from below by the circle of the spirit. To many sci-fi fans, Uranus looks like an orbiting satellite.

Uranus channels the highest energy of all, the white electrical light of the universal spiritual force that holds the cosmos together. This pure electrical energy is gathered from all over the universe. Because Uranus energy doesn't follow any ordinary celestial drumbeat, it can't be controlled or predicted (which is also true of those who are strongly influenced by this eccentric planet). In the symbol, this energy is manifested through the balance of polarities (the two opposite arms of the glyph) like the two polarized wires of a lightbulb.

The Neptune Glyph ♆

Neptune's glyph is usually stylized to look like a trident, the weapon of the Roman god Neptune. However, on a more esoteric level, it shows the large upturned crescent of the soul pierced through by the cross of matter. Neptune nails down, or materializes, soul energy, bringing impulses from the soul level into manifestation. That is why Neptune is associated with imagination or "imagining in," making an image of the soul. Neptune works through feelings, sensitivity, and the mystical capacity to bring the divine into the earthly realm.

The Pluto Glyph ♀

Pluto is written two ways. One is a composite of the letters *PL,* the first two letters of the word Pluto and coincidentally the initials of Percival Lowell, one of the planet's discoverers. The other, more esoteric symbol is a small circle above a large open crescent that surmounts the cross of matter. This depicts Pluto's power to regenerate. Imagine a new little spirit emerging from the sheltering cup of the soul. Pluto rules the forces of life and death. After this planet has passed a sensitive point in your chart, you are transformed, reborn in some way.

Sci-fi fans might visualize this glyph as a small satellite (the circle) being launched. It was shortly after Pluto's discovery that we learned how to harness the nuclear forces that made space exploration possible. Pluto rules the transformative power of atomic energy, which totally changed our lives and from which there is no turning back.

The Glyphs for the Signs

On an astrology chart, the glyph for the sign will appear after that of the planet. For example, when you see the moon glyph followed first by a number and then by another glyph representing the sign, this means that the moon was passing over a certain degree of that astrological sign at the time of the chart. On the dividing lines between the houses on your chart, you'll find the symbol for the sign that rules the house.

Because sun sign symbols do not contain the same basic geometric components of the planetary glyphs, we must look elsewhere for clues to their meanings. Many have been passed down from ancient Egyptian and Chaldean civilizations with few modifications. Others have been adapted over the centuries.

In deciphering many of the glyphs, you'll often find that the symbols reveal a dual nature of the sign, which is not always apparent in the usual sun sign descriptions. For instance, the Gemini glyph is similar to the Roman numeral for two, and reveals this sign's longing to discover a twin soul. The Cancer glyph may be interpreted as resembling either the nurturing breasts or the self-protective claws of a crab, both symbols associated with the contrasting qualities of this sign. Libra's glyph embodies the duality of the spirit balanced with material reality. The Sagittarius glyph shows that the aspirant must also carry along the earthly animal nature in his quest. The Capricorn sea goat is another symbol with dual emphasis. The goat climbs high, yet is always pulled back by the deep waters of the unconscious. Aquarius embodies the double waves of mental detachment, balanced by the desire for connection with others, in a friendly way. Finally, the two fishes of Pisces, which are forever tied together, show the duality of the soul and the spirit that must be reconciled.

The Aries Glyph ♈

Since the symbol for Aries is the Ram, this glyph is obviously associated with a ram's horns, which characterize one aspect of the Aries personality—an aggressive, me-first, leaping-headfirst attitude. But the symbol can be interpreted in other ways as well. Some astrologers liken it to a fountain of energy, which Aries people also embody. The first sign of the zodiac bursts on the scene eagerly, ready to go. Another analogy is to the eyebrows and nose of the human head, which Aries rules, and the thinking power that is initiated by the brain.

One theory of this symbol links it to the Egyptian god Amun, represented by a ram in ancient times. As Amun-Ra, this god was believed to embody the creator of the universe, the leader of all the other gods. This relates easily to the position of Aries as the leader (or first sign) of the zodiac, which begins at the spring equinox, a time of the year when nature is renewed.

The Taurus Glyph ♉

This is another easy glyph to draw and identify. It takes little imagination to decipher the bull's head with long curving horns. Like its symbol the Bull, the archetypal Taurus is slow to anger but ferocious when provoked, as well as stubborn, steady, and sensual. Another association is the larynx (and thyroid) of the throat area (ruled by Taurus) and the eustachian tubes running up to the ears, which coincides with the relationship of Taurus to the voice, song, and music. Many famous singers, musicians, and composers have prominent Taurus influences.

Many ancient religions involved a bull as the central figure in fertility rites or initiations, usually symbolizing the victory of man over his animal nature. Another possible origin is in the sacred bull of Egypt, who embodied the incarnate form of Osiris, god of death and resurrection. In early Christian imagery, the Taurus Bull represented St. Luke.

The Gemini Glyph ♊

The standard glyph immediately calls to mind the Roman numeral for two (II) and the Twins symbol, as it is called, for Gemini. In almost all drawings and images used for this sign, the relationship between two persons is emphasized. Usually one twin will be touching the other, which signifies communication, human contact, the desire to share.

The top line of the Gemini glyph indicates mental communication, while the bottom line indicates shared physical space.

The most famous Gemini legend is that of the twin sons Castor and Pollux, one of whom had a mortal father while the other was the son of Zeus, king of the gods. When it came time for the mortal twin to die, his grief-stricken brother pleaded with Zeus, who agreed to let them spend half the year on earth in mortal form and half in immortal life, with the gods on Mount Olympus. This reflects a basic duality of humankind, which possesses an immortal soul yet is also subject to the limits of mortality.

The Cancer Glyph ♋

Two convenient images relate to the Cancer glyph. It is easiest to decode the curving claws of the Cancer symbol, the Crab. Like the crab's, Cancer's element is water. This sensitive sign also has a hard protective shell to protect its tender interior. The crab must be wily to escape predators, scampering sideways and hiding under rocks. The crab also responds to the cycles of the moon, as do all shellfish. The other image is that of two female breasts, which Cancer rules, showing that this is a sign that nurtures and protects others as well as itself.

In ancient Egypt, Cancer was also represented by the scarab beetle, a symbol of regeneration and eternal life.

The Leo Glyph ♌

Notice that the Leo glyph seems to be an extension of Cancer's glyph, with a significant difference. In the Cancer glyph, the lines curve inward protectively. The Leo glyph expresses energy outwardly. And there is no duality in the symbol, the Lion, or in Leo, the sign.

Lions have belonged to the sign of Leo since earliest times. It is not difficult to imagine the king of beasts with his sweeping mane and curling tail from this glyph. The upward sweep of the glyph easily describes the positive energy of Leo: the flourishing tail, the flamboyant qualities. Another analogy, perhaps a stretch of the imagination, is that of a heart leaping up with joy and enthusiasm, also very typical of Leo, which also rules the heart. In early Christian imagery, the Leo Lion represented St. Mark.

The Virgo Glyph ♍

You can read much into this mysterious glyph. For instance, it could represent the initials of "Mary Virgin," or a young woman holding a staff of wheat, or stylized female genitalia, all common interpretations. The M shape might also remind you that Virgo is ruled by Mercury. The cross beneath the symbol reveals the grounded, practical nature of this earth sign.

The earliest zodiacs link Virgo with the Egyptian goddess Isis, who gave birth to the god Horus after her husband Osiris had been killed, in the archetype of a miraculous conception. There are many ancient statues of Isis nursing her baby son, which are reminiscent of medieval Virgin and Child motifs. This sign has also been associated with the image of the Holy Grail, when the Virgo symbol was substituted with a chalice.

The Libra Glyph ♎

It is not difficult to read the standard image for Libra, the Scales, into this glyph. There is another meaning, however, that is equally relevant: the setting sun as it descends over the horizon. Libra's natural position on the zodiac wheel is the descendant, or sunset position (as the Aries natural position is the ascendant, or rising sign). Both images relate to Libra's personality. Libra is always weighing pros and cons for a balanced decision. In the sunset image, the sun (male) hovers over the horizontal earth (female) before setting. Libra is the space between these lines, harmonizing yin and yang, spiritual and material, male and female, ideal and real worlds. The glyph has also been linked to the kidneys, which are associated with Libra.

The Scorpio Glyph ♏

With its barbed tail, this glyph is easy to identify as the Scorpion for the sign of Scorpio. It also represents the male sexual parts, over which the sign rules. From the arrowhead, you can draw the conclusion that Mars was once its ruler. Some earlier Egyptian glyphs for Scorpio represent it as an erect serpent, so the Serpent is an alternate symbol.

Another symbol for Scorpio, which is not identifiable in this glyph, is the Eagle. Scorpios can go to extremes, either in soaring like the eagle or self-destructing like the scorpion. In early Christian imagery, which often used zodiacal symbols, the Scorpio Eagle was chosen to symbolize the intense apostle St. John the Evangelist.

The Sagittarius Glyph ♐

This is one of the easiest to spot and draw: an upward pointing arrow lifting up a cross. The arrow is pointing skyward, while the cross represents the four elements of the material world, which the arrow must convey. Elevating materiality into spirituality is an important Sagittarius quality, which explains why this sign is associated with higher learning, religion, philosophy, travel—the aspiring professions. Sagittarius can also send barbed arrows of frankness in the pursuit of truth, so the Archer symbol for Sagittarius is apt. (Sagittarius is also the sign of the supersalesman.)

Sagittarius is symbolically represented by the centaur, a mythological creature who is half man, half horse, aiming his arrow toward the skies. Though Sagittarius is motivated by spiritual aspiration, it also must balance the powerful appetites of the animal nature. The centaur Chiron, a figure in Greek mythology, became a wise teacher who, after many adventures and world travels, was killed by a poisoned arrow.

The Capricorn Glyph ♑

One of the most difficult symbols to draw, this glyph may take some practice. It is a representation of the sea goat: a mythical animal that is a goat with a curving fish's tail. The goat part of Capricorn wants to leave the waters of the emotions and climb to the elevated areas of life. But the fish tail is the unconscious, the deep chaotic psychic level that draws the goat back. Capricorn is often trying to escape the deep, feeling part of life by submerging himself in work, steadily ascending to the top. To some people, the glyph represents a seated figure with a bent knee, a reminder that Capricorn governs the knee area of the body.

An interesting aspect of this glyph is the contrast of the sharp pointed horns—which represent the penetrating, shrewd, conscious side of Capricorn—with the swishing tail—which represents its serpentine, unconscious, emotional force. One Capricorn legend, which dates from Roman times, tells of the earthy fertility god, Pan, who tried to save himself from uncontrollable sexual desires by jumping into the Nile. His upper body then turned into a goat, while the lower part became a fish. Later, Jupiter gave him a safe haven as a constellation in the skies.

The Aquarius Glyph ♒

This ancient water symbol can be traced back to an Egyptian hieroglyph representing streams of life force. Symbolized by the Water Bearer, Aquarius is distributor of the waters of life—the magic liquid of regeneration. The two waves can also be linked to the positive and negative charges of the electrical energy that Aquarius rules, a sort of universal wavelength. Aquarius is tuned in intuitively to higher forces via this electrical force. The duality of the glyph could also refer to the dual nature of Aquarius, a sign that runs hot and cold and that is friendly but also detached in the mental world of air signs.

In Greek legends, Aquarius is represented by Ganymede, who was carried to heaven by an eagle in order to become the cupbearer of Zeus and to supervise the annual flooding of the Nile. The sign later became associated with aviation and notions of flight. Like the other fixed signs (Taurus, Scorpio, and Leo), Aquarius is associated with an apostle, in this case St. Matthew.

The Pisces Glyph ♓

Here is an abstraction of the familiar image of Pisces, two Fishes swimming in opposite directions yet bound together by a cord. The Fishes represent the spirit—which yearns for the freedom of heaven—and the soul—which remains attached to the desires of the temporal world. During life on earth, the spirit and the soul are bound together. When they complement each other, instead of pulling in opposite directions, they facilitate the Pisces creativity. The ancient version of this glyph, taken from the Egyptians, had no connecting line, which was added in the fourteenth century.

In another interpretation, it is said that the left fish indicates the direction of involution or the beginning of a cycle, while the right fish signifies the direction of evolution, the way to completion of a cycle. It's an appropriate grand finale for Pisces, the last sign of the zodiac.

CHAPTER 8

Join the Astrology Community

Astrology fans love to share their knowledge and socialize. So why not join the community of astrologers online or at a conference? You might be surprised to find an astrology club in your local area. Connecting with other astrology fans and learning more about this fascinating subject has never been easier. In fact the many options available with just a click of your computer are mind-boggling.

You need only type the word *astrology* into any Internet search engine and watch hundreds of listings of astrology-related sites pop up. There are local meetings and international conferences where you can meet and study with other astrologers, and books and tapes to help you learn at home. You could even combine your vacation with an astrological workshop in an exotic locale, such as Bali or Mexico.

To help you sort out the variety of options available, here are our top picks of the Internet and the astrological community at large.

National Council for Geocosmic Research (NCGR)

Whether you'd like to know more about such specialties as financial astrology or techniques for timing events, or if you'd prefer the psychological or mythological approach, you'll meet the top astrologers at conferences sponsored by the National Council for Geocosmic Research. NCGR is dedicated to providing quality education, bringing astrologers and astrology fans together at conferences, and promoting fellowship. Their course structure provides a systematized study of the many facets of astrology. The organization sponsors educational workshops, taped lectures, conferences, and a directory of professional astrologers.

For an annual membership fee, you get their excellent publications and newsletters, plus the opportunity to network with other astrology buffs at local chapter events. At this writing there are chapters in twenty-six states and four countries.

To join NCGR and for the latest information on upcoming events and chapters in your city, consult their Web site: www.geocosmic.org.

American Federation of Astrologers (AFA)

Established in 1938, this is one of the oldest astrological organizations in the United States. AFA offers conferences, conventions, and a correspondence course. If you are looking for a reading, their interesting Web site will refer you to an accredited AFA astrologer.

6535 South Rural Road
Tempe, AZ 85283
Phone: (888) 301-7630 or (480) 838-1751
Fax: (480) 838-8293
Web site: www.astrologers.com

Association for Astrological Networking (AFAN)

Did you know that astrologers are still being harassed for practicing astrology? AFAN provides support and legal information, and works toward improving the public image of astrology. AFAN's network of local astrologers links with the international astrological community. Here are the people who will go to bat for astrology when it is attacked in the media. Everyone who cares about astrology should join!

8306 Wilshire Boulevard
PMB 537
Beverly Hills, CA 90211
Phone: (800) 578-2326
E-mail: info@afan.org
Web site: www.afan.org

International Society for Astrology Research (ISAR)

An international organization of professional astrologers dedicated to encouraging the highest standards of quality in the field of astrology with an emphasis on research. Among ISAR's benefits are quarterly journals, a weekly e-mail newsletter, and a free membership directory.

P.O. Box 38613
Los Angeles, CA 90038
Fax: (805) 933-0301
Web site: www.isarastrology.com

Astrology Magazines

In addition to articles by top astrologers, most have listings of astrology conferences, events, and local happenings.

Horoscope Guide
Kappa Publishing Group
6198 Butler Pike
Suite 200
Blue Bell, PA 19422-2600
Web site: www.kappapublishing.com/astrology

Dell Horoscope
Their Web site features a listing of local astrological meetings.

Customer Service
6 Prowitt Street
Norwalk, CT 06855
Phone: (800) 220-7443
Web site: www.dellhoroscope.com

The Mountain Astrologer
A favorite magazine of astrology fans, *The Mountain Astrologer* also has an interesting Web site featuring the latest news from an astrological point of view, plus feature articles from the magazine.

P.O. Box 970
Cedar Ridge, CA 95924
Web site: www.mountainastrologer.com

Astrology College

Kepler College of Astrological Arts and Sciences

A degree-granting college, which is also a center of astrology, has long been the dream of the astrological community and is a giant step forward in providing credibility to the profession. Therefore, the opening of Kepler College in 2000 was a historical event for astrology. It is the only college in the United States authorized to issue BA and MA degrees in astrological studies. Here is where to study with the best scholars, teachers, and communicators in the field. A long-distance study program is available for those interested.

Kepler College also offers online noncredit courses that anyone can take via the Kepler Community Learning Center. Classes range from two days to ten weeks in length, and the cost will vary depending upon the class taken. Students can access an online Web site to enroll in specific classes and interact with other students and instructors.

For more information, contact:

4630 200th Street SW
Suite P
Lynnwood, WA 98036
Phone: (425) 673-4292
Fax: (425) 673-4983
Web site: www.kepler.edu

Our Favorite Web sites

Of the thousands of astrological Web sites that come and go on the Internet, these have stood the test of time and are likely to still be operating when this book is published.

Astrodienst (www.astro.com)

Don't miss this fabulous international site, which has long been one of the best astrology resources on the Internet. It's a great place to view your own astrology chart. The world atlas on this site will give you the accurate longitude and latitude of your birthplace for setting up your horoscope. Then you can print out your free chart in a range of easy-to-read formats. Other attractions: a list of famous people born on your birth date, a feature that helps you choose the best vacation spot, and articles by world-famous astrologers.

AstroDatabank (www.astrodatabank.com)

When the news is breaking, you can bet this site will be the first to get accurate birthdays of the headliners. The late astrologer Lois Rodden was a stickler for factual information and her meticulous research is being continued, much to the benefit of the astrological community. The Web site specializes in charts of current newsmakers, political figures, and international celebrities. You can also participate in discussions and analysis of the charts and see what some of the world's best astrologers have to say about them. Their AstroDatabank program, which you can purchase at the site, provides thousands of birthdays sorted into categories. It's an excellent research tool.

StarIQ (www.stariq.com)

Find out how top astrologers view the latest headlines at the must-see StarIQ site. Many of the best minds in astrology comment on the latest news, stock market ups and downs, and political contenders. You can sign up to receive e-mail forecasts at the most important times keyed to your individual chart. (This is one of the best of the online forecasts.)

Astro-Noetics (www.astro-noetics.com)

For those who are ready to explore astrology's interface with politics, popular culture, and current events, here is a sophisticated site with in-depth articles and personality profiles. Lots of depth and content here for the astrology-savvy surfer.

Astrology Books (www.astroamerica.com)

The Astrology Center of America sells a wide selection of books on all aspects of astrology, from the basics to the most advanced, at this online bookstore. Also available are many hard-to-find and used books.

Astrology Scholars' Sites

See what Robert Hand, one of astrology's great teachers, has to offer on his site at www.robhand.com. A leading expert on the history of astrology, he's on the cutting edge of the latest research.

The Project Hindsight group of astrologers is devoted to restoring the astrology of the Hellenistic period, the primary source for all later Western astrology. There are fascinating articles for astrology fans on this site at www.projecthindsight.com.

Financial Astrology Sites

Financial astrology is a hot specialty, with many tipsters, players, and theorists. There are online columns, newsletters, specialized financial astrology software, and mutual funds run by astrology seers. One of the more respected financial astrologers is Ray Merriman, whose market comments on www.mmacycles.com are a must for those following the bulls and bears.

Explore Your Relationships (www.topsynergy.com)

Ever wondered how you'd get along with Brad Pitt, Halle Berry, or another famous hottie? TopSynergy offers a clever tool called a relationship analyst that will help you use astrology to analyze past, present, or possible future relationships. There's a database of celebrity horoscopes for you to partner with your own as well. It's free for unlimited use.

How to Zoom Around the Sky

If you haven't already discovered the wonders of Google Earth (www.earth.google.com), then you've been missing close-up aerial views of anyplace on the planet from your old hometown to the beaches of Hawaii. Even more fascinating for astrology buffs is the newest feature called Google Sky, a marvel of computer technology that lets you view the sky overhead from anyplace you choose. Want to see the stars over Paris at the moment? A few clicks of your mouse will take you there. Then you can follow the tracks of the sun, moon, and planets or check astronomical information and beautiful Hubble images. Go to the Google Web site to download this free program. Then get ready to take a cosmic tour around the earth and sky.

Listen to the Sounds of Your Sign

Astrology Weekly (www.astrologyweekly.com) is a Web site from Romania, with lots to offer astro surfers. Here you can check all the planetary placements for the week, get free charts, join an international discussion group, and check out charts for countries and world leaders. Of special interest is the chart generator, an easy-to-use feature that will create a natal chart. Just click on *new chart* and enter the year, month, day, time, longitude, and latitude of your birth place. Select the Placidus or Koch house system and click on *show it*. Your chart should come right up on the screen. You can then copy the link to your astrology chart, store it, and later share your chart with friends. If you don't have astrology software, this is a good way to view charts instantly. This site also has some fun ways to pass the time, such as listening to music especially chosen for your sun sign.

Stellar Gifts

If you've ever wondered what to give your astrology buddies, here's the place to find foolproof gifts. How about a mug, mouse pad, or plaque decorated with someone's chart? Would a special person like a pendant personalized with their planets? Check out www.milestonegifts.co.uk for some great ideas for putting those astrology charts to decorative use.

CHAPTER 9

The Best Astrology Software: Take Your Knowledge to the Next Level

Are you ready to begin looking at charts of friends and family? Would you like to call up your favorite celebrity's chart or check the aspects every day on your BlackBerry? Perhaps you'd like to study astrology in depth and would prefer a more comprehensive program that adapts to your needs as you learn. If you haven't discovered the wonders of astrology software, you're missing out!

Astrology technology has advanced to the point where even a computerphobe can call up a Web site on a BlackBerry browser and put a chart on the screen in seconds. It does help to have some basic knowledge of the signs, houses, planets, and especially the glyphs for the planets and the signs. Then you can practice reading charts and relating the planets to the lives of friends, relatives, and daily events, the ideal way to get more involved with astrology.

There's a program for every level of interest at all price points—starting with free. For the dabbler, there are the affordable Winstar Express, Know, and Time Passages. For the serious student, there are Astrology (free), Solar Fire, Kepler, Winstar Plus—software that does every technique on the planet and gives you beautiful chart printouts. If you're a MAC user, you'll be satisfied with the wonderful IO and Time Passages software.

However, since all the programs use the astrology symbols, or glyphs, for planets and signs, rather than written words, you should learn the glyphs before you purchase your software. Chapter 7 will help you do just that. Here are some software options for you to explore.

Easy for Beginners

Time Passages

Designed for either a Macintosh or Windows computer, Time Passages is straightforward and easy to use. It allows you to generate charts and interpretation reports for yourself or friends and loved ones at the touch of a button. If you haven't yet learned the astrology symbols, this might be the program for you. Just roll your mouse over any symbols of the planets, signs, or house cusps, and you'll be shown a description in plain English below the chart. Then click on the planet, sign, or house cusp and up pops a detailed interpretation. Couldn't be easier. A new Basic Edition, under fifty dollars at this writing, is bargain priced and ideal for beginners.

Time Passages
(866) 772-7876 (866-77-ASTRO)
Web site: www.astrograph.com

The "Know Thru Astrology" Series

This new series is designed especially for the nonastrologer. There are four programs in the series: KNOW Your Self, KNOW Your Future, KNOW Your Lover, and KNOW Your Child, each priced at an affordable $49.95 (at this writing). Though it is billed as beginner software, the KNOW series offers many sophisticated options, such as a calendar to let you navigate future or past influences, detailed chart interpretations, built-in pop-ups to show you what everything means. You'll need a PC running current Windows versions starting with Windows 98 SE, with 512 Mb RAM, and a hard drive with 170–300 Mb free space.

Matrix Software
126 South Michigan Avenue
Big Rapids, MI 49307
(800) 752-6387
Web site: www.astrologysoftware.com

Growth Opportunities

Astrolabe

Astrolabe is one of the top astrology software resources. Check out the latest version of their powerful Solar Fire software for Windows. It's a breeze to use and will grow with your increasing knowledge of astrology to the most sophisticated levels. This company also markets a variety of programs for all levels of expertise and a wide selection of computer-generated astrology readings. This is a good resource for innovative software as well as applications for older computers.

The Astrolabe Web site is a great place to start your astrology tour of the Internet. Visitors to the site are greeted with a chart of the time you log on. And you can get your chart calculated, also free, with a mini interpretation e-mailed to you.

Astrolabe
Box 1750-R
Brewster, MA 02631
Phone: (800) 843-6682
Web site: www.alabe.com

Matrix Software

You'll find a wide variety of software at student and advanced levels in all price ranges, demo disks, lots of interesting readings. Check out Winstar Express, a powerful but reasonably priced program suitable for all skill levels. The Matrix Web site offers lots of fun activities for Web surfers, such as free readings from the I Ching, the runes, and the tarot. There are many free desktop backgrounds with astrology themes.

Matrix Software
126 South Michigan Avenue
Big Rapids, MI 49307
Phone: (800) 752-6387
Web site: www.astrologysoftware.com

Astro Computing Services (ACS)

Books, software, individual charts, and telephone readings are offered by this company. Their freebies include astrology greeting cards and new moon reports. Find technical astrology materials here such as *The American Ephemeris* and PC atlases. ACS will calculate and send charts to you, a valuable service if you do not have a computer.

Starcrafts Publishing
334 Calef Hwy.
Epping, NH 03042
Phone: (866) 953-8458
Web site: www.astrocom.com

Air Software

Here you'll find powerful, creative astrology software, plus current stock market analysis. Financial astrology programs for stock market traders are a specialty. There are some interesting freebees at this site. Check out the maps of eclipse paths for any year and a free astrology clock program.

Air Software
115 Caya Avenue
West Hartford, CT 06110
Phone: (800) 659-1247
Web site: www.alphee.com

Kepler: State of the Art

Here's a program that's got everything. Gorgeous graphic images, audio-visual effects, and myriad sophisticated chart options are built into this fascinating software. It's even got an astrological encyclopedia, plus diagrams and images to help you understand advanced concepts. This program is pricey, but if you're serious about learning astrology, it's an investment that will grow with you! Check out its features at www.astrosoftware.com.

Timecycles Research: For Mac Users

Here's where Mac users can find astrology software that's as sophisticated as it gets. If you have a Mac, you'll love their beautiful graphic IO Series programs.

Time Cycles Research
P.O. Box 797
Waterford, CT 06385
(800) 827-2240
Web site: www.timecycles.com

Shareware and Freeware: The Price Is Right!

Halloran Software: A Super Shareware Program

Check out Halloran Software's Web site, which offers several levels of Windows astrology software. Beginners should consider their Astrology for Windows shareware program, which is available in unregistered demo form as a free download and in registered form for a very reasonable price.

Halloran Software
P.O. Box 75713
Los Angeles, CA 90075
(800) 732-4628
Web site: www.halloran.com

ASTROLOG

If you're computer-savvy, you can't go wrong with Walter Pullen's amazingly complete Astrology program, which is offered absolutely free at the site. The Web address is www.astrolog.org/astrolog.htm.

Astrolog is an ultrasophisticated program with all the features of much more expensive programs. It comes in versions for all formats: DOS, Windows, Mac, and UNIX. It has some cool features, such as a revolving globe and a constellation map. If you are looking for astrology software with all the bells and whistles that doesn't cost big bucks, this program has it all!

Buying a Computer with Astrology in Mind?

The good news is that astrology software is becoming more sophisticated and fun to use. However, if you've inherited an old computer, don't despair. You don't need the fastest processor and all the newest bells and whistles to run perfectly adequate astrology software. It is still possible to find programs for elder systems, including many new exciting programs.

To take full advantage of all the options, it is best to have a system that runs versions of Windows starting with Windows 98 SE. If you're buying a new computer, invest in one with as much RAM as possible, at least 1 GB. A CD drive will be necessary to load programs or an Internet connection, if you prefer to download programs online.

Mac fans who want to run Windows astrology software should invest in dual boot computers that will operate both the Mac and the Windows XP and Vista platforms.

CHAPTER 10

Ask the Expert: A Personal Reading Could Help

In these changing times, preparing ourselves for challenges ahead becomes a top priority as new issues surface in our lives. This could be the ideal time to add an astrologer to your dream team of advisers. Horoscopes can offer general advice to all members of your sign, but a personal reading can deal with what matters most to you. It can help you sort out a problem, find and use the strengths in your horoscope, set you on a more fulfilling career path, give you insight into your romantic life, or help you decide where to relocate. Many people consult astrologers to find the optimum time to schedule an important event, such as a wedding or business meeting.

Another good reason for a reading is to refine your knowledge of astrology by consulting with someone who has years of experience analyzing charts. You might choose an astrologer with a specialty that intrigues you. Armed with the knowledge of your chart that you have acquired so far, you can then learn to interpret subtle nuances or gain insight into your talents and abilities.

How do you choose when there are so many different kinds of readings available, especially since the Internet has brought astrology into the mainstream? Besides individual one-on-one readings with a professional astrologer, there are personal readings by mail, telephone, Internet, and tape. Well-advertised computer-generated reports and celebrity-sponsored readings are sure to attract your attention on commercial Web sites and in magazines. You can even purchase a reading that is incorporated into an expensive handmade fine art book. Then there are astrologers who specialize in specific areas such as finance or medical astrology. And unfortunately, there are many questionable practitioners who range from streetwise Gypsy fortune-tellers to unscrupulous scam artists.

The following basic guidelines can help you sort out your options to find the reading that's right for you.

One-on-One Consultations with a Professional Astrologer

Nothing compares to a one-on-one consultation with a professional astrologer who has analyzed thousands of charts and can pinpoint the potential in yours. During your reading, you can get your specific questions answered and discuss possible paths you might take. There are many astrologers who now combine their skills with training in psychology and are well-suited to help you examine your alternatives.

To give you an accurate reading, an astrologer needs certain information from you: the date, time, and place where you were born. (A horoscope can be cast about anyone or anything that has a specific time and place.) Most astrologers will then enter this information into a computer, which will calculate a chart in seconds, and interpret the resulting chart.

If you don't know your exact birth time, you can usually locate it at the Bureau of Vital Statistics at the city hall of the town or the county seat in the state where you were born. If you still have no success in getting your time of birth, some astrologers can estimate an approximate birth time by using past events in your life to determine the chart. This technique is called rectification.

How to Find an Astrologer

Choose your astrologer with the same care as you would any trusted adviser, such as a doctor, lawyer, or banker. Unfortunately, anyone can claim to be an astrologer—to date, there is no licensing of astrologers or universally established professional criteria. However, there are nationwide organizations of serious, committed astrologers that can help you in your search.

Good places to start your investigation are organizations such as the American Federation of Astrologers (AFA) or the National Council for Geocosmic Research (NCGR), which offer a program of study and certification. If you live near a major city, there is sure to be an active NCGR chapter or astrology club in your area; many are listed in astrology magazines available at your local newsstand. In response to many requests for referrals, both the AFA and the NCGR have directories of professional astrologers listed on their Web sites; these directories include a glossary of terms and an explanation of specialties within the astrological field. Contact the NCGR and AFA headquarters for information. (See also Chapter 8.)

What Happens in a Reading

As a potentially lucrative freelance business, astrology has always attracted self-styled experts who may not have the knowledge or the counseling experience to give a helpful reading. These astrologers can range from the well-meaning amateur to the charlatan or street-corner Gypsy who has for many years given astrology a bad name. Be very wary of astrologers who claim to have occult powers or who make pretentious claims of celebrated clients or miraculous achievements. You can often tell from the initial phone conversation if the astrologer is legitimate. He or she should ask for your birthday time and place and then conduct the conversation in a professional manner. Any astrologer who gives a reading based only on your sun sign is highly suspect.

When you arrive at the reading, the astrologer should be prepared. The consultation should be conducted in a private, quiet place. The astrologer should be interested in your problems of the moment. A good reading is interactive and involves feedback on your part, so if the reading is not relating to your concerns, you should let the astrologer know. You should feel free to ask questions and get clarifications of any technical terms. The more you actively participate, rather than expecting the astrologer to carry the reading or come forth with oracular predictions, the more meaningful your experience will be. An astrologer should help you validate your current experience and be frank about possible negative happenings, but also suggest a positive course of action.

In their approach to a reading, some astrologers may be more literal and others more intuitive. Those who have had counseling training may take a more psychological approach. Though some astrologers may seem to have an almost psychic ability, extrasensory perception or any other parapsychological talent is not essential. A very accurate picture can be drawn from the data in your horoscope chart.

An astrologer may do several charts for each client, including one for the time of birth and a progressed chart, showing the evolution from birth to the present time. According to your individual needs, there are many other possibilities, such as a chart for a different location if you are contemplating a change of place. Relationships between any two people, things, or events can be interpreted with a chart that compares one partner's horoscope with the other's. A composite chart, which uses the midpoint between planets in two individual charts to describe the relationship, is another commonly used device.

An astrologer will be particularly interested in transits, those times when cycling planets activate the planets or sensitive points in your birth chart. These indicate important events in your life.

Many astrologers offer readings recorded on tape or CD, which is another option to consider, especially if the astrologer you choose lives at a distance from you. In this case, you'll be mailed a recorded reading based on your birth chart. This type of reading is more personal than a computer printout and can give you valuable insights, though it is not equivalent to a live dialogue with the astrologer when you can discuss your specific interest and issues of the moment.

The Telephone Reading

Telephone readings come in two varieties: a dial-in taped reading, usually recorded in advance by an astrologer, or a live consultation with an "astrologer" on the other end of the line. The recorded readings are general daily or weekly forecasts, applied to all members of your sign and charged by the minute. The quality depends on the astrologer. Be aware that these readings can run up quite a telephone bill, especially if you get into the habit of calling every day. Be sure that you are aware of the per-minute cost of each call beforehand.

Live telephone readings also vary with the expertise of the astrologer. Ideally, the astrologer at the other end of the line enters your birth data into a computer, which then quickly calculates your chart. This chart will be referred to during the consultation. The advantage of a live telephone reading is that your individual chart is used and you can ask about a specific problem. However, before you invest in any reading, be sure that your astrologer is qualified and that you fully understand in advance how much you will be charged. There should be no unpleasant financial surprises later. The best astrologer is one who is recommended to you by a friend or family member.

Computer-Generated Reports

Companies that offer computer programs (such as ACS, Matrix, and Astrolabe) also offer a variety of computer-generated horoscope readings. These can be quite comprehensive, offering a beautiful printout of the chart plus many pages of detailed information about each planet and aspect of the chart. You can then study it at your convenience. Of course, the interpretations will be general, since there is no personal input from you, and might not cover your immediate concerns. Since computer-generated horoscopes are much lower in cost than live consultations, you might consider them as either a supplement or a preparation for an eventual live reading. You'll then be more familiar with your chart and able to plan specific questions in advance. They also make a terrific gift for astrology fans. In chapter 9, there are listed several companies that offer computerized readings prepared by reputable astrologers.

Whichever option you decide to pursue, may your reading be an empowering one!

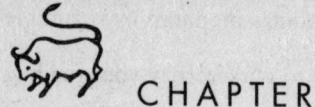

CHAPTER 11

Loving Every Sign in the Zodiac

In times of change, we crave the comfort of a loving partner more than ever. If we don't have love, we want to know how and where to find it; and if we already have a loving relationship, we want to know how to make it last forever. You can use astrology to find a lover, understand the one you have, or add excitement to your current relationship. Here are sun-sign seduction tips for romancing every sign in the zodiac.

Aries: Play Hard to Get

This highly physical sign is walking dynamite with a brief attention span. Don't be too easy to get, ladies. A little challenge, a lively debate, and a merry chase only heat them up. They want to see what you're made of. Once you've lured them into your lair, be a challenge and a bit of a daredevil. Pull out your X-rated tricks. Don't give your all—let them know there's more where that came from. Make it exciting; show you're up for adventure. Wear bright red somewhere interesting. Since Aries rules the head and face, be sure to focus on these areas in your lovemaking. Use your lips, tongue, breath, and even your eyelashes to the max. Practice scalp massages and deep kissing techniques. Aries won't wait, so when you make your move, be sure you're ready to follow through. No head games or teasing!

To keep you happy, you've got to voice your *own* needs, because this lover will be focused on *his*. Teach him how to please, or this could be a one-sided adventure.

Taurus: Appeal to All Their Senses

Taurus wins as the most sensual sign, with the most sexual stamina. This man is earthy and lusty in bed; he can go on all night. This is not a sign to tease. Like a bull, he'll see red, not bed. So make him comfortable, and then bombard all his senses. Good food gets Taurus in the mood. So do the right music, fragrance, revealing clothes, and luxurious bedlinens. Give him a massage with delicious-smelling and -tasting oils; focus on the neck area.

Don't forget to turn off the phone! Taurus hates interruptions. Since they can be very vocal lovers, choose a setting where you won't be disturbed. And don't ever rush; enjoy a long, slow, delicious encounter.

Gemini: Be a Playmate

Playful Gemini loves games, so make your seduction fun. Be their lost twin soul or confidante. Good communication is essential, so share deep secrets and live out fantasies. This sign adores variety. Nothing bores Gemini more than making love the same way all the time, or bringing on the heavy emotions. So trot out all the roles you've been longing to play. Here's the perfect partner. But remember to keep it light and fun. Gemini's turn-on zone is the hands, and this sign gives the best massages. Gadgets that can be activated with a touch amuse Gemini. This sign is great at doing two things at once, like making love while watching an erotic film. Turn the cell phone off unless you want company. On the other hand, Gemini is your sign for superhot phone sex.

Gemini loves a change of scene. So experiment on the floor, in the shower, or on the kitchen table. Borrow a friend's apartment or rent a hotel room for variety.

Cancer: Use the Moon

The key to Cancer is to get this moon child in the mood. Consult the moon—a full moon is best. Wining, dining, old-fashioned courtship, and breakfast in bed are turn-ons. Whatever makes your Cancer feel secure will promote shedding inhibitions in the sack. (Don't try any of your Aries daredevil techniques here!) Cancer prefers familiar, comfortable, homey surroundings. Cancer's turn-on zone is the breasts. Cancer women often have naturally inflated chests. Cancer men may fantasize about a well-endowed playmate. If your breasts are enhanced, show them off. Cancer will want to know all your deepest secrets, so invent a few good ones. But lots of luck delving into *their* innermost thoughts!

Take your Cancer near water. The sight and sound of the sea can be their aphrodisiac. A moonlit beach, a deserted swimming pool, a Jacuzzi, or a bubble bath are good seduction spots. Listen to the rain patter on the roof in a mountain cabin.

Leo: Offer the Royal Treatment

Leo must be the best and hear it from you often. In return, they'll perform for you, telling you just what you want to hear (true or not). They like a lover with style and endurance, and to be swept off their feet and into bed. Leos like to go first-class all the way, so build them up with lots of attention, wining and dining, and special gifts.

Never mention other lovers or make them feel second-best. A sure signal for Leo to look elsewhere is a competitive spouse. Leos take great pride in their bodies, so you should pour on the admiration. A few well-placed mirrors could inspire them. So would a striptease with beautiful lingerie, expensive fragrance on the sheets, and, if female, an occasional luxury hotel room, with champagne and caviar delivered by room service. Leo's erogenous zone is the lower back, so a massage with expensive oils would make your lion purr with pleasure.

Virgo: Let Them Be the Teacher

Virgo's standards are so sky-high that you may feel intimidated at first. The key to pleasing fussy Virgo lovers is to look for the hot fantasy beneath their cool surface. They're really looking for someone to make over. So let Virgo play teacher, and you play the willing student; the doctor-patient routine works as well. Be Eliza Doolittle to his Henry Higgins.

Let Virgo help you improve your life, quit smoking, learn French, and diet. Read an erotic book together, and then practice the techniques. Or study esoteric, erotic exercises from the Far East.

The Virgo erogenous zone is the tummy area, which should be your base of operations. Virgo likes things pristine and clean. Fall onto crisp, immaculate white sheets. Wear a sheer virginal white nightie. Smell shower-fresh with no heavy perfume. Be sure your surroundings pass the hospital test. A shower together afterward (with great-smelling soap) could get the ball rolling again.

Libra: Look Your Best

Libra must be turned on aesthetically. Make sure you look as beautiful as possible, and wear something stylishly seductive but never vulgar. Have a mental affair first, as you flirt and flatter this sign. Then proceed to the physical. Approach Libra like a dance partner, ready to waltz or tango.

Libra must be in the mood for love; otherwise, forget it. Any kind of ugliness is a turnoff. Provide an elegant and harmonious atmosphere, with no loud noise, clashing colors, or uncomfortable beds. Libra is not an especially spontaneous lover, so it is best to spend time warming them up. Libra's back is his erogenous zone, your cue to provide back rubs with scented potions. Once in bed, you can be a bit aggressive sexually. Libra loves strong, decisive moves. Set the scene, know what you want, and let Libra be happy to provide it.

Scorpio: Be an All-or-Nothing Lover

Scorpio is legendary in bed, often called the sex sign of the zodiac. But seducing them is often a power game. Scorpio likes to be in control, even the quiet, unassuming ones. Scorpio loves a mystery, so don't tell all. Keep them guessing about you, offering tantalizing hints along the way. The hint of danger often turns Scorpio on, so you'll find members of this sign experimenting with the exotic and highly erotic forms of sex. Sadomasochism, bondage, or anything that tests the limits of power could be a turn-on for Scorpio.

Invest in some sexy black leather and some powerful music. Clothes that lace, buckle, or zip tempt Scorpio to untie you. Present yourself as a mysterious package just waiting to be unwrapped.

Once in bed, there are no holds barred with Scorpio. They'll find your most pleasurable pressure points, and touch you as you've never been touched before. They are quickly aroused (the genital area belongs to this sign) and are willing to try anything. But they can be possessive. Don't expect your Scorpio to share you with anyone. It's all or nothing for them.

Sagittarius: Be a Happy Wanderer

Sagittarius men are the Don Juans of the zodiac—love-'em-and-leave-'em types who are difficult to pin down. Your seduction strategy is to join them in their many pursuits, and then hook them with love on the road. Sagittarius enjoys sex in venues that suggest movement; planes, SUVs, or boats. But a favorite turn-on place is outdoors, in nature. A deserted hiking path, a field of tall grass, or a remote woodland glade—all give the centaur sexy ideas. Athletic Sagittarius might go for some personal training in an empty gym. Join your Sagittarius for amorous aerobics, meditate together, and explore the tantric forms of sex. Lovemaking after hiking and skiing would be healthy fun.

Sagittarius enjoys lovers from exotic ethnic backgrounds, or lovers met in spiritual pursuits or on college campuses. Sagittarius are great cheerleaders and motivators, and will enjoy feeling that they have inspired you to be all that you can be.

There may be a canine or feline companion sharing your Sagittarius lover's bed with you, so check your allergies. And bring Fido or Felix a toy to keep them occupied.

Capricorn: Take Their Mind off Business

The great news about Capricorn lovers is that they improve with age. They are probably the sexiest seniors. So stick around, if you have a young one. They're lusty in bed (it's not the sign of the goat for nothing), and can be quite raunchy and turned on by X-rated words and deeds. If this is not your thing, let them know. The Capricorn erogenous zone is the knees. Some discreet fondling in public places could be your opener. Capricorn tends to think of sex as part of a game plan for the future. They are well-organized, and might regard lovemaking as relaxation after a long day's work. This sign often combines business with pleasure. So look for a Capricorn where there's a convention, trade show, or work-related conference.

Getting Capricorn's mind off his agenda and onto yours could take some doing. Separate him from his buddies by whispering sexy secrets in his ear. Then convince him you're an asset to his image and a boon to his health. Though he may seem uptight at first, you'll soon discover he's a love animal who makes a wonderful and permanent pet.

Aquarius: Give Them Enough Space

This sign really does not want an all-consuming passion or an all-or-nothing relationship. Aquarius needs space. But once they feel free to experiment with a spontaneous and exciting partner, Aquarius can give you a far-out sexual adventure.

Passion begins in the mind, so a good mental buildup is key. Aquarius is an inventive sign who believes love is a playground without rules. Plan surprise, unpredictable encounters in unusual places. Find ways to make love transcendental, an extraordinary and unique experience. Be ready to try anything Aquarius suggests, if only once. Calves and ankles are the special Aquarius erogenous zone, so perfect your legwork.

Be careful not to be too possessive. Your Aquarius needs lots of space and tolerance for friends (including old lovers) and their many outside interests.

Pisces: Live Their Fantasies

Pisces is the sign of fantasy and imagination. This sign has great theatrical talent. Pisces looks for lovers who will take care of them. Pisces will return the favor! Here is someone who can psych out your deepest desires without mentioning them. Pisces falls for sob stories and is always ready to empathize. It wouldn't hurt to have a small problem for Pisces to help you overcome. It might help if you cry on his shoulder, for this sign needs to be needed. Use your imagination when setting the scene for love. A dramatic setting brings out Pisces theatrical talents. Or creatively use the element of water. Rain on the roof, waterfalls, showers, beach houses, water beds, and Jacuzzis could turn up the heat. Experiment with pulsating jets of water. Take midnight skinny-dips in deserted pools.

The Pisces erogenous zone is the feet. This is your cue to give a sensuous foot massage using scented lotions. Let him paint your toes. Beautiful toenails in sexy sandals are a special turn-on.

Your Hottest Love Match

Here's a tip for finding your hottest love match. If your lover's Mars sign makes favorable aspects to your Venus, is in the same element (earth, air, fire, water), or is in the same sign, your lover will do what you want done! Mars influences how we act when we make love, while Venus shows what we like done to us. Sometimes fighting and making up is the sexiest fun of all. If you're the type who needs a spark to keep lust alive (you know who you are!), then look for Mars and Venus in different signs of the same quality (fixed or cardinal or mutable). For instance, a fixed sign (Taurus, Leo, Scorpio, Aquarius) paired with another fixed sign can have a sexy tug-of-war before you finally surrender. Two cardinal signs (Aries, Cancer, Libra, Capricorn) set off passionate fireworks when they clash. Mutable signs (Gemini, Virgo, Sagittarius, Pisces) play a fascinating game of cat and mouse, never quite catching each other.

Your Most Seductive Time

The best time for love is when Venus is in your sign, making you the most desirable sign in the zodiac. This only lasts about three weeks (unless Venus is retrograde) so don't waste time! And find out the time this year when Venus is in your sign by consulting the Venus chart at the end of chapter 5.

What's the Sexiest Sign?

It depends on what sign you are. Astrology has traditionally given this honor to Scorpio, the sign associated with the sex organs. However, we are all a combination of different signs (and turn-ons). Gemini's communicating ability and manual dexterity could deliver the magic touch. Cancer's tenderness and understanding could bring out your passion more than regal Leo.

Which Is the Most Faithful Sign?

The earth signs of Capricorn, Taurus, and Virgo are usually the most faithful. They tend to be more home- and family-oriented, and they are usually choosy about their mates. It's impractical, inconvenient, and probably expensive to play around, or so they think.

Who'll Play Around?

The mutable signs of Gemini, Pisces, and Sagittarius win the playboy or playgirl sweepstakes. These signs tend to be changeable, fickle, and easily bored. But they're so much fun!

CHAPTER 12

Financial Tips from the Stars

Getting the most bang from our buck will be our personal challenge this year, as we continue to learn to live within our means and balance our budgets. One of the advantages of astrology is that we can know the natural direction of the cosmic forces in advance and make financial plans accordingly.

Over the past few years, we've experienced a dramatic shift from the expansive risk taking of Pluto in Sagittarius to the conservative, thrift-promoting Pluto in Capricorn. This influence should continue for several years. Financially savvy astrologers also look to the movement of Jupiter, the planet of luck and expansion, for growth opportunities. Jupiter gives an extra boost to the sign it is passing through. Jupiter moves through Pisces, a sign that Jupiter especially favors, so Pisces and fellow water signs, Cancer and Scorpio, receive extra-lucky rays. Most of us could benefit from using some Pisces-inspired creativity, insight, and imagination especially in the area of our horoscope where Jupiter will be giving us growth opportunities. Pisces will give us the imaginative ideas; then Jupiter enters Aries briefly over the summer and for a lengthy stay next year, which should give us the courage and pioneering spirit to pursue them.

Aries

You've got a taste for fast money, quick turnover, and edgy investments, with no patience for gradual, long-term gains.

You're an impulse buyer with the nerve for risky tactics that could backfire. On the other hand, you're a pioneer who can see into the future, who dares to take a gamble on a new idea or product that could change the world ... like Sam Walton of the Wal-Mart stores, who changed the way we shop. You need a backup plan in case one of your big ideas burns out. To protect your money, get a backup plan you can follow without thinking about it. Have a percentage of your income automatically put into a savings or retirement account. Then give yourself some extra funds to play with. Your weak point is your impatience; so you're not one to wait out a slow market or watch savings slowly accumulate. When Jupiter moves into Aries temporarily this summer, you'll want to move full steam ahead. However, you may have to reevaluate your goals in the fall. Save your big moves for next year, when Jupiter reenters Aries and you can make real progress.

Taurus

You're a saver who loves to see your cash, as well as your possessions, accumulate. You have no qualms about steadily increasing your fortune. You're a savvy trader and a shrewd investor, in there for long-term gains. You have low toleration for risk; you hate to lose anything. But you do enjoy luxuries, and may need to reward yourself frequently. You might pass up an opportunity because it seems too risky, but you should take a chance once in a while. Since you're inspired by Jupiter in Pisces and Aries this year, it's time to support your long-range goals and ideals by exploring socially conscious investments, especially in the clean-energy field and the creative arts. You're especially lucky in real estate or any occupation that requires appraising and trading, as well as earth-centered businesses like organic farming and conservation.

Gemini

With Gemini, the cash can flow in and then out just as quickly. You naturally multi-task, and you are sure to have several projects going at once, as well as several credit cards, which can easily get out of hand. Saving is not one of your strong points—too boring. You fall in and out of love with different ideas; you have probably tried a round of savings techniques. Diversification is your best strategy. Have several different kinds of investments—at least one should be a long-term plan. Set savings goals and then regularly deposit small amounts into your accounts. Follow the lead of Gemini financial adviser Suze Orman and get a good relationship going with your money! With lucky Jupiter accenting your public image, there should be new career opportunities this year. Investigate careers in communications and the media.

Cancer

You can be a natural moneymaker with your peerless intuition. You can spot a winner that everyone else misses. Consider Cancer success stories like those of cosmetics queen Estee Lauder and Roxanne Quimby, of Burt's Bees, who turned her friend's stash of beeswax into a thriving cosmetics business. Who knew? So trust your intuition. You are a saver who always has a backup plan, just in case. Remember to treat and nurture yourself as well as others. Investments in the food industry, restaurants, hotels, shipping, and water-related industries are Cancer territory. You're one of the luckiest signs this year, so keep your antennae tuned for new investment opportunities.

Leo

You love the first-class lifestyle, but may not always have the resources to support it. Finding a way to fund your extravagant tastes is the Leo challenge. Some courses in money management or an expert financial coach could set you on the right track. However, you're also a terrific salesperson, and you're fabulous in high-profile jobs that pay a lot. You're the community tastemaker; you satisfy your appetite for "the best" by working for a quality company that sells luxury goods, splendid real estate, dream vacations, and first-class travel—that way you'll have access to the lifestyle without having to pay for it. This year, Jupiter brings luck through fortunate partnerships and travel.

Virgo

Your sign is a stickler for details, which includes your money management. You like to follow your spending and saving closely; you enjoy planning, budgeting, and price comparison. Your sign usually has no problem sticking to a savings or investment plan. You have a critical eye for quality, and you like to bargain and to shop to get the best value. In fact, Warren Buffet, a Virgo billionaire, is known for value investing. You buy cheap and sell at a profit. Investing in health care, organic products, and food could be profitable for you. With Jupiter in Pisces accenting partnerships, you might want to team up for investing purposes this year.

Libra

Oh, do you ever love to shop! And you often have an irresistible urge to acquire an exquisite object or a designer dress you can't really afford or to splurge on the perfect antique armoire. You don't like to settle for second-rate or bargain buys. Learning to prioritize your spending is especially difficult for your sign, so try to find a good money manager to do it for you. Following a strictly balanced budget is your key to financial success. With Libra's keen eye for quality and good taste, you are a savvy picker at auctions and antiques fairs, so you might be able to turn around your purchase for a profit. With Jupiter accenting the care and maintenance part of your life, this is an excellent year to put your finances in order and balance the budget.

Scorpio

Scorpios prefer to stay in control of their finances at all times. You're sure to have a financial-tracking program on your computer. You're not an impulse buyer, unless you see something that immediately turns you on. Rely on your instincts! Scorpio is the sign of credit cards, taxes, and loans, so you are able to use these tools cleverly. Investing for Scorpio is rarely casual. You'll do extensive research and track your investments by reading the financial pages, annual reports, and profit-loss statements. Investigate the arts, media, and oil and water projects for Jupiter-favored investments this year.

Sagittarius

Sagittarius is a natural gambler, with a high tolerance for risk. It's important for you to learn when to hold 'em, and when to fold 'em, as the song goes, by setting limits on your risk taking and covering your assets. You enjoy the thrill of playing the stock market, where you could win big and lose big. Money itself is rarely the object for Sagittarius—it's the game that counts. Since your sign rarely saves for a rainy day, your best strategy might be a savings plan that transfers a certain amount into a savings account. Regular bill-paying plans are another strategy to keep you on track. Jupiter favors investing in home improvements and family-related businesses this year.

Capricorn

You're one of the strongest money managers in the zodiac, which should serve you well this year when Jupiter, the planet of luck and expansion, is blessing your house of finance. You're a born bargain hunter and clever negotiator—a saver rather than a spender. You are the sign of self-discipline, which works well when it comes to sticking with a budget and living frugally while waiting for resources to accumulate. You are likely to plan carefully for your elder years, profiting from long-term investments. You have a keen sense of value, and you will pick up a bargain and then turn it around at a nice profit. Jupiter favors the communications industry and opportunities in your local area this year.

Aquarius

There should be many chances to speculate on forward-looking ventures this year. The Aquarius trait of unpredictability extends to your financial life, where you surprise us all with your ability to turn something totally unique into a money spinner. Consider your wealthy sign mates Oprah Winfrey and Michael Bloomberg, who have been able to intuit what the public will buy at a given moment. Some of your ideas might sound far-out, but they turn out to be right on the money. Investing in high-tech companies that are on the cutting edge of their field is good for Aquarius. You'll probably intuit which ones will stay the course. You'll feel good about investing in companies that improve the environment, such as new types of fuel, or ones that are related to your favorite cause.

Pisces

Luck is with you this year! The typical Pisces is probably the sign least interested in money management. However, there are many billionaires born under your sign, such as Michael Dell, David Geffen, and Steve Jobs. Generally they have made money from innovative ideas and left the details to others. That might work for you. Find a Scorpio, Capricorn, or Virgo to help you set a profitable course and systematically save (which is not in your nature). Sign up for automatic bill paying so you won't have to think about it. If you keep in mind how much less stressful life will be and how much more you can do when you're not worried about paying bills, you might be motivated enough to stick to a sensible budget. Investment-wise, consider anything to do with water—off-shore drilling, water conservation and purifying, shipping, and seafood. Petroleum is also ruled by your sign, as are institutions related to hospitals.

CHAPTER 13

Children of 2010

Parents of several children may see a marked difference between children born in 2010 and those born more than two years ago, because the cosmic atmosphere has changed, which should imprint the personalities of this year's children.

Astrologers look to the slow-moving outer planets—Uranus, Neptune, and Pluto—to describe a generation. When an outer planet changes signs, this indicates a significant shift in energy, which is the case in 2010. In the first half of the year, Uranus and Jupiter in Pisces continue the visionary and creative influence of that sign, which will be reflected in the children born then. However, Uranus moves briefly into fiery Aries in June, which will be accompanied by Jupiter, the planet of expansion, indicating a very astrologically active summer of 2010. Children born during the warm months will reflect this with more drive and energy. After Uranus retrogrades back into Pisces in mid-August for the remainder of the year, the atmosphere becomes somewhat calmer. Neptune still passing through Aquarius and Pluto in Capricorn should add vision and practicality to the personality of this year's children. This generation will be focused on saving the planet and on making things work in order to clear the path for the future. Saturn in Libra will enter the mixture, teaching them diplomacy in getting along with others.

Astrology can be an especially helpful tool when used to design an environment that enhances and encourages each child's positive qualities. Some parents start before conception, planning the birth of their child as far as possible to harmonize with the signs of other family members. However, each baby has its own schedule, so if yours arrives a week early or late, or elects a different sign than you'd planned, recognize that the new sign may be more in line with the mission your child is here to accomplish. In other words, if you were hoping for a Libra child and he arrives during Virgo, that Virgo energy may be just what is needed to stimulate or complement your family. Remember that there are many astrological elements besides the sun sign that indicate strong family ties. Usually each child will share a particular planetary placement, an emphasis on a particular sign or house, or a certain chart configuration with his parents and other family members. Often there is a significant planetary angle that will define the parent-child relationship, such as family sun signs that form a T-square or a triangle.

One important thing you can do is to be sure the exact moment of birth is recorded. This will be essential in calculating an accurate astrological chart. The following descriptions can be applied to the sun or moon sign (if known) of a child—the sun sign will describe basic personality and the moon sign indicates the child's emotional needs.

The Aries Child

Baby Aries is quite a handful. This energetic child will walk—and run—as soon as possible, and perform daring feats of exploration. Caregivers should be vigilant. Little Aries seems to know no fear (and is especially vulnerable to head injuries). Many Aries children, in their rush to get on with life, seem hyperactive, and they are easily frustrated when they can't get their own way. Violent temper tantrums and dramatic physical displays are par for the course with this child, requiring a time-out mat or naughty chair.

The very young Aries should be monitored carefully, since he is prone to take risks and may injure himself. Aries love to take things apart and may break toys easily, but with encouragement, the child will develop formidable coordination. Aries's bossy tendencies should be molded into leadership qualities, rather than bullying, which should be easy to do with this year's babies. Encourage these children to take out aggressions and frustrations in active, competitive sports, where they usually excel. When young Aries learns to focus energies long enough to master a subject and learns consideration for others, the indomitable Aries spirit will rise to the head of the class.

Aries born in 2010 will be a more subdued version of this sign, but still loaded with energy. The Capricorn effect should make little Aries easier to discipline and more focused on achievement. A natural leader!

The Taurus Child

This is a cuddly, affectionate child who eagerly explores the world of the senses, especially the senses of taste and touch. The Taurus child can be a big eater and will put on weight easily if not encouraged to exercise. Since this child likes comfort and gravitates to beauty, try coaxing little Taurus to exercise to music, or take him or her out of doors, with hikes or long walks. Though Taurus may be a slow learner, this sign has an excellent retentive memory and generally masters a subject thoroughly. Taurus is interested in results and will see each project patiently through to completion, continuing long after others have given up. This year's earth sign planets will give him a wonderful sense of support and accomplishment.

Choose Taurus toys carefully to help develop innate talents. Construction toys, such as blocks or erector sets, appeal to their love of building. Paints or crayons develop their sense of color. Many Taurus have musical talent and love to sing, which is apparent at a young age.

This year's Taurus will want a pet or two, and a few plants of his own. Give little Taurus a small garden, and watch the natural green thumb develop. This child has a strong sense of acquisition and an early grasp of material value. After filling a piggy bank, Taurus graduates to a savings account, before other children have started to learn the value of money.

Little Taurus gets a bonanza of good luck from Jupiter in compatible Pisces, supported by Pluto in Capricorn and Saturn retrograding back into Virgo, a compatible earth sign. These should give little Taurus an especially easygoing disposition and provide many opportunities to live up to his sign's potential.

The Gemini Child

Little Gemini will talk as soon as possible, filling the air with questions and chatter. This is a friendly child who enjoys social contact, seems to require company, and adapts quickly to different surroundings. Geminis have quick minds that easily grasp the use of words, books, and telephones, and will probably learn to talk and read at an earlier age than most. Though they are fast learners, Gemini may have a short attention span, darting from subject to subject. Projects and games that help focus the mind could be used to help them concentrate. Musical instruments, typewriters, and computers help older Gemini children combine mental with manual dexterity. Geminis should be encouraged to finish what they start before they go on to another project. Otherwise, they can become jack-of-all-trade types who have trouble completing anything they do. Their disposition is usually cheerful and witty, making these children popular with their peers and delightful company at home.

This year's Gemini baby is impulsive and full of energy, with a strong Aries influence in his life. He will be highly independent and original, a go-getter. When he grows up, Gemini may change jobs several times before he finds a position that satisfies his need for stimulation and variety.

The Cancer Child

This emotional, sensitive child is especially influenced by patterns set in early life. Young Cancers cling to their first memories as well as their childhood possessions. They thrive in calm emotional waters, with a loving, protective mother, and usually remain close to her (even if their relationship with her was difficult) throughout their lives. Divorce and death—anything that disturbs the safe family unit—are devastating to Cancers, who may need extra support and reassurance during a family crisis.

They sometimes need a firm hand to push the positive, creative side of their personality and discourage them from getting swept away by emotional moods or resorting to emotional manipulation to get their way. If this child is praised and encouraged to find creative expression, Cancers will be able to express their positive side consistently, on a firm, secure foundation.

This year's Cancer baby may run against type, thanks to a meeting of Jupiter and Uranus in hyperactive Aries, which might make him much more outgoing and energetic than usual. He should have natural leadership tendencies, which should be encouraged, and the parents' challenge will be to find positive outlets for his energy.

The Leo Child

Leo children love the limelight and will plot to get the lion's share of attention. These children assert themselves with flair and drama, and can behave like tiny tyrants to get their way. But in general, they have a sunny, positive disposition and are rarely subject to blue moods.

At school, they're the types voted most popular, head cheerleader, or homecoming queen. Leo is sure to be noticed for personality, if not for stunning looks or academic work; the homely Leo will be a class clown, and the unhappy Leo can be the class bully.

Above all, a Leo child cannot tolerate being ignored for long. Drama or performing-arts classes, sports, and school politics are healthy ways for Leo to be a star. But Leos must learn to take lesser roles occasionally, or they will have some painful putdowns in store. Usually, their popularity is well earned; they are hard workers who try to measure up to their own high standards—and usually succeed.

This year's Leo should be a highly active version of the sign, with Saturn in Libra teaching lessons of balance and diplomacy in relationships, while Jupiter and Uranus in Aries amp up the energy level and Pluto in Capricorn demands focus and results. Good use of this energy could produce pioneers, fearless natural leaders who could change the world for the better.

The Virgo Child

The young Virgo can be a quiet, rather serious child, with a quick, intelligent mind. Early on, little Virgo shows far more attention to detail and concern with small things than other children. Little Virgo has a built-in sense of order and a fascination with how things work. It is important for these children to have a place of their own, which they can order as they wish and where they can read or busy themselves with crafts and hobbies. This child's personality can be very sensitive. Little Virgo may get hyper and overreact to seemingly small irritations, which can take the form of stomach upsets or delicate digestive systems. But this child will flourish where there is mental stimulation and a sense of order. Virgos thrive in school, especially in writing or language skills, and they seem truly happy when buried in books. Chances are, young Virgo will learn to read ahead of classmates. Hobbies that involve detail work or that develop fine craftsmanship are especially suited to young Virgos.

Baby Virgo of 2010 is likely to be an early talker, and will show concern for the welfare of others. This child should be a natural communicator and may show an interest in the arts or the legal profession.

The Libra Child

The Libra child learns early about the power of charm and appearance. This is often a very physically appealing child with an enchanting dimpled smile, who is naturally sociable and enjoys the company of both children and adults. It is a rare Libra child who is a discipline problem, but when their behavior is unacceptable, they respond better to calm discussion than displays of emotion, especially if the discussion revolves around fairness. Because young Libras without a strong direction tend to drift with the mood of the group, these children should be encouraged to develop their unique talents and powers of discrimination, so they can later stand on their own.

In school, this child is usually popular and will often have to choose between social invitations and studies. In the teen years, social pressures mount as the young Libra begins to look for a partner. This is the sign of best friends, so Libra's choice of companions can have a strong effect on his future direction. Beautiful Libra girls may be tempted to go steady or have an unwise early marriage. Chances are, both sexes will fall in and out of love several times in their search for the ideal partner.

Little Libra of 2010 is an especially creative, expressive child, who may have strong artistic talents. This child is endowed with much imagination, as well as social skills.

The Scorpio Child

The Scorpio child may seem quiet and shy, but will surprise others with intense feelings and formidable willpower. Scorpio children are single-minded when they want something and intensely passionate about whatever they do. One of a caregiver's tasks is to teach this child to balance activities and emotions, yet at the same time to make the most of his great concentration and intense commitment.

Since young Scorpios do not show their depth of feelings easily, parents will have to learn to read almost imperceptible signs that troubles are brewing beneath the surface. Both Scorpio boys and girls enjoy games of power and control on or off the playground. Scorpio girls may take an early interest in the opposite sex, masquerading as tomboys, while Scorpio boys may be intensely competitive and loners. When her powerful energies are directed into work, sports, or challenging studies, Scorpio is a superachiever, focused on a goal. With trusted friends, young Scorpio is devoted and caring—the proverbial friend through thick and thin, loyal for life.

Scorpio 2010 has a strong emphasis on achievement and success. Uranus and lucky Jupiter in Pisces in their house of creativity should put them on the cutting edge of whichever field they choose.

The Sagittarius Child

This restless, athletic child will be out of the playpen and off on explorative adventures as soon as possible. Little Sagittarius is remarkably well-coordinated, attempting daredevil feats on any wheeled vehicle from scooters to skateboards. These natural athletes need little encouragement to channel their energies into sports. Their cheerful friendly dispositions earn them popularity in school, and once they have found a subject where their talent and imagination can soar, they will do well academically. They love animals, especially horses, and will be sure to have a pet or two, if not a home zoo. When they are old enough to take care of themselves, they'll clamor to be off on adventures of their own, away from home, if possible.

This is a child who loves to travel, who will not get homesick at summer camp, and who may sign up to be a foreign-exchange student or spend summers abroad. Outdoor adventure appeals to little Sagittarius, especially if it involves an active sport, such as skiing, cycling or mountain climbing. Give them enough space and encouragement, and their fiery spirit will propel them to achieve high goals.

Baby Sagittarius of 2010 has a natural generosity of spirit and an optimistic, social nature. Home and family will be especially important to him, though he may have an unconventional family life. He'll have an ability to look past the surface of things to seek out what has lasting value.

The Capricorn Child

These purposeful, goal-oriented children will work to capacity if they feel this will bring results. They're not ones who enjoy work for its own sake—there must be a goal in sight. Authority figures can do much to motivate these children, but once set on an upward path, young Capricorn will mobilize his energy and talent and work harder, and with more perseverance, than any other sign. Capricorn has built-in self-discipline that can achieve remarkable results, even if lacking the flashy personality, quick brainpower, or penetrating insight of others. Once involved, young Capricorn will stick to a task until it is mastered. This child also knows how to use others to his advantage and may well become the team captain or class president.

A wise parent will set realistic goals for the Capricorn child, paving the way for the early thrill of achievement. Youngsters should be encouraged to express their caring, feeling side to others, as well as their natural aptitude for leadership. Capricorn children may be especially fond of grandparents and older relatives, and will enjoy spending time with them and learning from them. It is not uncommon for young Capricorns to have an older mentor or teacher who guides them. With their great respect for authority, Capricorn children will take this influence very much to heart.

The Capricorn born in 2010 should be a good talker, with sharp mental abilities. He is likely to be social and outgoing, with lots of friends and closeness to brothers and sisters.

The Aquarius Child

The Aquarius child has a well-focused, innovative mind that often streaks so far ahead of peers that this child seems like an oddball. Routine studies never hold the restless youngster for long; he or she will look for another, more experimental place to try out his ideas and develop his inventions. Life is a laboratory to the inquiring Aquarius mind. School politics, sports, science, and the arts offer scope for their talents. But if there is no room for expression within approved social limits, Aquarius is sure to rebel. Questioning institutions and religions comes naturally, so these children may find an outlet elsewhere, becoming rebels with a cause. It is better not to force these children to conform, but rather to channel forward-thinking young minds into constructive group activities.

This year's Aquarius will have special financial talent. Luck and talent are his and fame could be in the stars!

The Pisces Child

Give young Pisces praise, applause, and a gentle, but firm, push in the right direction. Lovable Pisces children may be abundantly talented, but may be hesitant to express themselves, because they are quite sensitive and easily hurt. It is a parent's challenge to help them gain self-esteem and self-confidence. However, this same sensitivity makes them trusted friends who'll have many confidants as they develop socially. It also endows many Pisces with spectacular creative talent.

Pisces adores drama and theatrics of all sorts; therefore, encourage them to channel their creativity into art forms rather than indulging in emotional dramas. Understand that they may need more solitude than other children may as they develop their creative ideas. But though daydreaming can be creative, it is important that these natural dreamers not dwell too long in the world of fantasy. Teach them practical coping skills for the real world.

Since Pisces are sensitive physically, parents should help them build strong bodies with proper diet and regular exercise. Young Pisces may gravitate to more individual sports, such as swimming, sailing, and skiing, rather than to team sports. Or they may prefer more artistic physical activities, like dance or ice-skating.

Born givers, these children are often drawn to the underdog (they quickly fall for sob stories) and attract those who might take advantage of their empathic nature. Teach them to choose friends wisely, to set boundaries in relationships, and to protect their emotional vulnerability—invaluable lessons in later life.

With the planet Uranus now in Pisces along with lucky Jupiter, the 2010 baby belongs to a generation of Pisces movers and shakers. This child may have a rebellious streak that rattles the status quo. But this generation also has a visionary nature, which will be much concerned with the welfare of the world at large.

CHAPTER 14

Give the Perfect Gift to Every Sign

So often we're in a quandary about what to give a loved one, someone who has everything, that hard-to-please friend, or a fascinating new person in your life, or about the right present for a wedding, birthday, or hostess gift. Why not let astrology help you make the perfect choice by appealing to each sun sign's personality. When you're giving a gift, you're also making a memory, so it should be a special occasion. The gift that's most appreciated is one that touches the heart, reminds you both of a shared experience, or shows that the giver has really cared enough to consider the recipient's personality.

In general, the water signs (Cancer, Pisces, Scorpio) enjoy romantic, sentimental, and imaginative gifts given in a very personal way. Write your loved one a poem or a song to express your feelings. Assemble an album of photos or mementos of all the good times you've shared. Appeal to their sense of fantasy. Scorpio Richard Burton had the right idea when he gave Pisces Elizabeth Taylor a diamond bracelet hidden in lavender roses (her favorite color).

Fire signs (Aries, Leo, Sagittarius) appreciate a gift presented with lots of flair. Pull out the drama, like the actor who dazzled his Aries sweetheart by presenting her with trash cans overflowing with daisies.

Air signs (Gemini, Libra, Aquarius) love to be surprised with unusual gifts. The Duke of Windsor gave his elegant Gemini duchess, Wallis Windsor, fabulous jewels engraved with love notes and secret messages in their own special code.

Earth signs (Taurus, Virgo, Capricorn) value solid, tangible gifts or ones that appeal to all the senses. Delicious gourmet treats, scented body lotions, the newest CDs, the gift of a massage, or stocks and bonds are sure winners! Capricorn Elvis Presley once received a gold-plated piano from his wife.

Here are some specific ideas for each sign:

Aries

These are the trendsetters of the zodiac, who appreciate the latest thing! For Aries, it's the excitement that counts, so present your gift in a way that will knock their socks off. Aries is associated with the head, so a jaunty hat, hair ornaments, chandelier earrings, sunglasses, and hair-taming devices are good possibilities. Aries love games of any kind that offer a real challenge, like war video games, military themes, or rousing music with a beat. Anything red is a good bet: red flowers, red gems, and red accessories. How about giving Aries a way to let off steam with a gym membership or aerobic-dancing classes? Monogram a robe with a nickname in red.

Taurus

These are touchy-feely people who love things that appeal to all their senses. Find something that sounds, tastes, smells, feels, or looks good. And don't stint on quality or comfort. Taurus know the value of everything and will be aware of the price tag. Taurus foodies will appreciate chef-worthy kitchen gadgets, the latest cookbook, and gourmet treats. Taurus is a great collector. Find out what their passion is and present them with a rare item or a beautiful storage container such as an antique jewelry box. Green-thumb Taurus would love some special plants or flowers, garden tools, beautiful plant containers. Appeal to their sense of touch with fine fabrics—high-thread-count sheets, cashmere, satin, and mohair. One of the animal-loving signs, Taurus might appreciate a retractable leash or soft bed for the dog or cat. Get them a fine wallet or checkbook cover. They'll use it often.

Gemini

Mercury-ruled Gemini appreciates gifts that appeal to their mind. The latest book or novel, a talked-about film, a CD from a hot new singer, or a high-tech gadget might appeal. A beautiful diary or a tape recorder would record their adventures. Since Geminis often do two things at once, a telephone gadget that leaves their hands free would be appreciated. In fact, a new telephone device or superphone would appeal to these great communicators. Gloves, rings, and bracelets accent their expressive hands. Clothes from an interesting new designer appeal to their sense of style. You might try giving Gemini a variety of little gifts in a beautiful box or a Christmas stocking. A tranquil massage at a local spa would calm Gemini's sensitive nerves. Find an interesting way to wrap your gift. Nothing boring, please!

Cancer

Cancer is associated with home and family, so anything to do with food, entertaining at home, and family life is a good bet. Beautiful dishes or serving platters, silver items, fine crystal and linen, gourmet cookware, cooking classes or the latest DVD from a cooking teacher might be appreciated. Cancer designers Vera Wang and Giorgio Armani have perfected the Cancer style and have many home products available, as well as their elegant designer clothing. Naturally, anything to do with the sea is a possibility: pearls, coral, or shell jewelry. Boat and water-sports equipment might work. Consider cruise wear for traveling Cancers. Sentimental Cancer loves antiques and silver frames for family photos. Cancer people are often good photographers, so consider frames, albums, and projectors to showcase their work. Present your gift in a personal way with a special note.

Leo

Think big with Leo and appeal to this sign's sense of drama. Go for the gold (Leo's color) with gold jewelry, designer clothing, or big attention-getting accessories. Follow their signature style, which could be superelegant, like Jacqueline Onassis, or superstar, like Madonna or Jennifer Lopez. This sign is always ready for the red carpet and stays beautifully groomed, so stay within these guidelines when choosing your gift. Feline motifs and animal prints are usually a hit. The latest grooming aids, high-ticket cosmetics, and mirrors reflect their best image. Beautiful hairbrushes tame their manes. Think champagne, high-thread-count linens, and luxurious loungewear or lingerie. Make Leo feel special with a custom portrait or photo shoot with your local star photographer. Be sure to go for spectacular wrapping, with beautiful paper and ribbons. Present your gift with a flourish!

Virgo

Virgo usually has a special subject of interest and would appreciate relevant books, films, lectures, or classes. Choose health-oriented things: gifts to do with fitness and self-improvement. Virgo enjoys brainteasers, crossword puzzles, computer programs, organizers, and digital planners. Fluffy robes, bath products, and special soaps appeal to Virgo's sense of cleanliness. Virgo loves examples of good, practical design: efficient telephones, beautiful briefcases, computer cases, desk accessories. Choose natural fibers and quiet colors when choosing clothes for Virgo. Virgo has high standards, so go for quality when choosing a gift.

Libra

Whatever you give this romantic sign, go for beauty and romance. Libra loves accessories, decorative objects, whatever makes him or his surroundings more aesthetically pleasing. Beautiful flowers in pastel colors are always welcome. Libras are great hosts and hostesses, who might appreciate a gift related to fine dining: serving pieces, linens, glassware, flower vases. Evening or party clothes please since Libra has a gad-about social life. Interesting books, objets d'art, memberships to museums, and tickets to cultural events are good ideas. Fashion or home-decorating magazine subscriptions usually please Libra women. Steer away from anything loud, garish, or extreme. Think pink, one of their special colors, when giving Libra jewelry, clothing, or accessories. It's a very romantic sign, so be sure to remember birthdays, holidays, and anniversaries with a token of affection.

Scorpio

Scorpios love mystery, so bear that in mind when you buy these folks a present. You could take this literally and buy them a good thriller DVD, novel, or video game. Scorpios are power players, so a book about one of their sign might please. Bill Gates, Jack Welch, Condoleezza Rice, and Hillary Clinton are hot Scorpio subjects. Scorpios love black leather, suede, fur, anything to do with the sea, power tools, tiny spy tape recorders, and items with secret compartments or intricate locks. When buying a handbag for Scorpio, go for simple shapes with lots of interior pockets. Sensuous Scorpios appreciate hot lingerie, sexy linens, body lotions, and perfumed candles. Black is the favored color for Scorpio clothing—go for sexy textures like cashmere and satin in simple shapes by designers like Calvin Klein. This sign is fascinated with the occult, so give them an astrology or tarot-card reading, beautiful crystals, or an astrology program for the computer.

Sagittarius

For these outdoor people, consider adventure trips, designer sportswear, gear for their favorite sports. A funny gift or something for their pets pleases Sagittarius. For clothing and accessories, the fashionista of this sign tends to like bright colors and dramatic innovative styles. Otherwise, casual sportswear is a good idea. These travelers usually have a favorite getaway place; give them a travel guide, DVD, novel, or history book that would make their trip more interesting. Luggage is also a good bet. Sleek carry-ons, travel wallets, ticket holders, business-card cases, and wheeled computer bags might please these wanderers. Anything that makes travel more comfortable and pleasant is good for Sagittarius, including a good book to read en route. This sign is the great gambler of the zodiac, so gifts related to their favorite gambling venue would be appreciated.

Capricorn

For this quality-conscious sign, go for a status label from the best store in town. Get Capricorns something good for their image and career. They could be fond of things Spanish, like flamenco or tango music, or of country-and-western music and motifs. In the bookstore, go for biographies of the rich and famous, or advice books to help Capricorn get to the top. Capricorns take their gifts seriously, so steer away from anything too frivolous. Garnet, onyx, or malachite jewelry, Carolina Herrera fragrance and clothing, and beautiful briefcases and wallets are good ideas. Glamorous status tote bags carry business gear in style. Capricorns like golf, tennis, and sports that involve climbing, cycling, or hiking, so presents could be geared to their outdoor interests. Elegant evening accessories would be fine for this sign, which often entertains for business.

Aquarius

Give Aquarius a surprise gift. This sign is never impressed with things that are too predictable. So use your imagination to present the gift in an unusual way or at an unexpected time. With Aquarius, originality counts. When in doubt, give them something to think about, a new electronic gadget, perhaps a small robot, or an advanced computer game. Or something New Age, like an amethyst-crystal cluster. Aquarius like innovative materials with a space-age look. They are the ones with the wraparound glasses, the titanium computer cases. This air sign loves to fly—an airplane ticket always pleases. Books should be on innovative subjects, politics, or adventures of the mind. Aquarius goes for unusual color combinations—especially electric blue or hot pink—and abstract patterns. They like the newest, coolest looks on the cutting edge of fashion and are not afraid to experiment. Think of Paris Hilton's constantly changing looks. Look for an Aquarius gift in an out-of-the-way boutique or local hipster hangout. They'd be touched if you find out Aquarius's special worthy cause and make a donation. Spirit them off to hear their favorite guru.

Pisces

Pisces respond to gifts that have a touch of fantasy, magic, and romance. Look for mystical gifts with a touch of the occult. Romantic music (a customized CD of favorite love songs) and love stories appeal to Pisces sentimentalists. Pisces is associated with perfume and fragrant oils, so help this sign indulge with their favorite scent in many forms. Anything to do with the ocean, fish, and water sports appeals to Pisces. How about a whirlpool, a water-therapy spa treatment, or a sea salt rub. Appeal to this sign with treats for the feet: foot massages, pedicures, ballet tickets, and dance lessons. Cashmere socks and metallic evening sandals are other Pisces pleasers. A romantic dinner overlooking the water is Pisces paradise. A case of fine wine or another favorite liquid is always appreciated. Write a love poem and enclose it with your gift.

CHAPTER 15

Your Pet-Scope for 2010: How to Choose Your Best Friend for Life

With Jupiter, the planet of luck and expansion, in compassionate Pisces, this is a great time to bring joy into your life by adopting an animal friend. At this writing, 63 percent of all American households have at least one pet, according to a recent survey by the American Pet Product Manufacturers Association. And we spend billions of dollars on the care and feeding of our beloved pets. Our pets are counted as part of the family, often sharing our beds and accompanying us on trips.

Whether you choose to adopt an animal from a local shelter or buy a Thoroughbred from a breeder, try for an optimal time of adoption and sun sign of your new friend. If you're rescuing an animal, however, it's difficult to know the sun sign of the animal, but you can adopt on a day when the moon is compatible with yours, which should bless the emotional relationship. Using the moon signs listed in the daily forecasts in this book, choose a day when the moon is in your sign, a sign of the same element, or a compatible element. This means fire and air signs should go for a day when the moon is in fire signs Aries, Leo, Sagittarius or air signs Gemini, Libra, or Aquarius. Water and earth signs should choose a day when the moon is in water signs Cancer, Scorpio, or Pisces or earth signs Taurus, Virgo, or Capricorn. If possible, aim for a new moon, good for beginning a new relationship.

Here are some sign-specific tips for adopting an animal that will be your best friend for life.

Aries: The Rescuer

Aries gets special pleasure from rescuing animals in distress and rehabbing them, so do check your local shelters if you're thinking of adopting an animal. As an active fire sign, you'd be happiest with a lively animal that can accompany you, and you might do well with a rescue animal such as a German shepherd or Labrador retriever. You'd also enjoy training such an animal. Otherwise look for intelligence, alertness, playfulness and obedience in your friend. Since Aries tend to have an active life, look for a sleek, low maintenance coat on your dog or cat. Cat lovers would enjoy the more active breeds such as the Siamese or Abyssinian.

An Aries sun-sign dog or cat would be ideal. Aries animals have a brave, energetic, rather combative nature. They can be mischievous, so the kittens and puppies should be monitored for safety. They'll dare to jump higher, run faster, and chase more animals than their peers. They may require stronger words and more obedience training than other signs. Give them plenty of toys and play active games with them often.

Taurus: The Toucher

Taurus is a touchy-feely sign, and this extends to your animal relationships. Look for a dog or cat that enjoys being petted and groomed, is affectionate, and adapts well to family life. As one of the great animal-loving signs, Taurus is likely to have several pets, so it is important that they all get along together. Give each one its own special safe space to minimize turf wars.

Taurus animals are calm and even tempered, but do not like being teased and could retaliate, so be sure to instruct children in the proper way to handle and play with their pet. Since this sign has strong appetites and tends to put on weight easily, be careful not to overindulge them in caloric treats and table snacks. Sticking to a regular feeding schedule could help eliminate between-meal snacking.

Taurus female animals are excellent mothers and make good breeders. They tend to be clean and less destructive of home furnishings than other animals.

Gemini: The Companion

A bright, quick-witted sign like yours requires an equally interesting and communicative pet. Choose a social animal that adapts well to different environments, since you may travel or have homes in different locations.

Gemini animals can put up with noise, telephones, music, and different people coming and going. They'll want to be part of the action, so place a pillow or roost in a public place. They do not like being left alone, however, so, if you will be away for long periods, find them an animal companion to play with. You might consider adopting two Gemini pets from the same litter.

Animals born under this sign are easy to teach and some enjoy doing tricks or retrieving. They may be more vocal than other animals, especially if they are confined without companionship.

Cancer: The Nurturer

Cancer enjoys a devoted, obedient animal who demonstrates loyalty to its master. An affectionate, home-loving dog or cat who welcomes you and sits on your lap would be ideal. The emotional connection with your pet is most important; therefore, you may depend on your powerful psychic powers when choosing an animal. Wait until you feel that strong bond of psychic communication between you both. The moon sign of the day you adopt is very important for moon-ruled Cancer, so choose a water sign, if possible.

Cancer animals need a feeling of security; they don't like changes of environment or too much chaos at home. If you intend to breed your animal, the Cancer pet makes a wonderful and fertile mother.

Leo: The Prideful Owner

The Leo owner may choose a pet that reminds you of your own physical characteristics, such as similar coloring or build. You'll be proud of your pet, keep the animal groomed to perfection, and choose the most spectacular example of the breed. Noble animals with a regal attitude, beautiful fur, or striking markings are often preferred, such as the Himalayan or red tabby Persian cat, the standard poodle, the chow chow dog. An attention getter is a must.

Under the sign of the King of Beasts, Leo-born animals have proud noble natures. They usually have a cheerful, magnanimous disposition and rule their domains regardless of their breed, holding their heads with pride and walking with great authority. They enjoy grooming, like to show off and be the center of attention. Leo animals are naturals for the show ring, thriving in the spotlight and applause. They'll thrive with plenty of petting, pampering, and admiration.

Virgo: The Caregiver

Virgo owners will be very particular about their pets, paying special attention to requirements for care and maintenance. You need a pet who is clean, obedient, intelligent, yet rather quiet. A highly active, barking or meowing pet that might get on your nerves is a no-no.

Cats are usually very good pets for Virgo. Choose one of the calm breeds, such as a Persian. Though this is a high-maintenance cat, its beauty and personality will be rewarding.

You are compassionate with animals in need, and you might find it rewarding to volunteer at a local shelter or veterinary clinic or to train service dogs.

Virgo animals can be fussy eaters, very particular about their environment. They are gentle and intelligent, and respond to kind words and quiet commands, never harsh treatment.

Virgo is an excellent sign for dogs that are trained to do service work, since they seem to enjoy being useful and are intelligent enough to be easily trained.

Libra: The Beautifier

The Libra owner responds to beauty and elegance in your pet. You require a well-mannered, but social companion, who can be displayed in all of nature's finery. An exotic variety such as a graceful curly-haired Devon Rex cat would be a showstopper. Libra often prefers the smaller varieties, such as a miniature schnauzer, a mini-greyhound or a teacup poodle.

Pets born under Libra are usually charming, well-mannered gentlemen who love the comforts of home life. They tend to be more careful than other signs, not rushing willfully into potentially dangerous situations. They'll avoid confrontations and harsh sounds, responding to words of love and gentle corrections.

Scorpio: The Powerful

Scorpios enjoy a powerful animal with a strong character. They enjoy training animals in obedience, would do well with service dogs, guard dogs, or police animals. Some Scorpios enjoy the more exotic, edgy pets, such as hairless Sphynx cats or Chinese chin dogs. Scorpios could find rescuing animals in dire circumstances and finding them new homes especially rewarding, as Matthew McConaughey did during Hurricane Katrina.

Animals born under this sign tend to be one-person pets, very strongly attached to their owners and extremely loyal and possessive. They are natural guard animals who will take extreme risks to protect their owners. They are best ruled by love and with consistent behavior training. They need to respect their owners and will return their love with great devotion.

Sagittarius: The Jovial Freedom Lover

Sagittarius is a traveler and one of the great animal lovers of the zodiac. The horse is especially associated with your sign, and you could well be a "horse whisperer." You generally respond most to large, active animals. If a small animal, like a Chihuahua, steals your heart, be sure it's one that travels well or tolerates your absence. Outdoor dogs like hunting dogs, retrievers, and border collies would be good companions on your outdoor adventures.

Sagittarius animals are freedom-loving, jovial, happy-go-lucky types. They may be wanderers, however, so be sure they have the proper identification tags and consider embedded microchip identification. These animals tend to be openly affectionate, companionable, untemperamental. They enjoy socializing and playing with humans and other animals and are especially good with active children.

Capricorn: The Thoroughbred

Capricorn is a discriminating owner, with a great sense of responsibility toward your animal. You will be concerned with maintenance and care, will rarely neglect or overlook any health issues with your pet. You will also discipline your pet wisely, not tolerating any destructive or outrageous antics. You will be attracted to good breeding, good manners, and deep loyalty from your pet.

The Capricorn pet tends to be more quiet and serious than other pets, perhaps a lone wolf who prefers the company of its owner, rather than a sociable or mischievous type. This is another good sign for a working dog, such as a herder, as Capricorn animals enjoy this outlet for their energy.

Aquarius: The Independent Original

Aquarius owners tend to lead active, busy lives and need an animal who can either accompany them cheerfully or who won't make waves. Demanding or high-maintenance dogs are not for you. You might prefer unusual or oddball types of pets, such as dressed-up Chihuahuas who travel in your tote bag or scene-stealing, rather shocking hairless cats. Or you will acquire a group of animals who can play with one another when you are pursuing outside activities, as Oprah Winfrey does. You can relate to the independence of cats, who require relatively little care and maintenance.

Aquarius animals are not loners—they enjoy the companionship of humans or groups of other animals. They tend to be more independent and may require more training to follow the house rules. However, they can have unique personalities and endearing oddball behavior.

Pisces: The Soul Mate

This is the sign that can "talk to the animals." Pisces owners enjoy a deep communication with their pets, love having their animals accompany them, sleep with them, and show affection. Tenderhearted Pisces will often rescue an animal in distress or adopt an animal from a shelter.

Tropical fish are often recommended as a Pisces pet, and seem to have a natural tranquilizing effect on this sign. However, Pisces may require an animal that shows more affection than their fish friends.

Pisces animals are creative types, can be sensually seductive and mysterious, mischievous and theatrical. They make fine house pets, do not usually like to roam far from their owners, and have a winning personality, especially with the adults in the home. Naturally sensitive and seldom vicious, they should be treated gently and given much praise and encouragement.

CHAPTER 16

Your Taurus Personality and Potential: The Roles You Play in Life

The more you understand your Taurus personality and potential, the more you'll benefit from using your special solar power to help create the life you want. There's a life coach, personal trainer, career adviser, fashion expert, and matchmaker all built into your Taurus sun sign. Whether you want to make a radical change in your life or simply chose a new wardrobe or paint a room, your sun sign can help you discover new possibilities and make good decisions. You could tap into your Taurus power to deal with relationship issues, such as getting along with your boss or spicing up your love life. Maybe you'll be inspired by a celebrity sign mate who shares your special traits.

Let the following chapters help you move in harmony with your natural Taurus gifts. As the ancient oracle of Delphi advised, "Know theyself." To know yourself, as astrology helps you to do, is to gain confidence and strength.

You may wonder how astrologers determine what a Taurus personality is like. To begin with, we use a type of recipe, blending several ingredients. First there's your Taurus element: earth. Earth signs are practical, down-to-earth, solid. Taurus functions in a fixed way—it is a builder, a sign of growth and abundance, single-mindedness, and it can be stubborn. Then there's your sign's polarity, which adds a feminine, receptive, yin dimension. Let's not forget your planetary rules: Venus, the planet of love and beauty. Add your sign's location in the zodiac: in the second house of values, material possessions, what you own. Finally, stir in your symbol, the strong and solid Bull.

But all Taurus are not alike! This recipe influences everything we say about Taurus. For example, you could easily deduce that a fixed earth sign with Venus as a ruler will love the sensual goodies of life. And that Taurus will be good with money, possessive, and a bit stubborn. But your individual astrological personality contains a blend of many other planets, colored by the signs they occupy, plus factors such as the sign coming over the horizon at the exact moment of your birth. However, the more Taurus planets in your horoscope, the more likely you'll follow your sun sign's prototype. On the other hand, if many planets are grouped together in a different sign, they will color your horoscope accordingly, sometimes making a low-key, mellow sun sign come on much stronger. So if the Taurus traits mentioned here don't describe you, there could be other factors flavoring your cosmic stew. (Look up your other planets in the tables in this book to find out what they might be!)

The Taurus Man: The Material Guy

The Taurus man has a sharp eye for quality and value. You're interested in the tangible side of life, which can be fully experienced with all your senses. You'll work hard to provide yourself and your loved ones with material comforts. Born under a fixed, earth sign, you like solid, secure ground under your feet. Not for you is restless shifting from place to place (unless you have a strong Gemini influence in your horoscope). Taking frequent risks is not your cup of tea, either. Instead, each step is carefully considered before you make your move. Slow to commit and equally slow to let go, you are known for physical and emotional endurance, a tremendous asset in a business where you are required to be a judge of lasting value.

Endowed with stamina and persistence, you move steadily toward your goal, maintaining focus and control at all times. Like the strong, silent hero portrayed by Gary Cooper, rather than the swashbuckling extrovert on the fast track, you'll stick to your guns, rarely changing horses in midstream. Once you are committed, no one robs you easily of your rightful possessions or position. Taurus has so much patience that it takes a lot of pushing to make you angry. But one sure way of turning you into a raging Bull is to threaten your well-established territory or your hard-won material security. You make a formidable enemy, and your sign has produced several of the world's fiercest dictators.

The average Taurus male is usually uncomplicated in wants and needs. What you see is what you get with Taurus. You are usually quite predictable and take life literally, preferring to think in terms of direct experience rather than abstract concepts. Not one for a spartan lifestyle, Venus-ruled Taurus likes to enjoy the fruits of your labors to the fullest. You're susceptible to physical comfort, if not outright luxury: good food on your plate, the aroma of full-bloom roses or a simmering stew, the feel of beautiful fabrics. An atmosphere of plenty appeals to Taurus. Even the most pared-down Taurus lifestyle has comfort, sensual texture, carefully chosen objects, and an affectionate pet or two.

Because you love to be surrounded by comfort and beauty, you may overindulge in good food or accumulate collections of objects d'art. You'll devote much time and effort to making your beloved home as comforting and welcoming as possible. It may be very difficult to lure you away from your well-feathered nest. You prefer to entertain at home, remaining on secure, familiar turf, where you can enjoy your treasures and pleasures to the fullest rather than venturing out to explore new territory.

In a Relationship

The physical side of a relationship is high priority for the sensual Taurus man. You need to be touched, held, and hugged. You love to look at the beauty of the human form. Romantically, you'll tumble hard and fast for physical beauty, especially if combined with a voluptuous, well-sculpted body. The combination of sensuality and endurance makes Taurus one of the great lovers of the zodiac, though your outward appearance is more wholesome and easygoing, like heartthrob George Clooney or vintage movie heroes Jimmy Stewart, Bing Crosby, James Mason, and Gary Cooper.

Letting go of anything, whether it's a threadbare, once-beloved old sweater or your first love, is especially difficult for you. You can carry the torch for years after a romance has faded, sometimes staying in an unhappy or abusive relationship long after another sign would have departed. In the extreme, this becomes an obsession—Taurus never forgets, especially a broken promise.

Once you have established a loving, cozy, secure home base, you can be one of the most devoted husbands. You're happiest with a domestic, earth-mother woman who won't interfere in your equally comfortable work routines. Before committing yourself, however, you may experiment with different erotic adventures. Such is your fondness for beauty of all kinds that you could easily fall for a flirtatious charmer or a glamorous independent career woman.

Ultimately, though, you'd prefer having your wife nearby. A partner who is too self-sufficient will either send you off to greener pastures or make you see red. Since you have such a long memory for discomfort or grief, you may let grievances accumulate until you are pushed too far, then end the relationship with an explosion. However, when you do find a compatible mate, you can be the stable, secure, and sensual husband of most women's dreams.

The Taurus Woman: Sensible and Sensual

You are the earth mother of the zodiac, an unabashed, uninhibited sensualist who revels in beauty in all its earthly manifestations. An animal lover and green-thumbed gardener, you see divinity in nature and respond almost spiritually to physical beauty in all its forms. You feel a surge in your heart when you find a full-bloom rose, when an animal does something lovable or charming. Nature-loving Taurus takes an especially protective attitude toward the environment and the welfare of animals (you're sure to have at least one beloved pet).

You're also conscious of what things cost, both in terms of talent and cold cash. No one can tell the "real thing" from the fake as well as you can. You never underestimate the worth of your own talent, either. It was Taurus supermodel Linda Evangelista who once proclaimed: "I never get out of bed for less than $10,000."

Another famous Taurus beauty was described: "She moves like a storm through life, and in the end, she gets just what she wants." A pronounced Taurus trait is stubbornness. When a Taurus woman sets her mind to something, there is no stopping her. With blinders on, you'll bulldoze ahead until you get what you want, disregarding public opinion or advice to the contrary. You'll patiently wait until your infallible instincts tell you the time is right to take action. Once on track, you won't be derailed by other options, no matter how tempting.

Taurus is slow to make changes. You'll find the particular style or image that works best for you and make it your own. Many Taurus women in show business remain memorable, with a style that others try to copy but few can imitate. Think of Audrey Hepburn, Carol Burnett, Barbra Streisand, Cher, Candice Bergen—each unique, memorable, and much imitated. While other stars fade, these talented Taurus go from strength to strength, improving with age as they build on their previous success.

One of your greatest gifts is your common sense. You're a realist who brings ideas down to earth. Though you may be less gifted in judging the complexities of other people, you do understand what really works. You drive a hard bargain, and you're the least likely of any sign to fall for a puffed-up sales pitch.

You'll hold people to their commitments, with little regard for those who change their minds or promise what they cannot deliver. Therefore, fire signs (Aries, Sagittarius, Leo) and air signs (Gemini, Libra, Aquarius) will present special difficulties for you. Their idea of commitment is often negotiable. Though you love their glamour and dash, you're not always willing to grant the flexibility these signs demand, or to leave your comfortable abode to accompany them to more exciting places. (Many Taurus have "fear of flying," of losing control of their environment.) You'll also give short shrift to the playboy who changes his women frequently and to the loser who doesn't produce.

In a Relationship

You rarely marry on a whim. Many of you give special consideration to a man's ability to provide the lifestyle of your dreams, or to create it with you. Because you dislike change or instability, you tend to stick with a marriage even after it has deteriorated. The most successful Taurus relationships are those where both partners have similar goals and a mutual agreement on the lifestyle they wish to achieve. You often make a particularly good partner for a sensitive, artistic man who appreciates the warm, stable, nurturing atmosphere you can provide.

You're usually a talented homemaker, though you may delegate some or most of the mundane chores to others. You prize your secure home turf and family life above all. Whether you stay rooted in the same place for decades or change homes on a whim, each nest will be beautifully and comfortably, if not luxuriously, appointed.

A wizard with money, you have a talent for budgeting, investing, and finding a bargain. You'll be a full-time mother, if necessary, devoting time and attention to your brood—though you may run a business on the side from your home.

Taurus in the Family

The Taurus Parent

Taurus takes to parenting naturally. You provide the ideal atmosphere and qualities to nurture a growing child, as you love to nurture all living things. Taurus is an especially effective parent for young children, who benefit most from your calm, patient qualities. You provide a secure foundation of love, and a stable family atmosphere.

Your heart goes out to children who are growing up in difficult circumstances, and you can be a tireless charity worker on their behalf.

You thoroughly enjoy the early childhood stages, when your demonstrative, affectionate nature seems designed to give the child a sense of security. Later, as the child grows more independent, it may be difficult for you to let go. You may find it especially difficult to deal with the rebellious teenager who has a stubborn streak to match yours. Indeed, many children of Taurus remain in the family nest into adulthood. A Taurus mom is a tough act to follow, as many young wives have discovered! And there is no one as protective of his children throughout their lives as a Taurus dad.

The song "There's No Place Like Home" was surely written by a Taurus. Images of Mother baking chocolate-chip cookies in the kitchen and Daddy comfortably lodged in his favorite chair with a big dog lounging at his feet are Taurus stereotypes. Though few Taurus can manage the Norman Rockwell fantasy in today's world, this ideal is close to Taurus hearts. Rare is the Taurus who doesn't long for a place in the country with swings on the trees, fragrant rosebushes, and a well-stocked kitchen.

The Taurus Stepparent

Your steady, calm nature can be reassuring to stepchildren longing for a stable atmosphere. Patiently, you'll wait for the children to become accustomed to the new family structure. When they do, you'll be warm and affectionate. However, when you must assert your disciplinary authority, do so with calm control. Understand that youngsters with strong wills may resent your position.

Stepchildren will teach you to develop flexibility, and can expand your horizons if given the chance. Be open to an extended family situation that may not follow the traditional rules. Children will appreciate your allowing them time alone with their biological parent to share mutual interests and strengthen bonds.

The Taurus Grandparent

In spirit, Taurus grandparents are picture-book elders of a Norman Rockwell painting, even if they look young and glamorous. By this time, you've established a warm, comfortable home and are content to gather all the family round. The Taurus grandma is the archetypal matriarch with a large brood to nurture, whether they are your own or other children in need. Chances are, your extended family will include all the relatives of your in-laws.

Yours will be the home where all the family gathers for holiday feasts, the garden of prizewinning flowers and fresh vegetables, and the special recipes no one else can quite duplicate. You'll be concerned about the children's future and may provide a trust fund or nest egg to finance their education. As the years go by, you'll strengthen family ties by planning celebrations, sending thoughtful notes, and making frequent phone calls. Your grandchildren will remember gratefully how you taught them the true meaning of family traditions by providing them with a strong sense of their own roots.

CHAPTER 17

Taurus Fashion and Decor Tips: Elevate Your Mood with Taurus Style!

In this year of serious concerns, why not put joy and imagination into your life by creating a harmonious environment and expressing your sun sign's natural flair in everything you do and wear. There are colors, sounds, fashion, and decor tips that fit Taurus like the proverbial glove and that could brighten every day. Even small changes in decor could make you feel "home at last." A simple change of color in your walls or curtains, your special music in the air, and a wardrobe makeover inspired by a Taurus designer or celebrity are natural mood elevators that boost your confidence and energy level. Even your vacations might be more fun if you tailor them to your natural Taurus inclinations. Try these tips to enhance your lifestyle and express the Taurus in you.

Taurus Fashion Secrets

Taurus is known for a unique unforgettable style that remains consistent over the years. You know what you like and ignore the rest of the pack. You tend to evolve into your own look, be it dramatic (Cher), softly feminine (Andie MacDowell), high fashion (Audrey Hepburn), or classic (Renée Zellweger and Penelope Cruz). There is always an element of sensuality to the way you dress, regardless of whether you're voluptuous or slender. Luxurious fabrics and sensuous textures are a Taurus trademark. Many Taurus like to wear body-revealing looks, favored by Cate Blanchett and Uma Thurman.

Taurus women have especially lovely necks and throats, emphasized with beautiful necklaces, as Barbra Streisand and Candice Bergen do. You probably have an impressive jewelry collection, and have special flair with dramatic neckwear.

Like Kimora Lee Simmons, model and designer of the Baby Phat collection, you may be an Olympic shopper who accumulates overstuffed closets crammed with clothes and accessories. Some of these you regard as clothing investments to be retained for years. Your best strategy is to stick to simple shapes in luxurious fabrics. Avoid anything fussy, especially if you've overindulged your Taurus appetite for good food.

Taurus Colors

Sensual Taurus, one of the best colorists in the zodiac, is sure to have strong opinions about what you do not like. The colors of the countryside in the springtime are sure to be favorites, and look well on you. Usually you prefer pastels and quiet calm shades to more vibrant hues. Emerald green, the color of your birthstone, is also second nature to Taurus.

Your Taurus Fashion Role Models

Donatella Versace, a Taurus designer with a sexy edge, has posed her models in sumptuous mansions wearing clothes that glorify and expose the body beautiful. Valentino dresses the A-list of socialites and movie stars who appreciate the way his designs play up their natural elegance and femininity. Jean-Paul Gaultier shows the sexy side of Taurus in his avant-garde clothes for rock stars like Madonna. Michelle Pfeiffer, Candice Bergen, Cate Blanchett, and Uma Thurman are classic Taurus beauties whose looks should inspire you to make the most of yours.

Aim to be distinctively and consistently you. Create your own styles, rather than latch on to a look for the sake of being in. And finally, be sure to play up your femininity with a signature perfume.

Taurus Home Makeover Tips

You're the original earth mother or nature girl. Chances are you've got a jungle of green plants in your city window, or a beautiful garden in the backyard. So take a leaf or a flower from nature, and you'll be right on target when planning your home. The luxurious look of English or French country houses or the comfortable warmth of a cozy farmhouse suits you well. If you must live in the city, try to live near a park, use floral prints (or gutsy earthy colors), and fill your windows with plants (even indoor trees) to bring nature indoors, especially if you are looking out on a brick wall. Flowers spilling from antique containers are another wonderful Taurus touch. Your furniture should be roomy and comfortable, upholstered in a feel-good fabric.

You're one of the great collectors of the zodiac; you do it for both pleasure and investment. Perhaps you'll accumulate a trove of pottery or delicate porcelain, artworks, sculpture, records, jewelry, and antiques. Be sure there are enough shelves to display your treasures beautifully. All those bargains you've scored on eBay may take up a lot of room, however. Use your Taurus creativity to devise some decorative storage solutions, ones that will protect your finds, yet make them accessible. Antique chests and armoires can be filled to capacity with your latest acquisitions. Taurus decorator Carolyne Roehm might inspire you with her lovely ideas.

Since you love good food and entertain at home, you'll want a large, well-equipped kitchen. The Taurus kitchen is usually the family gathering place, so you may want to combine it with a family room or use an open plan in order to socialize with your family while you cook.

Your animal companions should be considered also, with spaces to roam and places to roost. Provide an indoor carpeted cat tree for your feline friends and some comfortable dog beds for Rover.

Taurus Sounds

One of the most musical signs, you respond to rich, sensual sounds of all kinds, especially vocal music, because Taurus is associated with the voice. Perhaps you have a well-tuned piano or guitar for at-home musical entertainment. Family sing-alongs are a Taurus specialty. Since you are sensitive to the slightest distortion in tone, invest in an excellent sound system. You may collect the great vocalists like Barbra Streisand, Cher, Willie Nelson, and Ella Fitzgerald. Or rock to Janet Jackson, Stevie Wonder, and David Byrne. Taurus songwriters like Burt Bacharach, Oscar Hammerstein, and Irving Berlin created sensuous sounds that glorify the human voice.

Taurus Getaways

If turf-loving Taurus travels, it's usually for the following reasons: gourmet food, fantastic bargain shopping, or luxurious pampering. Sometimes, you just have to get away from it all, so look for a home away from home when you travel. A comfortable bed-and-breakfast or a familiar hotel with a good restaurant where the owners know your preferences would be best. A luxurious cruise ship on which you can travel without a constant change of rooms or a pampering spa with spectacular views of fragrant gardens will soothe you when you are away from familiar turf. Or rent your own romantic castle somewhere like Tuscany or Provence, with a pastoral landscape and a town famous for its cuisine.

When you pack, be sure to include a few comfort items, such as a fragrant candle to take away the stale smell of hotel rooms, a favorite scarf to drape over a lamp, some framed photos of loved ones, your own special scented bath oils and shower gels, and some delicious little snacks. You might even want to bring a small travel-size coffee press with your special coffee blend. A touch of luxury when you travel can make a world of difference, especially after a long day of sightseeing or shopping. For evenings on the road, a DVD you've been longing to see could buffer any feelings of homesickness. Don't forget your favorite bathrobe, and pamper yourself with breakfast in bed.

You'll need an extra bag—or two—for all the goodies you accumulate on shopping trips to the local markets. Invest in featherweight ballistic nylon suitcases and tote bags that fold up in their own little cases, perfect for stashing your cache of souvenirs. Always carry an extra shopping bag with you. You never know when or where a bargain will appear!

CHAPTER 18

The Taurus Way to Stay Healthy and Age Well

This year we'll be focused on staying healthy to avoid the high costs of health care and to cope with stressful events. Some signs have an easier time than others committing to a health and diet regimen. Taurus usually enjoys a structured routine with clear health goals. It's important to design a unique program that incorporates health-building activities into your busy life and provides plenty of enjoyable activities and delicious diet alternatives. Astrology can clue you in to the specific Taurus tendencies that contribute to good or ill health. So follow these sun-sign tips to help yourself become the healthiest Taurus possible.

Downsize Portions

Taurus loves food, all kinds of food, in quantity. Especially rich, creamy desserts and fried goodies. (Once you start eating rich food, you find it almost impossible to stop.) Deprivation in any form is not going to work for you, so find a diet that allows you healthy variations of the foods you love most. First, raid your refrigerator and eliminate any foods that are not on your diet. If it's there, you'll find it and eat it. Aim for smaller portions and fill up on skinny foods like salads. Once in a while, give yourself a day off and indulge in the treats you love so you won't feel deprived.

Exercise for Pleasure

Pleasure is the key to your exercise routine. You need an attractive place to work out, not a sweaty gym. Why not plan your workout to take place in one of the scenic areas of your town? Jogging or biking along a river or through a park, exploring the woodlands and seashore in your area with long nature hikes, or horseback riding along a scenic trail can make you look forward to exercising. Or plant an extensive garden that requires lots of active maintenance. Weeding, shoveling, and mowing are great Taurus ways to exercise. If you live in an appropriate setting, get a dog that requires lots of active play. Working with horses or other large animals can also be a joy for Taurus.

Protect Your Neck

Pay special attention to the Taurus area of the body: the neck. Yoga exercises, head rolls, the proper pillow, and a good masseuse can make a big difference here. Though Taurus is a hardy sign with great stamina and endurance, you can become sluggish if you're overweight or if you have a thyroid problem. So, if you can barely drag yourself off the couch, be sure to check your thyroid. If you're not getting enough sleep, it could be due to tension in your neck. Try changing your pillow to one specially designed to support your neck area.

Massage is one way to soothe the raging bull in you, especially if tension is lodging in your neck. Try shiatsu massage targeted to the acupressure points in the neck area. Neck massages are a sybaritic way to release tension and promote more restful sleep.

Stay Forever Young

As the zodiac's gourmet, Taurus needs to monitor your diet and craving for sweets as you grow older, since you're more likely to overindulge and gain weight. If you've become a couch potato, trick yourself into motion by combining a workout with a walk in a beautiful nature preserve or on a bike path, or take along one of your favorite companions. Walking an adorable dog could get you outdoors and in motion. Since you are a great shopper, why not combine bargain hunting with a power walk in your local mall? Or get a workout playing with young grandchildren—volunteering to do some extra babysitting could be a fun way to work off a few pounds as you keep up with the youngsters.

CHAPTER 19

Add Taurus Star Power to Your Career: What It Takes to Succeed in 2010

In today's tight job market, you'll need to pull out all the stops to land a great job. Taurus has a combination of talents and abilities that can make you a natural winner. Tops on the list is your keen sense of value. You're a natural trader, with financial savvy, who understands true worth. You respond to beauty in all its forms and are an excellent judge of quality, which serves you well in appraisal or design careers. Your love of nature could lead you into a highly lucrative environmental or agricultural field. If you develop and nurture your Taurus talents, you'll be more likely to find a career you truly enjoy, as well as one that rewards you financially. Here's to your success!

Where to Look for Your Perfect Job

Taurus prefers a slow, steady rise to the top, so look for an initial job that offers strong growth potential. A company that promotes from within would be ideal. Taurus is a long-term survivor in the working world, with more endurance and persistence than any other sign. You thrive in a career with staying power and work best when you stick to one career direction. In the riskier professions, you often succeed because you simply hang in there the longest, weathering the storms.

The downside is that you may vegetate in a job that has no challenges, because you value the steady income.

Since Taurus is the sign of buying, appraising, and accumulating, you thrive in careers such as retailing, trading of any sort, auctions, dealing in art or collectibles, banking, or real estate. You might do very well in the online-auction field, especially if you have access to antiques or collectibles. Your love of nature could lead you into farming, landscape gardening, horticulture, or animal breeding. Taurus is a natural builder, so consider architecture, construction, or engineering. Your sensual side could gravitate to careers in music, culinary arts, fashion, photography, jewelry design, or the fragrance industry.

Live Up to Your Leadership Potential

Taurus are natural empire builders who go into business for long-term gains, rarely switching careers. To find a field you like and develop a career slowly and steadily is the Taurus style. If you have dreams of running a business, be inspired by those who achieved phenomenal success, such as William Randolph Hearst, who founded a newspaper empire, and Hollywood's Aaron Spelling, who developed series like *Dynasty*.

When you're supervising others, you like total control of your turf, which can make you a steady and wise leader or, more negatively, a benevolent dictator or tyrant. You like the last word on each aspect of your business, rarely changing your mind once you have made a decision. Though you might nurture underlings and reward loyalty generously, you may hesitate to give them the independence they need to grow by trial and error. You tend to promote from within, working with people you have known for some time, with the goal of building a solid structure for your organization. You'll value that structure rather than flashy ideas or flash-in-the-pan products. Try to be more flexible and open to new ideas.

How to Work with Others

Once you are comfortable in a steady job, you tend to settle in for the long term and rise steadily through the ranks. You are oriented toward seeing concrete results rather than speculating; therefore, you may not be the most ambitious employee, especially when rising to the top involves taking many risks. But as a valued member of the team, you're the one who can be counted on to ride out storms, handle crises with common sense, negotiate cleverly, and come through in a pinch.

The Taurus Way to Get Ahead

Your Taurus gifts can bring you the highest return on the investment of your time and energy. Pick a company that offers a steady rise to the top and promotes from within. Then play up your best Taurus attributes:
- Loyalty
- Thoroughness
- Financial savvy
- Patience and perseverance
- Reliability
- Steadiness
- Evaluation and appraisal skills
- Practicality
- Negotiation skills

CHAPTER 20

Learn from Taurus Celebrities

You know how much fun it is when you find a famous person who shares your sun sign—and even your birthday! Why not turn your brush with fame into an education in astrology? Celebrities who capture the media's attention relfect the current planetary influences, as well as the unique star quality of their sun sign. Who's in this year may be out next year. You can learn from the hottest stellar spotlight stealers what the public is responding to and what this says about our current values.

If one of your famous sign mates intrigues you, explore his personality further by looking up his other planets using the tables in this book. You may even find his horoscope posted on astrology-related Internet sites like www.astrodatabank.com or www.stariq.com, which have charts of world events and headline makers. Then apply the effects of Venus, Mars, Saturn, and Jupiter to his sun-sign traits. It's a way to get up close and personal with your famous friend, and maybe learn some secrets not revealed to the public.

You're sure to have lots in common with your famous signmates. Consider how Jack Nicholson, Candice Bergen, Cher, and Al Pacino have forged long-lasting careers in show business. Do you have the classic Taurus style of Cate Blanchett and the fashion designer Valentino, or are you an over-the-top Taurus like Donatella Versace? There are many heroes born under Taurus whose success stories can inspire you, such as Michael Moore and Coretta Scott King.

Get to know these famous Taureans better and learn what makes their stars shine brightly.

Taurus Celebrities

Ryan O'Neal (4/20/41)
Jessica Lange (4/20/49)
Luther Vandross (4/20/51)
Carmen Electra (4/20/72)
Anthony Quinn (4/21/15)
Queen Elizabeth II (4/21/26)
Charles Grodin (4/21/35)
Patti Lupone (4/21/49)
Tony Danza (4/21/51)
Andie MacDowell (4/21/58)
Tony Romo (4/21/80)
Aaron Spelling (4/22/28)
Jack Nicholson (4/22/37)
Peter Frampton (4/22/50)
Lee Majors (4/23/39)
Sandra Dee (4/23/42)
Michael Moore (4/23/54)
Valerie Bertinelli (4/23/60)
Melina Kanadaredes (4/23/67)
Shirley MacLaine (4/24/34)
Barbra Streisand (4/24/42)
Eric Bogosian (4/24/53)
Kelly Clarkson (4/24/82)
Al Pacino (4/25/39)
Talia Shire (4/25/46)
Hank Azaria (4/25/64)
Renée Zellweger (4/25/69)
Jason Lee (4/25/70)
Carol Burnett (4/26/33)
Coretta Scott King (4/27/27)
Anouk Aimee (4/27/34)
Sheena Easton (4/27/59)
Saddam Hussein (4/28/37)
Ann-Margret (4/28/41)
Jay Leno (4/28/50)
Penelope Cruz (4/28/74)
Jessica Alba (4/28/81)

William Randolph Hearst (4/29/1863)
Duke Ellington (4/29/1899)
Jerry Seinfeld (4/29/55)
Daniel Day-Lewis (4/29/57)
Michelle Pfeiffer (4/29/57)
Carnie Wilson (4/29/68)
Andre Agassi (4/29/70)
Uma Thurman (4/29/70)
Cloris Leachman (4/30/30)
Willie Nelson (4/30/33)
Jill Clayburgh (4/30/44)
Kirsten Dunst (4/30/82)
Pierre Teilhard de Chardin (5/1/1881)
Kate Smith (5/1/1909)
Satyajit Ray (5/1/21)
Bing Crosby (5/2/1904)
Earl Blackwell (5/2/13)
Bianca Jagger (5/2/45)
Christine Baranski (5/2/52)
David Beckham (5/2/75)
Doug Henning (5/3/47)
Wynonna (5/3/64)
Kimora Lee Simmons (5/3/75)
Audrey Hepburn (5/4/29)
Pia Zadora (5/4/55)
Randy Travis (5/4/59)
Ann B. Davis (5/5/20)
Tammy Wynette (5/5/42)
Rudolph Valentino (5/6/1895)
George Clooney (5/6/61)
Melania Trump (5/6/70)
Robert Browning (5/7/1812)
Darren McGavin (5/7/22)
Rick Nelson (5/8/40)
Melissa Gilbert (5/8/64)
Enrique Iglesias (5/8/75)
Candice Bergen (5/9/46)
Billy Joel (5/9/49)
Rosario Dawson (5/9/79)
Bono (5/10/60)

Linda Evangelista (5/10/65)
Martha Graham (5/11/1894)
Valentino (5/11/32)
Louis Farrakhan (5/11/33)
Natasha Richardson (5/11/63)
Katharine Hepburn (5/12/1907)
Gabriel Byrne (5/12/50)
Tom Snyder (5/12/36)
Stephen Baldwin (5/12/66)
Bea Arthur (5/13/26)
Harvey Keitel (5/13/39)
Peter Gabriel (5/13/50)
Stevie Wonder (5/13/50)
Dennis Rodman (5/13/61)
Cate Blanchett (5/13/69)
David Byrne (5/14/52)
Jasper Johns (5/15/30)
Chazz Palminteri (5/15/51)
Jamie Lynn Sigler (5/15/81)
Muktananda (5/16/1908)
Liberace (5/15/19)
Pierce Brosnan (5/16/52)
Janet Jackson (5/16/66)
Tori Spelling (5/16/73)
Perry Como (5/18/12)
Margot Fonteyn (5/18/19)
Janet Jackson (5/18/66)
David Hartman (5/19/35)
Nora Ephron (5/19/41)
Adela Rogers St. Johns (5/20/1894)
Cher (5/20/46)

CHAPTER 21

Your Taurus Relationships with Every Other Sign: The Green Lights and Red Flags

Are you looking for insight into a relationship? Perhaps it's somone you've met online, a new business partner, a roommate, or the proverbial stranger across a crowded room. After an initial attraction, you may be wondering if you'll still get along down the line. Or why supposedly incompatible signs sometimes have a magical attraction to each other. If things aren't working out, astrology could give you some clues as to why he or she is "not that into you."

Astrology has no magic formula for success in love, but it does offer a better understanding of the qualities each person brings to the relationship and how your partner is likely to react to your sun-sign characteristics. Knowing your potential partner's sign and how it relates to yours could give you some clues about what to expect down the line.

There is also the issue of the timing of a new relationship. From an astrological perspective, the people you meet at any given time provide the dynamic that you require at that moment. If you're a practical, home-loving Taurus, for instance, you might benefit from a more social Gemini or globe-trotting Sagittarius at a certain time in your life.

The celebrity couples in this chapter can help you visualize each sun-sign combination. You'll note that some legendary lovers have stood the test of time, while others blazed, then broke up, and still others existed only in the fantasy world of film or television (but still captured our imagination).

Traditional astrological wisdom holds that signs of the same element are naturally compatible. For Taurus, that would be fellow earth signs Virgo and Capricorn. Also favored are signs of complementary elements, such as earth signs with water signs (Cancer, Scorpio, Pisces). In these relationships communication supposedly flows easily, and you'll feel most comfortable together.

As you read the following matches, remember that there are no hard-and-fast rules; each combination has perks as well as peeves. So when sparks fly and an irresistible magnetic pull draws you together, when disagreements and challenges fuel intrigue, mystery, passion, and sexy sparring matches, don't rule the relationship out. That person may provide the diversity, excitement, and challenge you need for an unforgettable romance, stimulating friendship, or a successful business partnership!

Taurus/Aries

THE GREEN LIGHTS:

Aries gets slow-moving Taurus up and at 'em, waving a red flag before the Bull. Taurus is excited and ready to charge. Aries gets direction, follow-through, and solid backup support, as well as a warm, loving sensual companion who is devoted and loyal.

THE RED FLAGS:

Adapting to each other's pace calls for compromise, as Aries learns that you cannot be pushed, and you learn that Aries wants everything now. You could lock horns over short-term versus long-term goals. You'll prefer comfortable, luxurious surroundings, while Aries happily sacrifices comfort for adventure. Separate vacations might be the only solution.

SIGN MATES:

Taurus Katharine Hepburn and Aries Spencer Tracy

Taurus/Taurus

THE GREEN LIGHTS:

Loyalty and emotions run deep with these sign mates. Here is the cozy, familiar, comfortable kind of love, spiced by strong sensuality. In this solid, secure relationship, you could be so contented, you never leave home!

THE RED FLAGS:

Disagreements, if they occur, can be devastating. You two lock horns and never let go. Or there's a permanent stand-off. The other possibility is you'll bore, rather than gore, each other to death, or look for stimulation elsewhere.

SIGN MATES:

Tauruses Carmen Electra and Dennis Rodman

Taurus/Gemini

THE GREEN LIGHTS:

Next-door signs may be best friends as well as lovers. In this case, Gemini gets you out of the house and into the social scene, adding laughter to love. Taurus has a soothing, stabilizing quality that can make nervous Gemini bloom.

THE RED FLAGS:

Homebody Taurus usually loves one-on-one relationships, while social Gemini loves to flirt with a crowd. Geminis need to curb their roving eyes and bodies. Infidelity can be serious business with Taurus. The balance scales between freedom and license swing and sway here.

SIGN MATES:

Taurus Andre Agassi and Gemini Steffi Graf
Taurus Queen Elizabeth II and Gemini Prince Philip

Taurus/Cancer

THE GREEN LIGHTS:

In theory, this should be one of the best combinations. Taurus can't ever get too much affection, which Cancer happily provides. And Taurus protects Cancer from the cold world with solid, secure assets. Both are home loving, emotional, and sensual.

THE RED FLAGS:

Cancer dark moods plus Taurus stubbornness could create some muddy moments. Both partners should look for constructive ways to let off steam rather than brood and sulk over grievances.

SIGN MATES:

Taurus Barbra Streisand and Cancer James Brolin
Taurus Tony Romo and Cancer Jessica Simpson

Taurus/Leo

THE GREEN LIGHTS:

Leo passion meets Taurus sensuality, and there's a volcanic physical attraction as you test each other's strength. Both lovers of beauty and comfort, you also have high ideals, fidelity, good food, and music going for you. Taurus money management could provide Leo with a royal lifestyle. The Leo confidence makes Taurus bloom.

THE RED FLAGS:

Tensions between these two fixed signs are inevitable. The Leo extravagance and your Taurus possessiveness could be bones of contention. Leo plays dangerous games here, such as denying affection or sex. Focus on building emotional security and avoiding no-win emotional showdowns.

SIGN MATES:

Taurus Bianca Jagger and Leo Mick Jagger

Taurus/Virgo

THE GREEN LIGHTS:

Taurus admires the Virgo analytical mind, while Virgo admires Taurus concentration and goal orientation. Virgo feels secure with predictable Taurus. You enjoy taking care of each other. Relaxed, soothing Taurus brings out Virgo sensuality. Virgo brings the world of ideas home to Taurus.

THE RED FLAGS:

Virgo nagging can cause Taurus self-doubt, which can show up in bullheaded stubbornness. The Taurus slow pace and ideal of deep-rooted comfort could feel like constraint to Virgo, who needs the stimulation of diversity and lively communication.

SIGN MATES:

Taurus Tim McGraw and Virgo Faith Hill

Taurus/Libra

THE GREEN LIGHTS:

Both Venus-ruled signs, who are turned on by beauty and luxury, you are happy to indulge each other. Libra brings intellectual sparkle, style, and social savvy to Taurus. Taurus gives Libra financial stability and adoration. And Libra profits from your strong Taurus sense of direction and decisiveness.

THE RED FLAGS:

Taurus is possessive and enjoys staying at home. Libra loves social life and flirting. Curb your jealousy, Taurus, because Libra flirtations are rarely serious, only part of the social game. Libra can be extravagant, while Taurus sticks to a budget and loves to watch money pile up in the bank—another cause for resentment.

SIGN MATES:

Taurus Evita and Libra Juan Peron

Taurus/Scorpio

THE GREEN LIGHTS:

Many marriages happen when these opposites attract. Taurus has a calming effect on the Scorpio innate paranoia. And Taurus responds to Scorpio intensity and fascinating air of mystery. Together, these signs have the perfect complement of sensuality and sexuality.

THE RED FLAGS:

Problems of control are inevitable when you both want to run the show. Avoid long and bitter battles or silent stand-offs by drawing territorial lines from the start. Then stick to them!

SIGN MATES:

Taurus Jessica Lange and Scorpio Sam Shepard
Taurus Tori Spelling and Scorpio Dean McDermott

Taurus/Sagittarius

THE GREEN LIGHTS:

Sagittarius energizes Taurus and gets this sign to take calculated risks and dare to think big. Taurus provides the solid support and steady income that can make Sagittarius ideas happen. Sagittarius will be challenged to produce, Taurus to stretch and grow.

THE RED FLAGS:

You are very different types who are not especially sympathetic to each other's needs. Taurus believes in hard work, Sagittarius in luck and seizing the moment of opportunity. Sagittarius is a rolling stone; Taurus is a quiet meadow. Sagittarius appreciates freedom; Taurus appreciates substance.

SIGN MATES:

Taurus Kirsten Dunst and Sagittarius Jake Gyllenhaal

Taurus/Capricorn

THE GREEN LIGHTS:

Your similar traditional values can make communication easy. This is a combination that works well on all levels. You find it easy to set goals, to organize and support each other. There are earthy passion and instinctive understanding.

THE RED FLAGS:

There may be too much earth here. The relationship can become too dutiful, practical, and unromantic. You both need to expand your horizons occasionally, and may look for stimulation elsewhere. Taurus may resent the Capricorn devotion to career, since home and family are top priority.

SIGN MATES:

Taurus Jack Nicholson and Capricorn Diane Keaton

Taurus/Aquarius

THE GREEN LIGHTS:

This is an uncomfortable, but stimulating, partnership between the conventional Taurus and the rule-breaking Aquarius. Taurus takes care of the practical, while Aquarius provides the inspiration and social involvement that shake Taurus out of a rut.

THE RED FLAGS:

Resolution of conflicts can wear this one out. Taurus is predictable. Aquarius is unpredictable. Taurus loves privacy. Aquarius is a people person. Taurus wants to settle down. Aquarius needs space. Taurus is possessive. Aquarius is detached.

SIGN MATES:

Taurus Cher and Aquarius Sonny Bono

Taurus/Pisces

THE GREEN LIGHTS:

This could be your dream lover. You both love the good things in life and can indulge each other sensually and sexually. Your Taurus focus adds stability and direction to Pisces, while Pisces creativity is lovingly encouraged by Taurus.

THE RED FLAGS:

Taurus wants Pisces to produce, not just dream, and will try to corral the slippery fish into steady employment. Not a good idea! Pisces can't be bossed or caged, and will swim off, leaving Taurus with the dotted line unsigned!

SIGN MATES:

Taurus Tony Parker and Pisces Eva Longoria
Taurus Penelope Cruz and Pisces Javier Bardem

CHAPTER 22

The Big Picture for Taurus in 2010

Welcome to 2010! You'll be delighted to know this is your year to define and enjoy your freedom. You'll experience things that will force you to think outside the box. You'll have opportunities to take risks and to add greater variety to your life.

Your ruler, Venus, begins the year in Capricorn, your ninth house, increasing the likelihood of romance with someone from another country or whose belief system is vastly different from yours. On January 18, Venus enters Aquarius, your tenth house, and for the next three weeks you have a wonderful window of opportunity for professional matters. In fact, each month until October, Venus enters a new sign, lighting up and facilitating the affairs of that house. Then, on October 8, Venus turns retrograde in Scorpio, where it remains until the end of the year. The dates for Venus transits are noted in both the daily readings and in the annual guide for your sign.

Mars, the planet that symbolizes our sexuality and aggression, begins the year retrograde in Leo, your fourth house, and turns direct again on March 10. Until then, there may be disagreements and heated discussions at home. You may also be thinking about how you would like to refurbish or change your home in some way. After March 10, you'll speed ahead on your renovation plans and much of what you do will be a reflection of who you are. Mars makes it through six signs this year, and the meaning of its transits are noted in the dailies and in the annual for your sign.

On January 13, Saturn turns retrograde in Libra, your sixth house, then moves back into Virgo and finally enters Libra again on July 21. During its transit through Virgo, Saturn urges you to assume responsibility and meet your obligations concerning children and creativity. The things you do for fun and pleasure during this time are likely to be structured in some way. In other words, instead of deciding on the spur of the moment to head to Greece, you'll plan it out to the last detail. When Saturn is in Libra, your daily work and health routines are likely to become more stringent, laden with more responsibility. You'll begin to find great support in networks of friends and coworkers, and the people with whom you work may compose a large part of your social life. This transit will last about two and a half years.

Pluto, the planet of profound transformation, continues its long journey through Capricorn, your ninth house, and keeps bringing about change in your worldview, your educational status, and your love for foreign travel and people. Pluto turns retrograde on April 6 and doesn't turn direct again until September 13. During this retrograde period, pay close attention to everything that happens related to education, publishing, and foreign travel. Follow synchronicities; listen to your intuition.

Neptune—the planet that symbolizes our illusions, idealism, all forms of escapism, and our higher selves—continues its journey through Aquarius and your tenth house. Neptune has been in this position since 1998, so by now you're well aware of how it impacts professional matters. When it turns retrograde between May 31 and November 6, your career may not be functioning quite as smoothly as usual. But you'll be injecting plenty of compassion and idealism into your career.

Uranus—the planet that symbolizes our individualism and sudden and unexpected change—enters Aries on May 27, for a period of about seven years. Check your birth chart to find out exactly what area of your life will be affected by this transit. That area will experience sudden, unexpected change, new and exciting experiences and insights. Uranus's job is to shake up the status quo and get us out of the comfortable ruts into which we often fall. The best way to navigate this seven-year transit is to embrace change. Try new things, go back to school, find a new career path, change jobs, and do whatever you feel will expand your universe and help you to evolve and achieve your potential.

Uranus turns retrograde on July 5 and doesn't turn direct again until December 5. During this period, it retrogrades back into Pisces, your eleventh house, and stirs up old issues with friends that you thought were resolved.

Jupiter, the planet of expansion and luck, enters Pisces on January 17, speeds through it without any retrogrades, and enters Aries on June 6. On July 23, it turns retrograde, slips back into Pisces in early September, and remains there throughout the rest of the year. It enters Aries again in late January 2011, where it remains until early June 2011.

So two different areas of your chart will get a taste of Jupiter's expansiveness this year. You'll have many new opportunities to expand who you are, what you're doing, and how you're doing it. If you have a copy of your natal chart, by all means check to see the house in which Aries falls in your chart. This will tell you a great deal about the specific area of your life where expansion is what you're doing.

Romance and Creativity

There are two notable time periods this year that favor romance and creative endeavors. Between March 31 and April 25, Venus will be in your sign. This transit increases your sex appeal, charisma, and general self-confidence. If you're uninvolved when the transit begins, you probably won't be when the transit ends. Venus in your sign accentuates all your normal traits and characteristics. If you get involved under this transit, your passions will be running the show!

The second great time period for romance falls between July 10 and August 6, when Venus is in fellow earth sign Virgo, transiting your fifth house of romance and creativity. This period should be very romantic if you're already involved, and incredibly exciting if you're just getting involved. It's also a creative time, when your muse is so up close and personal that you feel you simply have to do something creative. So dust off those manuscripts and portfolios!

A third period occurs between August 8 and the end of the year, when Venus transits Scorpio, your seventh house of partnerships. Venus will be retrograde part of the time—as will Mercury—but the period should be quite nice for romance!

Career

The best career dates this year occur when Venus transits your tenth house and Aquarius—from January 1 to January 18. Also, great backup dates for making sales pitches, selling manuscripts, scheduling auditions, and just about any other professional endeavor fall between January 1 and May 27, while Uranus is making its final passage (except for retrogrades) through Pisces. Pisces is compatible with your sun sign, so you have innovative ways of making a living and pushing forward your own agenda.

Another great time falls around the new moon in Taurus on May 13. This moon happens just once a year and sets the tone for the next year. Both Jupiter and Uranus form harmonious angles to this moon, indicating that opportunities that somehow expand your professional venue appear out of nowhere.

Best Times For

Buying or selling a home: June 14 to July 10, when Venus transits Leo and your fourth house.

Family reunions: May 19 to July 14.

Financial matters: April 25 to May 19, and January 17 to June 6, while Jupiter is moving direct through Pisces.

Signing contracts: When Mercury is moving direct!

Overseas travel, publishing, and higher-education endeavors: January 1 to April 6, and after September 13, while Pluto is moving in direct motion through Capricorn and your ninth house.

Mercury retrogrades

Every year, Mercury—the planet of communication and travel—turns retrograde three times. During this period, it's wise not to sign contracts (unless you don't mind renegotiating when Mercury is moving direct), to check and recheck travel plans, and to communicate as succinctly as possible. Refrain from buying any big-ticket items or electronics during this time too. Often, computers and appliances go on the fritz, cars act up, data is lost—you get the idea. Be sure to back up all files before the dates below:

April 17—May 11: Mercury retrograde in Taurus. Your personal life may feel like it belongs to someone else!

August 20—September 12: Mercury retrograde in Virgo, your fifth house of romance, creativity, children, what you do for fun and pleasure.

December 10—December 30: Mercury retrograde in Capricorn, your ninth house of education, publishing, and overseas travel.

Eclipses

Solar eclipses tend to trigger external events that bring about change according to the sign and the house in which they fall. Lunar eclipses trigger inner, emotional events according to the sign and house in which they fall. Any eclipse marks both beginnings and endings. The solar and lunar eclipses in a pair fall in opposite signs.

If you were born under or around the time of an eclipse, it's to your advantage to take a look at your birth chart to find out exactly where the eclipses will impact you.

Most years feature four eclipses—two solar and two lunar, with the set separated by about two weeks. In 2009, there was a lunar eclipse in Cancer on December 31, so the first eclipse in 2010 is a solar eclipse in the opposite sign, Capricorn. Below are the dates for this year's eclipses:

January 15: solar, Capricorn, your ninth house. Events concerning the affairs of this house—education, worldview, foreign countries, travel, people, the law and judicial system—should be quite positive in nature. Venus is also close to the eclipse degree, adding a protective quality.

June 26: lunar, Capricorn. Your ninth house is hit again. Emotions stirred concerning all the areas mentioned above.

July 11: solar, Cancer, your third house. External events concerning your relatives, neighbors, your daily life, and how you think.

December 21: lunar, Gemini, your second house of money. Emotions surface concerning finances.

Luckiest Day of the Year

There's at least one day a year when the sun and Jupiter link up in some way. This year, March 2 looks to be that day, with a nice backup on July 26.

Now let's find out what's in store for you, day by day!

CHAPTER 23

Eighteen Months of Day-by-Day Predictions: July 2009 to December 2010

Moon sign times are calculated for Eastern Standard Time and Eastern Daylight Time. Please adjust for your local time zone.

JULY 2009

Wednesday, July 1 (Moon in Libra to Scorpio 1:20 a.m.) Uranus turns retrograde in Pisces, your eleventh house. This retrograde isn't felt with the same immediacy as a Mercury retrograde, but nonetheless could create some tension in your friendships. It also provides an opportunity to gain insight into some of your friendships.

Thursday, July 2 (Moon in Scorpio) Your partner or spouse—or even a business partner—has issues to discuss. It's mostly a need to vent and clear the air. On other fronts, it's an excellent day to conduct research of any kind. Keep good notes. You'll need them down the line.

Friday, July 3 (Moon in Scorpio to Sagittarius 11:12 a.m.) Mercury enters Cancer, your third house. This transit comes just in time for the Fourth of July weekend, when you may be getting together with family and friends. If you're traveling, there shouldn't be any snafus in your schedule—except for the usual hassles of holiday traveling.

Saturday, July 4 (Moon in Sagittarius) Happy Independence Day! Instead of setting off fireworks, spend a little time today reflecting on the Bill of Rights. Have your rights been compromised in the last several years? The moon in Sagittarius certainly allows you to see the big picture today.

Sunday, July 5 (Moon in Sagittarius to Capricorn 11:08 p.m.) Venus enters Gemini and your second house. This transit lasts until July 31 and should boost your income. A new job with higher pay is a possibility.

Monday, July 6 (Moon in Capricorn) You're building structures and laying foundations today. In-laws, teachers, publishers, and even attorneys may feature in the day's events. This moon forms a nice angle with Mars in your sign, adding a mental resolve to your physical energy.

Tuesday, July 7 (Moon in Capricorn) Today's lunar eclipse in Capricorn affects your ninth house. Expect an emotional reaction to a situation involving ninth-house matters and goals. Be sure you're keeping up on dental appointments; Capricorn is ruled by Saturn, which governs teeth and bones.

Wednesday, July 8 (Moon in Capricorn to Aquarius 12:04 p.m.) The moon enters your tenth house, joining Jupiter in Aquarius. Once again, you have a window of opportunity to expand professionally. Network with peers, touch base with bosses and superiors, and pitch your ideas as though it's your last time to do so. Your passion is convincing.

Thursday, July 9 (Moon in Aquarius) In a few days, Mars enters Gemini, leaving your sign. So for today and tomorrow, focus on projects that need a major push of energy to get them out of your life. You may be burning the midnight oil, but you achieve your goal.

Friday, July 10 (Moon in Aquarius) The moon will soon enter Pisces and your eleventh house. Uranus is here, too, and that usually makes for an interesting day. Sudden, unexpected emotional events could surface, but these events should be positive.

Saturday, July 11 (Moon in Aquarius to Pisces 12:44 a.m.) Mars enters Gemini, joining Venus in your second house. This combination bodes well for positive financial news and activities. It also points to a possible romantic relationship with someone who shares your values and concerns. So between now and July 31, when Venus enters Cancer, make the most of this energy.

Sunday, July 12 (Moon in Pisces) If you're between jobs, start sending out résumés and get leads through friends. It's a great time for possibilities, and if your résumé is in good shape, you should have the job you want and need before the end of the month. For now, resist large purchases.

Monday, July 13 (Moon in Pisces to Aries 11:40 a.m.) The moon enters Aries and your twelfth house. You stay out of the limelight today and are glad for it. It's easier to do whatever needs to be done at work and at home when there's a minimum of interference.

Tuesday, July 14 (Moon in Aries) You like things a certain way; this could have its roots in some incident in childhood. If you have kids, however, you're learning that flexibility is the key to cooperative living. Your passions may be running quite high today.

Wednesday, July 15 (Moon in Aries to Taurus 6:30 p.m.) The moon enters your sign, signaling the beginning of another power period. It forms a harmonious angle to Saturn in Virgo, in your fifth house, indicating that today is about structures. Perhaps you're discovering what personal power means.

Thursday, July 16 (Moon in Taurus) If a Cancer friend has a birthday or it's your anniversary, celebrate in a quiet but genuine way. Take in a movie or have dinner out. Show your appreciation for that person and watch it come back to you threefold.

Friday, July 17 (Moon in Taurus to Gemini 11:42 p.m.) Mercury enters Leo and your fourth house. This transit lasts until August 2, and during this time, you may be researching your genealogical roots and perhaps even visiting the place where you were born. This transit also favors communication with your family.

Saturday, July 18 (Moon in Gemini) The moon enters your second house. There's all sorts of activity surrounding finances. Even though it's a weekend, you may be trying to track down a check or deposit slip or rectifying your accounts in some way.

Sunday, July 19 (Moon in Gemini) Tomorrow, the moon enters Cancer, a water sign that's compatible with your earth sun. Tomorrow and most of the next day should be quite pleasant. However, there's a solar eclipse in Cancer on June 21, so you may have more contact than usual with relatives and neighbors.

Monday, July 20 (Moon in Gemini to Cancer 12:52 a.m.) Pay close attention to events. Their tone and pattern may hold strong clues about what tomorrow's solar eclipse has in store for you. If you're a writer or in the communications or travel business, be sure you've got things lined up exactly how you want them before proceeding to something else.

Tuesday, July 21 (Moon in Cancer) Solar eclipses always involve a new moon. So expect opportunities related to short-distance travel, neighbors and neighborhoods, and even relationships with siblings.

Wednesday, July 22 (Moon in Cancer to Leo 12:28 a.m.) With both Venus and Mars in Gemini, and the moon and Mercury in Leo, your magnetism is spectacular. Your communication skills are pretty incredible, too. If you're in sales, it's one of those times when you can sell anything to anyone. Regardless of your profession, you're convincing.

Thursday, July 23 (Moon in Leo) The moon will soon join Saturn in your fifth house. Play by the rules in your creative projects or with a romantic relationship. Everyone—including you—will be much happier.

Friday, July 24 (Moon in Leo to Virgo 12:24 a.m.) The devil is in the details—isn't that how the saying goes? It's definitely true today. Time to check in with your kids. Perhaps a family meeting is in order. Give everyone a chance to speak.

Saturday, July 25 (Moon in Virgo) Get out and do something just for the fun of it. If you're involved with someone, take him or her with you. If you're feeling especially creative, then close yourself away from other people and indulge your artistic self.

Sunday, July 26 (Moon in Virgo to Libra 2:26 a.m.) With the moon entering your sixth house of health and work, you're in rare form. Since it's Sunday, work isn't your focus, but your health and appearance are. Hit the gym, take a yoga class, or get a massage. Do anything that makes you feel fortified physically.

Monday, July 27 (Moon in Libra) The arts figure into the day's events. You are either creating or buying art or hanging out with artists. These individuals open your eyes to the aesthetic possibilities of one of your own creative projects.

Tuesday, July 28 (Moon in Libra to Scorpio 7:57 a.m.) With the moon entering your seventh house, you and your partner may be planning to get away this weekend. If you aren't involved at the moment, then an outing with friends is definitely in order.

Wednesday, July 29 (Moon in Scorpio) At the end of the month, Venus enters compatible water sign Cancer. Get ready for it by making sure all your relationships with relatives are in order. On other fronts today, a contract negotiation is possible.

Thursday, July 30 (Moon in Scorpio to Sagittarius 5:10 p.m.) With the moon entering your eighth house, make sure your insurance payments are up-to-date. If you've applied for a mortgage or a line of credit, you should hear after August 2, when Mercury enters Virgo.

Friday, July 31 (Moon in Sagittarius) Venus enters Cancer. During this transit, which lasts until August 26, love may be closer than you think. You may meet someone special through a brother or sister. Or a neighbor becomes something more than just the person next door.

AUGUST 2009

Saturday, August 1 (Moon in Sagittarius) You're looking for the broader scope today about cosmic questions: What happens when we die? Is reincarnation real? The quest is a good one. If and when you find the answers—and it probably will be a Taurus who does—let the rest of us know.

Sunday, August 2 (Moon in Sagittarius to Capricorn 5:09 a.m.) Mercury enters Virgo, joining Saturn in your fifth house. Between now and August 25, you and your romantic partner have a lot to say to each other. Get it all out in the open—your gripes, your observations, and your wishes, dreams, and hopes for the relationship.

Monday, August 3 (Moon in Capricorn) The moon forms a harmonious angle with the planets in your fifth house. This is excellent for your creative projects. Expect news, in fact, concerning one of your creative endeavors. If you have children, spend some time talking to them about their goals, wishes, and dreams.

Tuesday, August 4 (Moon in Capricorn to Aquarius 6:08 p.m.) The moon enters your tenth house. Synchronicities point the way to a new exploration of cosmic issues. Another possible exploration that begins today or tomorrow is alternative healing.

Wednesday, August 5 (Moon in Aquarius) The lunar eclipse in Aquarius highlights all career matters. Jupiter is within eight degrees of this moon, so whatever feelings you have might be blown out of proportion. Just don't make any decisions until the next new moon on August 20.

Thursday, August 6 (Moon in Aquarius) You've got a lot of air-sign friends around today—Gemini, Libra, even an Aquarius or two. You enjoy their mental input and camaraderie and gain insight through their lively imaginations. It could be that these people are your professional support team.

Friday, August 7 (Moon in Aquarius to Pisces 6:35 a.m.) The moon enters Pisces and joins Uranus in your eleventh house. Your emotional responses to friendship issues could be somewhat unusual today. But you gain insight into a particular friendship and realize that its shortcomings and strengths mirror your own.

Saturday, August 8 (Moon in Pisces) Your intuition and imagination are heightened. It's a perfect day to work on a group creative project. It could involve friends or family members. You may also be involved in a home-improvement project.

Sunday, August 9 (Moon in Pisces to Aries 5:24 p.m.) The moon enters your twelfth house. This can be a difficult transit for you, unless you have natal planets or a natal rising in Aries. Your best bet for today is to carve out as much private time as possible. This evening, you and a close friend may take in a movie or head over to the local bookstore.

Monday, August 10 (Moon in Aries) With Mercury and Saturn still in Virgo, your fifth house, there could be some delays or restrictions in terms of creative endeavors. However, discussions continue. If you're in a contract negotiation, be sure to sign before Mercury turns retrograde on September 6.

Tuesday, August 11 (Moon in Aries)   With the moon in your twelfth house, Uranus retrograde in your eleventh house, and Neptune retrograde in your tenth house, you've got your hands full trying to figure things out. A lot of your energy is turned inward, and your scrutiny of your ideals, friendships, and even your own motives happens unconsciously.

Wednesday, August 12 (Moon in Aries to Taurus 1:51 a.m.)   It's another power day, and you're at the top of your game. With Mercury and Saturn forming harmonious angles to the moon and your sun sign, you've got a solid foundation to your arguments. You've done your homework.

Thursday, August 13 (Moon in Taurus)   Your resolve wins out. You have a clear idea of what you want; don't surrender because of peer pressure. There're good reasons you're called the most stubborn sign in the zodiac.

Friday, August 14 (Moon in Taurus to Gemini 7:27 a.m.)   The moon enters your second house, placing your focus on finances and your values. With Mars also in this position, you've been working longer hours and doing more than your share of work. Pretty soon, you'll get a break when Mars enters Cancer.

Saturday, August 15 (Moon in Gemini)   Network today. Whether you're working with a political party or a theater group, touch base with like-minded individuals. Get on the Internet, and start sending out a newsletter to your database of clients.

Sunday, August 16 (Moon in Gemini to Cancer 10:14 a.m.)   The moon enters your third house. The intuitive flow of information is especially strong today, and you put it to use in your communications. Home, family, and neighborhood all play important roles in the day's events.

Monday, August 17 (Moon in Cancer) If you're doing more running around than usual, put the time to good use. Listen to an audio book. Or while you're sitting in parking lots, waiting for whomever you're driving around, return calls that have piled up in the last few days.

Tuesday, August 18 (Moon in Cancer to Leo 10:57 a.m.) The moon enters your fourth house. It's showtime at home! That means a gathering of people—perhaps kids, if you have them, or the children of friends—with lots of drama going on.

Wednesday, August 19 (Moon in Leo) Coworkers gather at your place for a meeting. The meeting may turn into a party unless you maintain structure. Listen to all sides, but don't make any major decisions until after tomorrow's new moon.

Thursday, August 20 (Moon in Leo to Virgo 11:01 a.m.) Today's new moon in Virgo brings opportunities related to your home and family. This moon could portend a pregnancy, a birth, a marriage, a move—anything related to your own family or to your parents. Mars forms a harmonious angle to this moon, indicating that you have plenty of energy to deal with whatever comes up. Uranus's angle to this moon indicates you'll need some fine-tuning in the attitude department.

Friday, August 21 (Moon in Virgo) The moon and Saturn are now your fifth house, bringing more structure to a romantic relationship. There can also be an increased sense of responsibility concerning children and creative projects. At the end of October, Saturn will enter Libra and your sixth house for a two-and-a-half-year transit. Prepare for this one; it may bring delays and restrictions related to your daily work.

Saturday, August 22 (Moon in Virgo to Libra 12:12 p.m.) The moon enters your sixth house. Gym, anyone? Yoga? Whenever the moon enters Libra and your sixth house, your thoughts turn to health, your personal appearance, your daily work, and how these various aspects combine. If you're the type who doesn't exercise because you claim you don't have the time, make the time.

Sunday, August 23 (Moon in Libra) As the days spin toward September and the beginning of fall, you may feel somewhat pressured to clear off your desk, meet deadlines, and generally consolidate your energy. You'll feel the pressure even a bit more in a couple days, when Mercury and Mars both change signs. Buckle your seat belt, Taurus. The ride is about to slam into overdrive.

Monday, August 24 (Moon in Libra to Scorpio 4:17 p.m.) The moon enters your seventh house. You're researching and investigating something. With your Taurus resolve and the ability of the Scorpio moon to dig for answers, you find your leads by the end of the day.

Tuesday, August 25 (Moon in Scorpio) Mercury enters Libra and your sixth house, and Mars slides into Cancer, your third house. The first transit lasts until late October because Mercury will turn retrograde on September 6. Tie up loose ends at work, and get ready to revise, review, and revisit projects and issues you thought were resolved. The Mars transit lasts until October 16 and provides all the energy you need to deal with a move, if that's on your agenda. If you're a writer, you'll be burning the midnight oil.

Wednesday, August 26 (Moon in Scorpio) Venus enters Leo and your fourth house. This transit lasts until September 20 and indicates that your love life at home should be humming along quite nicely for the next several weeks. You may be beautifying your home in some way, too.

Thursday, August 27 (Moon in Scorpio to Sagittarius 12:16 a.m.) The moon enters your eighth house, forming a beneficial angle to Mars, Uranus, and Pluto. You've got a lot of power on your side; other people sense it and come to you for help. Other people are also willing to share their time, energy, and resources with you.

Friday, August 28 (Moon in Sagittarius) Contact with relatives, attorneys or accountants, or even neighbors is heightened today. You may want to record some of the events with a video camera.

Saturday, August 29 (Moon in Sagittarius to Capricorn 11:45 a.m.) This evening, the moon joins Pluto in Capricorn, your ninth house. With a lineup of planets in earth and compatible water signs, you're in the lead. If you're planning a trip overseas—or anywhere else—don't travel between September 6 and 29.

Sunday, August 30 (Moon in Capricorn) You're building your worldview, your politics, or your spirtual beliefs. And there may be a major shift in your life in these areas. You could, in fact, return to college or decide to head to graduate school.

Monday, August 31 (Moon in Capricorn) The moon joins Neptune in your tenth house. This powerful and intuitive combination focuses on your ideals. If someone you know has a birthday, make it a wonderful celebration!

SEPTEMBER 2009

Tuesday, September 1 (Moon in Capricorn to Aquarius 12:43 a.m.) A boss or peer has advice for you. Decide by the full moon on September 4 whether you think the advice is sound or not. Just remember that you're in a period of your life where your ideals aren't just something you talk about. You're trying to implement them in all areas of your life.

Wednesday, September 2 (Moon in Aquarius) You're making your Labor Day plans. Be prepared, though, that if you travel on Sunday, the day Mercury turns retrograde, your plans will change. If that doesn't bother you, good. If it does, keep your options open. You may decide to stay close to home.

Thursday, September 3 (Moon in Aquarius to Pisces 12:59 p.m.) The moon enters Pisces and your eleventh house.

Friends are your focus today. You may be on the verge of completing a project with a group to which you belong. By tomorrow's full moon in Pisces, that project should be done.

Friday, September 4 (Moon in Pisces) The full moon in Pisces should be quite pleasant, even romantic for you. Something about your wishes and dreams snaps into clarity, too, perhaps as a result of a conversation with a close friend or partner.

Saturday, September 5 (Moon in Pisces to Aries 11:15 p.m.) The moon enters Aries and your twelfth house. Solitude and harmony. It sounds like a weekend in the country with a small group of friends, a partner, or family members. If your muse is whispering in your ear, however, you may want to get away by yourself and indulge your wild, creative side.

Sunday, September 6 (Moon in Aries) Mercury turns retrograde in Libra, your sixth house. This could mess up your holiday plans, but try to go with the flow. Remain flexible. Think of it as an adventure. It may play havoc with work on Tuesday, the first day back at the grind since the retrograde started.

Monday, September 7 (Moon in Aries) If the weather is beautiful where you are, get outside and enjoy it, doing whatever brings you the most pleasure. The moon goes into your sign tomorrow, marking the beginning of another power period. Good thing, too, since work is likely to be confusing.

Tuesday, September 8 (Moon in Aries to Taurus 7:19 a.m.) You ground your ideas so that they are accessible to others. You're seeking practical solutions to complex problems. Look for the simplest solution first.

Wednesday, September 9 (Moon in Taurus) Another power day for you, Taurus! Do something sensual and physical for yourself—get a massage, visit a foot reflexologist, join a gym, or go out for a gourmet meal. And take someone with you whose company you enjoy.

Thursday, September 10 (Moon in Taurus to Gemini 1:18 p.m.) The moon enters your second house. Thanks to the Mercury retrograde, your financial affairs could be confusing. Checks may be delayed, or there could be errors on your bank statements. Don't despair. It'll be over after September 29.

Friday, September 11 (Moon in Gemini) Pluto turns direct in your ninth house. This movement has a subtle effect, but you'll feel the impact in your perceptions about the larger world. You should have a clearer idea about your political and spiritual beliefs and how to implement them in your daily life.

Saturday, September 12 (Moon in Gemini to Cancer 5:20 p.m.) With the moon entering your third house, joining Mars there, you've got the intuitive energy to obtain information in nontraditional ways. If you don't already practice meditation, it's a good day to start.

Sunday, September 13 (Moon in Cancer) It's your turn to nurture someone else; a brother, a sister, or a neighbor may be in need of emotional support. Or it could be a friend who is like family. A Scorpio or a Pisces is helpful.

Monday, September 14 (Moon in Cancer to Leo 7:40 p.m.) If you feel that things at work are somewhat bumpy, then lie low and tend to your own business. Don't get involved in office drama or gossip. Just do your work and focus on getting through the day with minimum hassle.

Tuesday, September 15 (Moon in Leo) With Venus in your house of romance and love, things should be going well in that department. But your parents or other people you consider family may be acting out to get your attention. Deal with it.

Wednesday, September 16 (Moon in Leo to Virgo 8:56 p.m.) Whenever the moon is changing signs, you may feel it in your body somewhere. You feel the change this evening, but in a positive way. The moon, after all, is entering a fellow earth sign, lighting up your house of romance and love.

Thursday, September 17 (Moon in Virgo) The details of a creative partnership are important and beneficial to you. Don't hesitate to get what you feel you deserve. Your talent is remarkable, and the people around you recognize the fact. Tomorrow's new moon in Virgo should bring some positive surprises.

Friday, September 18 (Moon in Virgo to Libra 10:26 p.m.) Today's new moon in Virgo opens opportunities for romantic relationships and creative endeavors. Mercury and Saturn form beneficial angles to this moon, accentuating communication, travel, and playing by the rules. Events in these areas may happen suddenly and unexpectedly, however, because Uranus forms a nearly perfect opposition.

Saturday, September 19 (Moon in Libra) The moon joins Mercury retrograde in your sixth house. There may still be some miscommunication at work, but you've set up guidelines for yourself, so you know how to deal with these situations. In another ten days, Mercury turns direct again, so just hold on till then!

Sunday, September 20 (Moon in Libra) Venus enters Virgo and your fifth house, signaling the start of one of the most romantic and creative periods for you this year. If you're not involved in a committed relationship right now, that may change between now and October 14. And if it doesn't change, it won't matter because you'll be having too much fun to worry about it.

Monday, September 21 (Moon in Libra to Scorpio 1:52 a.m.) The moon enters your seventh house and forms a harmonious angle to Venus. Today you tackle a new creative project that really excites you. You may be doing this project with a partner.

Tuesday, September 22 (Moon in Scorpio) Intense emotions regarding a spouse or close partnership whip through you. Take a deep breath, and back off a little. When you have some perspective, you'll feel better, and so will the other person.

Wednesday, September 23 (Moon in Scorpio to Sagittarius 8:44 a.m.) The moon enters your eighth house. This transit usually puts your focus on insurance and taxes or on the esoteric. You may be looking for more end-of-the-year tax write-offs, so a business purchase could be in the offing. To nurture the other side of you, you sign up for a workshop in alternative healing.

Thursday, September 24 (Moon in Sagittarius) You've got the bigger picture related to your health care and insurance needs. Since Mercury is still retrograde, though, you should wait until after September 29 before changing any of your coverage.

Friday, September 25 (Moon in Sagittarius to Capricorn 7:19 p.m.) The moon joins Pluto in Capricorn, your ninth house. This puts you in the driver's seat for the day. But use your power wisely. If you overstep yourself, the repercussions could be severe.

Saturday, September 26 (Moon in Capricorn) Another power day. Any time a planet hooks up with Pluto as a conjunction or a trine, the meaning is power and power issues related to the combination of the two planets. With the moon, Pluto exerts its influence through your emotions and intuition.

Sunday, September 27 (Moon in Capricorn) You're building educational goals that span several years, not just next month. Strive to keep your goals realistic and tailored to your needs, desires, and interests, rather than to someone else's.

Monday, September 28 (Moon in Capricorn to Aquarius 8:07 a.m.) The moon joins Neptune and Jupiter in your tenth house. With both Neptune and Jupiter retrograde, you're scrutinizing your deeper needs and comparing them to your professional reality. If you don't like what you see, take steps to change things.

Tuesday, September 29 (Moon in Aquarius) Mercury turns direct, always a cause for celebration. From this point through the end of the year, things at the office ease up in terms of employee relations and work in general. Any miscommunications in your love life straighten out, too.

Wednesday, September 30 (Moon in Aquarius to Pisces 8:27 p.m.) With Mercury moving direct again, you can anticipate a much better month ahead. The atmosphere at work will seem less weighted and tense; any ideas you pitch should fly.

OCTOBER 2009

Thursday, October 1 (Moon in Pisces) The moon joins Uranus in your eleventh house. Today, friends offer insights and information that help you make a decision. The information could concern electronics, computers, weather phenomena, earthquakes, or communication with the dead.

Friday, October 2 (Moon in Pisces) Your imagination is running full-tilt. You should take time to indulge it, even if that means knocking off early from work. Mercury is moving direct, so the message you're trying to get out is clear and unfettered. In about ten days, Jupiter turns direct in your tenth house, which is very good news for your career. Get your ducks lined up before then.

Saturday, October 3 (Moon in Pisces to Aries 6:21 a.m.) The moon enters Aries. Get ready for tomorrow's full moon by deciding how you're going to use your time. Best advice? Settle in with a good book or a movie you've been wanting to see. Ask a couple of friends over, or snuggle up with your partner.

Sunday, October 4 (Moon in Aries) The full moon in your twelfth house brings into clarity an issue that you thought was resolved. This could be a long-standing issue from childhood or even from a past life. Keep your dream journal handy tonight. It will be easy to recall your dreams.

Monday, October 5 (Moon in Aries to Taurus 1:34 p.m.)
The moon enters your sign, always a good time of the month! Tackle anything that has seemed challenging, but hold off until early this afternoon, when the moon is firmly in your sign.

Tuesday, October 6 (Moon in Taurus) Yesterday's resolve to tackle a thorny relationship or situation pays off. No one in the zodiac is more stubborn and relentless than Taurus. When you set your sights on something—or someone—you usually get what you want.

Wednesday, October 7 (Moon in Taurus to Gemini 6:47 p.m.) The moon enters Gemini early this evening, highlighting information, networking, and ideas. Apply these attributes to your finances in some way, perhaps by opening an online money market that pays high interest rates or keeping tabs on your accounts online.

Thursday, October 8 (Moon in Gemini) It's a book day. Treat yourself to a novel or nonfiction book that you've been wanting to read but haven't due to time constraints. Make time today for your interests and passions.

Friday, October 9 (Moon in Gemini to Cancer 10:48 p.m.) The moon enters your third house, joining Mars and forming a harmonious angle to Uranus. Buckle up. It could be a wild, unpredictable day, with surprises related to a brother, a sister, or a neighbor. Keep in mind that on October 29, Saturn enters Libra for a run of two and a half years. For you, it could mean increased responsibility in your daily life.

Saturday, October 10 (Moon in Cancer) You're locked into an intuitive flow today that just won't quit. And part of this flow is a need to beautify your home, your backyard, or even your neighborhood. Whether it's a coat of fresh paint for a room or the outside of your house, a new fence, or spiffing up around the neighborhood, you lead the brigade.

Sunday, October 11 (Moon in Cancer) Your mother or her substitute has advice and wisdom that you should hear.

It may be kitchen-table wisdom, but you can apply it to an area of your life that is challenging you. Another earth sign is helpful.

Monday, October 12 (Moon in Cancer to Leo 2:03 a.m.) Jupiter turns direct in Aquarius, your tenth house. This is terrific news. Everything that you think has been stalled professionally moves forward rapidly, expanding your opportunities for advancement, recognition, or perhaps even a whole new career path.

Tuesday, October 13 (Moon in Leo) Venus moves into Libra tomorrow, and you may feel some of what that can bring today. Pay special attention to anything concerning romance, flirtations, or the arts. With the moon in your fourth house, your home may be the location for a large get-together.

Wednesday, October 14 (Moon in Leo to Virgo 4:46 a.m.) Venus enters Libra. Between now and November 7, things at work should move along rather peacefully. An office flirtation may take a sudden, unexpected turn and become something much deeper.

Thursday, October 15 (Moon in Virgo) The moon joins Saturn in Virgo. You're finding your way through a creative endeavor, and you like what you're seeing. Whether this project is writing, sculpture, photography, dance, or acting, you've got your finger on the pulse.

Friday, October 16 (Moon in Virgo to Libra 7:30 a.m.) Mars enters Leo and your fourth house, and forms a harmonious angle to Venus in Libra. Your love life picks up steam—either at home or at work! Between now and December 20, home-improvement projects take center stage.

Saturday, October 17 (Moon in Libra) The moon and Venus are in your sixth house. This pleasant combination makes for an interesting and relaxing day. You and your partner get involved in a joint artistic project. If you're not involved with anyone at the moment, then this combination could indicate getting together with friends, possibly for a creative project.

Sunday, October 18 (Moon in Libra to Scorpio 11:23 a.m.) Today's new moon in Scorpio ushers in opportunities related to your daily work. You could get a raise, a promotion, or even a new job. There may be social opportunities, too. The opportunities that surface may appeal to your idealism and cause you to adjust your attitude in some way.

Monday, October 19 (Moon in Scorpio) The moon enters your seventh house. Your intense emotions concerning a friendship, a relationship, or even a business partnership surprise you. It's time to take a couple steps back, breathe deep, and delay making decisions until the moon is in a fellow earth sign.

Tuesday, October 20 (Moon in Scorpio to Sagittarius 5:50 p.m.) The moon enters your eighth house, usually a weird time of the month for you. Joint resources are highlighted: money, property, or any kind of resources you hold with a partner. If you're in the midst of a divorce or separation, don't hesitate to ask for what you feel is fair.

Wednesday, October 21 (Moon in Sagittarius) With Mercury and Venus both in Libra, your sixth house, your communication with coworkers and employees is excellent. Your fairness is nearly legendary, and people turn to you today to mediate a dispute.

Thursday, October 22 (Moon in Sagittarius) In another few days, both Mercury and Venus will enter Scorpio, your seventh house, and Saturn will enter Libra. These transits will impact your partnerships—both romantic and business—and your daily work environment. Of the three, the Saturn transit lasts the longest—two and a half years—so it will have the greatest impact. Prepare by making sure you're on top of everything at work.

Friday, October 23 (Moon in Sagittarius to Capricorn 3:40 a.m.) The moon joins Pluto in your ninth house. This powerful combination lifts your intuitive awareness to a new height. It's easier to glean information in nontraditional ways, through unusual venues. Dreams, for instance, may be a source of information and insight.

Saturday, October 24 (Moon in Capricorn) Your educational goals may be changing. If you're in college and you have to declare a major soon, you may find that your interests have changed. The same goes with graduate school. And if you're not in school, you may decide to sign up for a course or a workshop.

Sunday, October 25 (Moon in Capricorn to Aquarius 3:08 p.m.) With Jupiter moving in direct motion, your professional opportunities and relationships should be expanding like crazy. You get help from peers concerning a project that you hope to launch. Support comes from unexpected places.

Monday, October 26 (Moon in Aquarius) With Neptune still moving retrograde in your tenth house, you continue to scrutinize your ideals and how they fit into what you do for a living. Before Jupiter's transit ends next year, you may be in a completely different line of work or doing something within your profession that suits your ideals and spiritual beliefs.

Tuesday, October 27 (Moon in Aquarius) Tomorrow Mercury enters Scorpio. Be prepared to research, investigate, and communicate more than you have in recent months. On another front, gather your supporters around you and take a vote. Is your pet project ready to launch?

Wednesday, October 28 (Moon in Aquarius to Pisces 3:46 a.m.) Mecury enters Scorpio and your seventh house and forms harmonious angles to the moon, Uranus, and Pluto. Use your intuition and your research skills to get the real scoop on an issue or a person that perplexes you. Chances are, when you dig through the upper layers, you're going to be surprised at what you find.

Thursday, October 29 (Moon in Pisces) Saturn enters Libra and your sixth house. For the next two and a half years, your responsibilities at work may increase, but you may not be recognized for the work you do. At times, it will seem that you work too hard for what you're paid. Don't despair. During this transit, you're learning to play by the rules and to acknowledge the voice of authority in your own life. At the same time, your love life improves considerably and your creative endeavors are unencumbered.

Friday, October 30 (Moon in Pisces to Aries 1:57 p.m.) The moon enters Aries and your twelfth house. Today and tomorrow are primarily about tying up loose ends for the month. You're preparing for November 1, when the moon enters your sign. So clean your closets, your garage, and your attic. Finish projects.

Saturday, October 31 (Moon in Aries) Sleep late, lounge around, and indulge yourself. Today is for you to explore your deeper self in solitude. If solitude isn't possible, then carve out a little time away from the rest of your household.

NOVEMBER 2009

Sunday, November 1—Daylight Saving Time Ends (Moon in Aries to Taurus 7:45 p.m.) A perfect start to a new month: The moon enters your sign! Tackle something that you've been putting off all autumn. Whether it's a new health regimen, a home-improvement project, college hunting, or virtual traveling, dive in.

Monday, November 2 (Moon in Taurus) The full moon in your sign lights up your personal life. Romance is featured. There could be some tension with a partner—romantic or business—but as long as you're open and honest about what you feel, things work out splendidly. You're setting the stage for the new moon in your seventh house on November 16. So act with conscious intent.

Tuesday, November 3 (Moon in Taurus to Gemini 11:53 p.m.) The moon enters your second house and forms harmonious angles with Neptune and Mars. Your values come home to roost in your career, at home, and in your family. It's a positive event, even if it initially seems troubling.

Wednesday, November 4 (Moon in Gemini) Neptune turns direct in Aquarius, your tenth house. The effects will be subtle, but the bottom line is simple. From now to the end of the year, you can begin implementing your idealism into your professional life, and you won't be challenged.

Thursday, November 5 (Moon in Gemini) Information is the keyword. Whether you're tracking down ratings on a business, gathering material for an overseas trip, or just doing your usual research, you shouldn't have to look too far. Serendipity brings you exactly what you need.

Friday, November 6 (Moon in Gemini to Cancer 2:43 a.m.) It's Friday. So kick back and relax. Don't worry about the stars, your job, or your future. See a movie or go out to dinner. The real world can wait till Monday.

Saturday, November 7 (Moon in Cancer) Venus enters Scorpio, your seventh house. This transit, lasting until December 1, brings intense emotions into a committed relationship. The relationship may evolve into something much deeper than it presently is. Perhaps you and your partner decide to move in together or to get married and start a family. If you're not in a relationship when the transit begins, you probably will be before the transit is done.

Sunday, November 8 (Moon in Cancer to Leo 5:23 a.m.) The moon joins Mars in Leo. You may be short-tempered or impatient with family members. So if you want a peaceful day, be prepared to bite your tongue and hold back impulsive remarks.

Monday, November 9 (Moon in Leo) You're gearing up for the Thanksgiving holidays, hearing from family and friends headed your way. Would you rather leave home and have someone else do the cooking? If so, you need to be clear about that now.

Tuesday, November 10 (Moon in Leo to Virgo 8:31 a.m.) The moon enters your fifth house. Very nice for romance and creativity, and this time you don't have Saturn sharing the house and restricting you. Pay attention to details in the relationship—taking into account, for instance, your partner's pet peeves and passions.

Wednesday, November 11 (Moon in Virgo) The moon forms a harmonious angle with Uranus, so expect the unexpected in romance, creativity, and friendships. You gain insights into a romantic relationship through a friend or into a friendship through a partner.

Thursday, November 12 (Moon in Virgo to Libra 12:23 p.m.) The moon joins Saturn in your sixth house. If you're beginning to feel delays or restrictions in your daily work life as a result of Saturn's presence, try to turn things around by using Saturn's energy to build or shore up structures. Play by the rules.

Friday, November 13 (Moon in Libra) It's Friday, and you've got a lot to do before you can knock off for the day. Get to it. If you're self-employed, start thinking about Christmas bonuses for the people who work for you.

Saturday, November 14 (Moon in Libra to Scorpio 5:25 p.m.) The moon joins Venus and Mercury in Scorpio, your seventh house. This puts a lot of emphasis on partnerships—specifically, to talk about your feelings, where each of you sees the relationship headed. And this holds true even if you're living together or married. The Scorpio moon always seeks the absolute bottom line.

Sunday, November 15 (Moon in Scorpio) Mercury enters Sagittarius and your eighth house. If you have natal planets in Sagittarius, then this transit should be good. It heightens your conscious awareness about shared resources—those you share with a partner and with the planet. If you don't have natal planets in Sagittarius, then all this fire energy could make things a tad uncomfortable for you.

Monday, November 16 (Moon in Scorpio) Today's new moon in Scorpio opens new chapters with friendships and partnerships. You may start a business with a partner. You could move in with your partner or tie the knot. Regardless, the new moon spells opportunities.

Tuesday, November 17 (Moon in Scorpio to Sagittarius 12:23 a.m.) The moon enters your eighth house. A mortgage or loan for which you've applied is approved. Or there's activity concerning insurance payments or inheritances. If you're in the process of moving, Mars in your fourth house helps the process enormously.

Wednesday, November 18 (Moon in Sagittarius) With the moon forming a harmonious angle to both Mercury and Mars, your physical energy is excellent and favors any kind of rigorous exercise. You're enthusiastic about a project you're involved in with another person, perhaps a spouse or a family member.

Thursday, November 19 (Moon in Sagittarius to Capricorn 10:01 a.m.) The moon joins Pluto and Jupiter in your ninth house and forms a beneficial angle to Uranus. There's an air of excitement that swirls around the approach of the holidays. Your plans are finally coming together. You may be heading overseas.

Friday, November 20 (Moon in Capricorn) Is Pluto really a planet? Regardless of what the astronomers say, astrologers understand the power of this planet, particularly when it's linked up with expansive Jupiter and the moon. Today, this powerful trio impacts your political and spiritual beliefs in some way.

Saturday November 21 (Moon in Capricorn to Aquarius 10:11 p.m.) The moon joins Neptune in your tenth house.

Now that Neptune is moving direct, you're able to integrate your ideals and spiritual beliefs into your profession or into your dealings with the public. This combination may also relate to dealings with your father or another authority figure.

Sunday, November 22 (Moon in Aquarius) Your cutting-edge ideas are put to excellent use. Your peers are definitely in your court and willing to support your ideas in front of the boss. There could be a little tension at home that should be dealt with as soon as possible.

Monday, November 23 (Moon in Aquarius) If friends or family members are arriving at your place ahead of Thanksgiving, today could be challenging. You've got a million things screaming for your attention at work, but what you would really like to be doing is hanging out with loved ones at home.

Tuesday, November 24 (Moon in Aquarius to Pisces 11:08 a.m.) The moon joins Uranus in your eleventh house. Social invitations arrive. You'll have your pick of places to go and people to see over the holidays. Select carefully, according to what your heart says, not your sense of obligation.

Wednesday, November 25 (Moon in Pisces) If you're on the road, pass the driving time with a book on tape or even a detour to some spot you've always wanted to explore. If you're traveling with your family, be sure to split the driving with someone else.

Thursday, November 26 (Moon in Pisces to Aries 10:11 p.m.) The moon enters your twelfth house. This position for the moon isn't especially social or people-oriented. So you may want to get off by yourself for a few hours today. Go for a hike or a drive.

Friday, November 27 (Moon in Aries) If you've taken today off, indulge your need for solitude. If you're working, do whatever you have to do to knock off early for the weekend. Inner tensions will ease up on November 29, when the moon enters your sign.

Saturday, November 28 (Moon in Aries) Your dream recall is excellent right now. Use your dreams to find insightful solutions to issues, relationships, and situations that puzzle or challenge you. Saturn forms a challenging angle to the moon in Aries, so be prepared to play by the rules in everything you do.

Sunday, November 29 (Moon in Aries to Taurus 5:35 a.m.) The day looms before you, and you can't wait to explore it. The moon is in your sign, and just about anything is possible today. So choose your activities wisely.

Monday, November 30 (Moon in Taurus) It's an ideal way to end the month. With the moon in your sign, making harmonious angles to Uranus and Pluto, you're in the driver's seat. Other earth signs—Virgo and Capricorn—figure prominently in the day's events.

DECEMBER 2009

Tuesday, December 1 (Moon in Taurus to Gemini 9:24 a.m.) A busy day! Venus enters Sagittarius, and Uranus in Pisces turns direct. Venus and Mars are now in favorable angles to each other, which certainly heats up both your love and sex life. With Uranus moving direct in your eleventh house, it's possible that a friendship suddenly becomes something much more.

Wednesday, December 2 (Moon in Gemini) The full moon in Gemini lights up your money house, allowing you to clearly see a financial issue that may have puzzled you. Don't make any rash decisions. Gather your information and wait until the moon is in Cancer before you make your move.

Thursday, December 3 (Moon in Gemini to Cancer 11:01 a.m.) The moon enters your third house late this morning. Wait until tomorrow to make important decisions. Today you should probe your options, perhaps through meditation.

Friday, December 4 (Moon in Cancer) Your neighbors and your community feature in the day's events. Someone in your community may be planning a holiday celebration and asks you to get involved. Commit only if you feel sure you have the time this celebration deserves.

Saturday, December 5 (Moon in Cancer to Leo 12:08 p.m.) Mercury joins Pluto in Capricorn, your ninth house. Well, if you weren't thinking of a long trip before, you certainly will be during the coming weeks. You also may be exploring your higher-education opportunities and how you could pay for them.

Sunday, December 6 (Moon in Leo) Let's take stock. All the planets are moving in direct motion, which means they're functioning the way they should be. Take advantage of this stellar energy to complete projects and tie up loose ends in all areas of your life. By December 20, things begin to slow down when Mars turns retrograde in Leo. On December 26, Mercury turns retrograde in Capricorn.

Monday, December 7 (Moon in Leo to Virgo 2:07 p.m.) The moon enters your fifth house. If you feel somewhat vulnerable in a romantic relationship, explore the possible reasons why. It could be a fear of separation during the holidays or, if you and your partner live together, a nostalgia for the bygone days.

Tuesday, December 8 (Moon in Virgo) You and a partner or close friend get a jump on holiday shopping. You also may be taking care of things you've postponed—like scheduling dentist and doctor appointments. Look to a Capricorn for help.

Wednesday, December 9 (Moon in Virgo to Libra 5:48 p.m.) The moon joins Saturn in your sixth house. You and a business partner are brainstorming for ways to expand your market overseas. Be sure to hire people with whom both you and your partner are compatible. You may want to gather up birthdates and have an astrologer compare charts for how personalities mesh.

Thursday, December 10 (Moon in Libra) You're after harmony and peace today. Both prove to be elusive, but part of the challenge is finding a place within yourself that the external world can't touch. Meditation helps.

Friday, December 11 (Moon in Libra to Scorpio 11:32 p.m.) The moon enters your seventh house. If you're awake when it happens, you may feel a palpable shift in energy. Your inner self suddenly seeks deeper answers. Tomorrow, start investigating and researching to find those deeper answers.

Saturday, December 12 (Moon in Scorpio) Your research yields results. Use the information you find to convince a partner that your ideas are sound and practical. No one is quite as proficient as a Taurus at making the abstract practical.

Sunday, December 13 (Moon in Scorpio) Kick back, relax, and take the day for yourself or for yourself and a partner. If you're not in a relationship, then spend time with a close friend or business partner. You may be doing touch-up projects at home, in preparation for the holidays. With Mars in your fourth house, it'll be easy to spend. Resist the urge!

Monday, December 14 (Moon in Scorpio to Sagittarius 7:25 a.m.) The moon enters your eighth house and forms a harmonious angle to Mars. Your emotions are running high today, but all that passion certainly gets things done. With the holidays now so close, you've got a million things to do, but you're able to make the time to do them.

Tuesday, December 15 (Moon in Sagittarius) When you look for the big picture concerning your life and where you're headed, a lot of factors come into play. But rather than approaching this with your left brain, let your intuitive right brain lead the way. On a more mundane level, you may be looking for last-minute tax deductions for 2009.

Wednesday, December 16 (Moon in Sagittarius to Capricorn 5:32 p.m.) The new moon is a perfect time to find that last-minute tax deduction. Whether it's a new computer or printer or a more expensive item, you've got a broader perspective with this new moon. Expect opportunities related to insurance, taxes, or joint finances.

Thursday, December 17 (Moon in Capricorn) On December 20, Mars will turn retrograde in Leo, followed on December 26 by Mercury retrograde in Capricorn. Both retrogrades will last into the New Year. The first will impact your love life, and the second, your communications and travel plans. Prepare for them now by having your affairs in order.

Friday, December 18 (Moon in Capricorn) It's never too early to start working on your New Year's resolutions, and with the moon in your ninth house, you've got the ideal window of opportunity. Make realistic resolutions, but don't hold back.

Saturday, December 19 (Moon in Capricorn to Aquarius 5:39 a.m.) The moon joins Jupiter and Neptune in your tenth house. Even if your mind isn't on work right now, it behooves you to have your ducks lined up, Taurus. You may be called upon to get involved in a project that advances your career in a major way.

Sunday, December 20 (Moon in Aquarius) Mars turns retrograde in Leo, your fourth house. This transit lasts into next year and, during the busy holiday season, could make you somewhat short-tempered and accident-prone. Things that normally wouldn't bother you seem more glaring and obvious. When you begin to feel antsy, take a deep breath and step back from the situation.

Monday, December 21 (Moon in Aquarius to Pisces 6:42 p.m.) This evening when the moon joins Uranus in Pisces, you feel more at home and comfortable within yourself again. The Pisces moon feeds your imagination, intuition, and artistic sensibilities. You'll need all this inner support.

Tuesday, December 22 (Moon in Pisces) On December 26, Mercury turns retrograde in your ninth house. So be sure that your travel plans are confirmed and paid for before December 26. Better yet, if at all possible, don't travel between December 26 and January 15, 2010.

Wednesday, December 23 (Moon in Pisces) You have a number of holiday invitations from which to choose. Maybe it's best to have a party at your place. If that's the route you go, be sure get the word out before December 26. You may be doing some last-minute holiday shopping, perhaps for coworkers or employees.

Thursday, December 24 (Moon in Pisces to Aries 6:40 a.m.) The moon enters Aries and your twelfth house. Hidden stuff that could be family-related or concern issues from your childhood surfaces. Your dream recall should be exceptionally vivid, so don't hesitate to ask for insight into situations and relationships that concern you.

Friday, December 25 (Moon in Aries) Merry Christmas! How appropriate that Venus enters Capricorn and your ninth house today, bringing a certain grace and peace to your spiritual beliefs. This transit lasts until January 19, 2010, and promises romance with a foreign-born individual or in a foreign culture. This transit also bodes well for an expansion of your business overseas.

Saturday, December 26 (Moon in Aries into Taurus 3:27 a.m.) Mercury turns retrograde today in Capricorn, your ninth house. The combination of retrograde Mercury with Venus can lead to some confusion in communication with a partner. The best way to mitigate the impact of this combination is to be clear and honest when you discuss anything. The fact that the moon enters your sign today helps soften any blows.

Sunday, December 27 (Moon in Taurus) With the moon in your sign, and Christmas two days behind you, you're now looking ahead to the New Year. What do you desire for yourself, your family, and your friends? How can you help these desires to manifest themselves in your life? Lay out a strategy, Taurus.

Monday, December 28 (Moon in Taurus to Gemini 8:15 p.m.) The moon enters your second house. Now you start worrying about your finances again, perhaps anticipating the arrival of holiday bills. Don't borrow trouble. After mid-January, when Mercury is moving direct again, things will be looking up.

Tuesday, December 29 (Moon in Gemini) If you're planning your New Year's Eve celebration, keep in mind that there will be a lunar eclipse in Cancer that night. This will stir up emotions related to home, hearth, siblings, or your neighborhood. It will be followed two weeks later by a solar eclipse in Capricorn. Stay tuned, Taurus. Pay attention to events that occur on New Year's Eve. They are harbingers of what could be headed your way in 2010.

Wednesday, December 30 (Moon in Gemini to Cancer 9:46 p.m.) The moon enters Cancer, your third house. If you're a writer or in the communications business, you're revising, re-writing, and rethinking. That's the best way to use the energy of a Mercury retrograde. Once the retrograde is finished, you emerge with a clearer sense of where you're headed.

Thursday, December 31 (Moon in Cancer) The lunar eclipse in Cancer may have you dreaming about bygone days. Rather than looking back, try to look forward. Remain upbeat and positive about what the future has to offer.

HAPPY NEW YEAR!

JANUARY 2010

Friday, January 1 (Moon in Cancer to Leo 10:42 p.m.) For most of today, you're doing just great, spending time with neighbors and relatives. You have your priorities and resolutions in place for the year. Even your ruler, Venus, is cooperating, since it's in fellow earth sign Capricorn and is smoothing over your love life. Then tonight, the moon slips into Leo, your fourth house, and you look around and realize what you have to get done before you hit the hay!

Saturday, January 2 (Moon in Leo) Good thing it's Saturday. Today you tend to all the things around your house that you have delayed doing. Complete home-improvement projects. Take down the Christmas tree, if you had one this year. Put away the holiday lights. You know the drill. You enjoy a fair amount of order in your life, and today you begin the process of restoring it.

Sunday, January 3 (Moon in Leo to Virgo 10:53 p.m.) The moon enters fellow earth sign Virgo, and yes, it's apparent in your love life and everything you do for fun and amusement. But because this moon is so emotionally precise, you may plan out the entire day. This probably suits your sun, and you end up doing more than you anticipated.

Monday, January 4 (Moon in Virgo) There's a lineup of planets in signs that are compatible with yours right now—from this moon to Mercury, Venus, and Pluto in Capricorn and to Uranus in Pisces. It makes for a fluid day, and if you allow yourself to go with the flow, you should have a ball. Unusual people continue to enter your life until late May, when Uranus moves into Aries.

Tuesday, January 5 (Moon in Virgo) Line up your Ps and Qs today at work. You know what has to be done, but may not be sure how to do it. You are a quick learner, and today you won't hesitate delegating. There are right ways and wrong ways. No middle ground right now!

Wednesday, January 6 (Moon in Virgo to Libra 12:59 a.m.) Your need for balance is reflected in your relationships with coworkers or employees. You rarely monopolize a conversation, and today you definitely won't. Use this energy to listen to what other people have to say—to listen with your heart as well as your mind.

Thursday, January 7 (Moon in Libra) You take in an art exhibit or a new art film, attend a concert, or do something creative and artistically pleasing for yourself. Or you may get lost in a good book, next to a fireplace if it's cold where you live—or on a beach, if you live someplace warm at this time of the year.

Friday, January 8 (Moon in Libra to Scorpio 6:01 a.m.) One more water sign planet in that interesting lineup of planets compatible with your sun sign. Your emotional focus shifts to partnerships—professional and personal—and how you can improve them. Your partner—or potential partner, perhaps—may be thinking of you as the type for whom still waters run deep.

Saturday, January 9 (Moon in Scorpio) Secrets are hidden within your past that you may not even be aware of consciously. But on an intuitive level, you know what they are and why you have them, and they may surface in your dreams and meditations. Be gentle with yourself. You have plenty of time to figure things out.

Sunday, January 10 (Moon in Scorpio to Sagittarius 2:10 p.m.) The moon enters your eighth house, that place of the weird and the strange and the inexplicable. This also happens to be the house that governs mundane issues like taxes and insurance. So take your pick. In which arena would you like to play today?

Monday, January 11 (Moon in Sagittarius) Aren't you the lucky one? Your upbeat mood hasn't gone unnoticed by bosses and higher ups. You may be in line for a promotion or raise. If you're self-employed, people are open to your services and products, and you're on a roll!

Tuesday, January 12 (Moon in Sagittarius) Mercury will be retrograde for another three days, in Capricorn, so if you're planning an overseas trips, don't buy your tickets until after January 15. Your deeper beliefs come into play today, perhaps through an encounter with a person whose beliefs differ from your own. Be patient.

Wednesday, January 13 (Moon in Sagittarius to Capricorn 12:54 a.m.) Saturn turns retrograde in Libra, your sixth house, until May 30. During this period, you'll be mulling over your goals in your daily work life. You may decide to take control of the maintenance of your health too, by joining a gym, taking yoga, or doing some other form of regular physical activity. Social relationships and obligations could feel somewhat burdensome.

Thursday, January 14 (Moon in Capricorn) You're able to plan and strategize today and are equally good at short- or long-range goals. As a fixed earth sign, you're known for completing what you start, a quality your bosses, coworkers, friends, and family appreciate. Mercury turns direct tomorrow in Capricorn. Wait a few days for the planet to stabilize before signing contracts or buying airline tickets!

Friday, January 15 (Moon in Capricorn to Aquarius 1:17 p.m.) Today's solar eclipse in Capricorn is like a double new moon. Mercury is exactly conjunct to the degree of this eclipse, so there will be lots of discussion about goals, overseas traveling, and higher education. Expect new opportunities to surface for expanding your business or products to overseas markets.

Saturday, January 16 (Moon in Aquarius) The moon links up with Neptune, in your tenth house. This combination, which happens once a month, brings compassion and a higher calling to your professional concerns. It can also bring blind spots, so follow your hunches today and tomorrow, and you won't take a wrong step forward.

Sunday, January 17 (Moon in Aquarius) Jupiter enters Pisces, your eleventh house. For the next six months, Jupiter should expand your network of friends and acquaintances, who will expand your opportunities in some way to achieve your dreams.

Monday, January 18 (Moon in Aquarius to Pisces 2:18 a.m.) Venus enters Aquarius and your tenth house and will be there until February 11. During this period, your career and professional life should move along smoothly. Career breaks of some kind are possible. And since Venus also symbolizes love and romance, there could be a flirtation or a romance with a peer or even a boss.

Tuesday, January 19 (Moon in Pisces) The moon joins Uranus in Pisces, bringing excitement and unpredictable events and insights. This won't happen much longer, though, because on May 27, Uranus enters Aries, your twelfth house. You and friends get together today to brainstorm, party, or just hang out. Keep a notebook handy. Your insights will come to you at odd times today.

Wednesday, January 20 (Moon in Pisces to Aries 2:37 p.m.) The moon enters your twelfth house, a transit that often brings up surprising insights from the past. You may want to spend some time alone pampering yourself!

Thursday, January 21 (Moon in Aries) You're doing internal cleaning, preparing yourself for the moon's entrance into your sign on Saturday. This is a process at which you actually excel. You can divest yourself of past baggage and issues by meditating, through dream work, or by journaling.

Friday, January 22 (Moon in Aries) Find a mental trunk into which you can put the past. Then go through everything inside and get rid of what no longer serves your best interests. And this evening, get together with friends or that special person in your life who makes you laugh!

Saturday, January 23 (Moon in Aries to Taurus 12:41 a.m.) The moon is in your sign, and don't be surprised if you sing the James Brown tune "I Feel Good." With that kind of positive emotion on your side today, you can accomplish anything you set your mind to. You just have to focus and dive in.

Sunday, January 24 (Moon in Taurus) You take on something large, perhaps something you've never done before. And while you're doing that, your love life is starting to heat up in a major way. Things may peak between February 11 and March 7, while Venus is transiting Pisces, a sign compatible with your sun sign.

Monday, January 25 (Moon in Taurus to Gemini 7:12 a.m.) Your emotional focus shifts to finances. Perhaps the holiday bills are starting to come in, and you're worried that a money crunch is on. Your bank account is fine, but you're most secure when your bills are paid promptly and your credit card debt is nonexistent.

Tuesday, January 26 (Moon in Gemini) Time to socialize and network. You feel a need for the company of others, a sense that you may be too isolated. You can always satisfy this need by creating your own blog and inviting friends to stop by for virtual coffee!

Wednesday, January 27 (Moon in Gemini to Cancer 10:02 a.m.) You may be working out of your house today, so don't get distracted. Get your work done first. Then have some fun!

Thursday, January 28 (Moon in Cancer) You get together or hear from relatives or neighbors today. You could be involved in some sort of neighborhood or community project too. If you have time to think about this before you dive in, be sure you have the time to commit.

Friday, January 29 (Moon in Cancer to Leo 10:10 a.m.) Is your home for sale? Is it on display in some way? Or is someone in your family on display? In some way, your home, your family, or even your genealogical roots play into the day's events. You're in a gregarious mood, and it's infectious.

Saturday, January 30 (Moon in Leo) Today's full moon in Leo should bring news concerning your home, family, romance, or something about which you're passionate. Mars is within a degree of this moon, indicating a lot of activity around this date. You may be doing more running around than usual, or your activities center around kids and creativity.

Sunday, January 31 (Moon in Leo to Virgo 9:23 a.m.) Fun, pleasure, and romance all figure into your activities today. You're very precise emotionally too, and if you're not careful, you could turn that precision on yourself, in the form of self-criticism. Resist criticizing yourself or others. Tomorrow, you'll be glad you did.

FEBRUARY 2010

Monday, February 1 (Moon in Virgo) As you enter the second month of the year, the moon, Mercury, Jupiter, and Uranus are in signs compatible with your own. So even if it's bleak winter where you live, your emotions and intellect remain grounded. Romance and pure enjoyment are your priorities today, so even though it's a Monday, be sure to get in your quota of fun today!

Tuesday, February 2 (Moon in Virgo to Libra 9:42 a.m.) The moon joins Saturn in your sixth house. This combination can make you feel that you're carrying more than your share of responsibility in some area of your life. It may be true, but your shoulders are wide and strong, and for now, just do what you have to and keep moving forward.

Wednesday, February 3 (Moon in Libra) Your social connections and contacts feature into the day's events. You may get together with coworkers or employees today to discuss a new program or product, and it's important that everyone contributes. Listen closely to what people *don't* say.

Thursday, February 4 (Moon in Libra to Scorpio 12:56 p.m.) Your passions run high today, particularly concerning a personal or business partnership. If you're ticked off about something, just say it rather than letting your anger build. Once you've said what's on your mind, the air is clearer.

Friday, February 5 (Moon in Scorpio) If you can sustain your present pace, you'll be able to finish what you're doing in record time. You're on a roll, locked into a creative groove where you seem to be the channel for a particular kind of information. Get it down; trust the process.

Saturday, February 6 (Moon in Scorpio to Sagittarius 8:04 p.m.) Other people are eager to share their time and expertise. You're in a reciprocal mood, and the results are beneficial to everyone involved. Isn't this how it would work in an ideal world?

Sunday, February 7 (Moon in Sagittarius) You may be itching to travel. Just be sure you do it before April 17 and after May 11, during Mercury's second retrograde of the year. You may decide to take a course or seminar in something that intrigues you. You tend to be a quick learner when the material intrigues you.

Monday, February 8 (Moon in Sagittarius) The moon and Venus form a beneficial angle to each other, increasing the likelihood that romance and love are on your mind today. If this is a new relationship, it's possible that you and this person were friends first or met through mutual friends. If you're involved already, then you and your partner reach a new level of understanding.

Tuesday, February 9 (Moon in Sagittarius to Capricorn 6:45 a.m.) The moon joins Pluto in your ninth house. This combination strengthens your resolve and brings some belief you have into stark relief so that it's as obvious to you as your own name. Is this belief truly your own or one you have adopted as your own? The difference is important.

Wednesday, February 10 (Moon in Capricorn) Mercury enters Aquarius, your tenth house, and will be there until March 7. This transit provides a window of opportunity for the discussion of career matters, sales pitches, even travel related to your professional life. Given the new moon in the same house and sign coming up on February 13, you're now laying the groundwork for new career opportunities, relationships, and events.

Thursday, February 11 (Moon in Capricorn to Aquarius 7:25 p.m.) Venus enters Pisces, a water sign compatible with your sun, where it will be until March 7. During this period, a romance with a friend is possible. It's also possible that you get involved in some sort of artistic project with a group of friends.

Friday, February 12 (Moon in Aquarius) Today's new moon in Aquarius should usher in career opportunities. Neptune is conjunct to this moon within a degree, adding compassion, idealism, and even beauty to the equation. One possibility is that music, photography, dance, acting, or fiction writing is part of the opportunity package!

Saturday, February 13 (Moon in Aquarius) You're on the cutting edge of something today—an idea as a way of doing something, a plan. It's best to keep your insights to yourself for now. You'll have plenty of time later to spread the word.

Sunday, February 14 (Moon in Aquarius to Pisces 8:24 a.m.) The moon hooks up with Venus, Uranus, and Jupiter, all in your eleventh house. The combination should bring about quite a bit of romantic excitement, and what better day for it than Valentine's Day?

Monday, February 15 (Moon in Pisces) You gain insight today about a friendship or a dream or a wish that you have. You and a friend or partner may be brainstorming for a new project. Regardless of what field you actually work in, this project is imaginative, different, and you may have found a niche for it in the market.

Tuesday, February 16 (Moon in Pisces to Aries 8:31 p.m.) With the moon in your twelfth house, you may be cleaning house. You're clearing away stuff that no longer serves you—from old clothes to old beliefs. It's all in preparation for the moon's entrance into your sign on February 19.

Wednesday, February 17 (Moon in Aries) You dabble in divination systems today. From the tarot to astrology and the I Ching to various online sites, you're sampling to find out which system works best for you. The value in these systems is that they can confirm what you sense already. Sometimes the best system is also the simplest.

Thursday, February 18 (Moon in Aries) Your dream recall now should be quite impressive. Keep a notebook and pen handy beside your bed and give yourself a suggestion to wake up when you have a particularly revealing or insightful dream. You're on to something unique and different. Don't hesitate to pursue it.

Friday, February 19 (Moon in Aries to Taurus 6:56 a.m.) The moon enters your sign, and you're ready to take on the world—or, at any rate, your part of the world! Gone is the angst you may feel when your head and heart are in conflict. Today, every part of you is on the same page.

Saturday, February 20 (Moon in Taurus) You're on a roll today, and your mood is infectious. You're able to garner all the support you could possibly need or want for a project or product. On a personal level, your love life is humming along quite nicely. And if it isn't, it will be soon.

Sunday, February 21 (Moon in Taurus to Gemini 2:47 p.m.) Your emotional focus shifts to finances and what you value. You're quite firm in your opinions and beliefs. But today calls for flexibility and thinking outside the box. If you have your natal chart, look to see where Uranus falls. That will tell you how you gain sudden insights.

Monday, February 22 (Moon in Gemini) Touch base with clients, friends, and family. If you're self-employed, it's particularly important to keep your client database updated and backed up. You may want to consider an external hard drive for your computer. That way, if your computer crashes, you've got all your data at your fingertips.

Tuesday, February 23 (Moon in Gemini to Cancer 7:29 p.m.) The moon enters your third house, highlighting your relationship with relatives and neighbors. One of your parents may need additional help or support today, perhaps nothing more than configuring a computer for the Internet. Events occur that make you more aware of how you nurture others as well as yourself.

Wednesday, February 24 (Moon in Cancer) If we are co-creators of our personal realities, then it's important to understand how we think on a daily basis. So for today, listen to the dialogue in your head. Is it primarily positive or negative? Each time you catch yourself thinking something negative, dismiss that thought and reach for something more positive.

Thursday, February 25 (Moon in Cancer to Leo 9:09 p.m.) There could be some tension with a romantic partner or friend today. It's nothing serious, but the Leo moon is rubbing Venus in Pisces the wrong way. It's a fire-water conflict. A part of you wants to be recognized for what you do and who you are, but at the heart of it all, your partner already appreciates you. So chill.

Friday, February 26 (Moon in Leo) Don't hesitate to toot your own horn. Sometimes you're too modest and reserved about your accomplishments. In fact, if you have a Web site or blog, that would be a good place to start. It's not boasting. You're simply patting yourself on the back for a job well done!

Saturday, February 27 (Moon in Leo to Virgo 8:53 p.m.) The moon enters Virgo, and is now opposite Venus. This combination can feel somewhat uncomfortable at times, creating irritation in a relationship over small, silly things. It's best to overlook irritants and wait until another day to talk about them.

Sunday, February 28 (Moon in Virgo) Today's full moon in Pisces should bring good news related to romance, creative endeavors, and your kids, if you have any. Pluto forms a powerful and beneficial angle to this moon, putting you squarely in the driver's seat. Enjoy your power.

MARCH 2010

Monday, March 1 (Moon in Virgo to Libra 8:32 p.m.) Mercury enters Pisces and joins Venus in your eleventh house. This combination, which lasts until March 7, when Venus enters Aries, should stimulate conversation with a partner, friends, and even with your muse! Your conscious mind is also very receptive to hunches and intuitions.

Tuesday, March 2 (Moon in Libra) Your social skills are in evidence today as you deal with a work-related issue. Employees or coworkers have issues they want addressed, and you're the person for the job. Say your piece; then listen closely to what others have to say. Teamwork is the key to resolution.

Wednesday, March 3 (Moon in Libra to Scorpio 10:12 p.m.) The moon enters your opposite sign, which could bring tension to a partnership, either romantic or business. But you're legendary for your patience, and that's really what this situation requires. So think before you speak, and bide your time.

Thursday, March 4 (Moon in Scorpio) You're on a hunt for something specific: information, illumination, insight. Take your pick. Your nose is to the ground, seeking the scent, and you won't stop until you find what you're seeking. Use your emotions as your measurement for whether you're on the right track. If it feels good, do it. If it doesn't feel good, run in the opposite direction.

Friday, March 5 (Moon in Scorpio) In a few days, Mars will turn direct in Leo, and things at home will run on a more even keel. A new romantic interest may enter your life too, and right now, you need to ask yourself what you're looking for in a partner. If you're involved already, then you and your partner may decide to take the relationship to a deeper level of commitment.

Saturday, March 6 (Moon in Scorpio to Sagittarius 3:37 a.m.) Other people ask for your support or help today.

You're wonderfully patient with these people, whoever they are, and you gladly give of your time and energy. Tomorrow, Venus enters Aries, your twelfth house, and you're going to keep an appointment with your unconscious!

Sunday, March 7 (Moon in Sagittarius) Venus enters Aries, where it will remain until March 31, when it goes into your sign. Think of this transit as the preparatory phase for one of the most romantic and creative times for you all year. Until March 31, you're exploring your hidden side. What motivates you? Who were you in previous lives?

Monday, March 8 (Moon in Sagittarius to Capricorn 1:15 p.m.) The moon enters fellow earth sign Capricorn. You feel like you're on solid ground today and with good reason. Your past planning is beginning to pay off. You can see the light at the end of the proverbial tunnel and feel confident that you're moving toward it right on schedule.

Tuesday, March 9 (Moon in Capricorn) Even on a bad day, your resolve is remarkable. But on a day like today, when the planets are lined up in your favor, your resolve to reach and achieve is extraordinary. You're able to organize your thoughts and actions effectively; don't hesitate to delegate.

Wednesday, March 10 (Moon in Capricorn) Mars turns direct in Leo, your fourth house. Any bumps and bruises you've been experiencing in your home life are now history. You're able to move forward on home-improvement projects. You may decide to refurbish your home office, or you may be redoing the guest room for visitors.

Thursday, March 11 (Moon in Capricorn to Aquarius 1:44 a.m.) The moon hooks up with Neptune, in your tenth house. Your emotional focus shifts to your career and professional matters. How can you be more visionary in your work? How can your ideals be more fully integrated into what you do? These are some of the questions you'll be asking yourself until the afternoon of March 13.

Friday, March 12 (Moon in Aquarius) Your emotions run the gamut today—from euphoria to a blue funk—and then finally straighten out when you find something to appreciate. As soon as you feel this appreciation, your mood lifts and more events and experiences that match that vibration pour in.

Saturday, March 13 (Moon in Aquarius to Pisces 2:44 p.m.) In two days, there will be a new moon in Pisces. Start preparing for it today by listing the experiences you would like to draw into your life. Every new moon represents an opportunity for new events, people, and emotions to enter your life. But a new moon is especially powerful when you're clear about what you want.

Sunday, March 14—Daylight Saving Time Begins (Moon in Pisces) The phase right before the new moon can bring up unsettled issues and emotions. Some of these feelings you're having may be related to events in past lives that were carried over into this life. Best to confront and deal with them now.

Monday, March 15 (Moon in Pisces) Today's new moon in Pisces receives a powerful and beneficial beam from Pluto in Capricorn. In some way, you become more aware of your personal power. This awareness is felt by others, who react to you as if you've got the answers.

Tuesday, March 16 (Moon in Pisces to Aries 3:32 a.m.) The moon enters your twelfth house, so it's time to clean out closets, attics, and your unconscious. There are ways to do this, of course, but you've got your own way of doing things. Pay close attention to your dreams tonight, and have a notebook handy! You'll gain insight and answers.

Wednesday, March 17 (Moon in Aries) Mercury joins the moon and Venus in Aries. This combination brings your conscious mind and your emotions into alignment. You're better able to extract what you need from your unconscious, and you're able to clear away issues through your conscious intent.

Thursday, March 18 (Moon in Aries to Taurus 1:30 p.m.) The moon is in your sign. You're now able to act on all the insights you have gained in the past few days and can effectively integrate these insights and new knowledge into your life. The process itself may be slow, but it's occurring at a deeper level. With so many planets in your twelfth house, this kind of information is more readily available to you.

Friday, March 19 (Moon in Taurus) You're particularly stubborn today when it comes to your personal life. And why shouldn't you be? It's *your* life. But you may want to tread gently with the people who may not grasp the full picture of what you're doing and why. In fact, it's a good time to sit down with these people and discuss your options.

Saturday, March 20 (Moon in Taurus to Gemini 9:29 p.m.) With the moon entering Gemini, your attention shifts to finances. The irony is that every time you think about money or obsess about it, your finances are in pretty good shape. The moon forms a harmonious angle with Mercury, Venus, and Uranus in Aries, your twelfth house, so you have access to answers for questions you haven't even asked!

Sunday, March 21 (Moon in Gemini) It's networking time again. This is sort of like a TV game show. If you answer the questions correctly, you win bonus points or money (a raise or promotion). If you garner the support you need, the payoff comes a bit down the road. So get out there and shake hands. Act like a politician.

Monday, March 22 (Moon in Gemini) Discussions ensue today. Whether it's through e-mail, phone, chat rooms, or instant messaging, you're able to use all the tools available to you to get out your message. You touch base with clients, employees, family, and friends. Sounds like you may be traveling.

Tuesday, March 23 (Moon in Gemini to Cancer 3:16 a.m.) The moon enters Cancer and your third house. This is a home day. It doesn't necessarily mean that you stay home, only that your emotions and focus are centered around home and family. And family can mean anything from the traditional concept to a house filled with animal companions.

Wednesday, March 24 (Moon in Cancer) You're nurturing someone else—or yourself—or someone is nurturing you. However it works, you're aware today of what nurturing means and how you do it. Even if you're not a parent, there are many other ways to nurture. Your techniques reveal a great deal about who you really are.

Thursday, March 25 (Moon in Cancer to Leo 6:40 a.m.) You're on exhibit today. Well, maybe not you personally, but your creative work, your home or family, or perhaps you as a teacher, mentor, or student. In some way, you are applauded or recognized for your knowledge or expertise.

Friday, March 26 (Moon in Leo) At the end of the month, Venus enters your sign, signaling the beginning of one of your most romantic and creative times this year. Prepare for this transit today by giving serious thought to what you would like to accomplish creatively and what you're looking for in a partner. If you're involved already, then how can you make the relationship better?

Saturday, March 27 (Moon in Leo to Virgo 7:58 a.m.) You're dotting Is and crossing Ts today. You also may be reflecting on your creative endeavors and love life. The Virgo moon enables you to perceive the details of a relationship or project more easily. How can you put what you learn to work in your daily life?

Sunday, March 28 (Moon in Virgo) If it's early spring where you are, then your blood should be humming with optimism and enthusiasm for warmer days ahead. This feeling translates into a surging self-confidence to which the people around you react. If you can tap into this feeling when the stars aren't stacked in your favor, you'll mitigate some of your angst.

Monday, March 29 (Moon in Virgo to Libra 8:22 a.m.) The full moon in Libra highlights your daily work routine, the maintenance of your health, social relationships, and your creative drive. Saturn forms a wide conjunction to this moon, indicating that obligations and responsibilities must be met. You also find structures that help you define who you are in the context of the larger world.

Tuesday, March 30 (Moon in Libra) Expect news concerning a relationship. It looks as if a partnership is about to be taken to a deeper level of commitment—but only if that's what you want. There are pros and cons, of course, but the best advice is to follow your heart.

Wednesday, March 31 (Moon in Libra to Scorpio 9:42 a.m.) Venus enters Taurus, where it will be until April 25. This should be a marvelously comfortable period for you. Not only does your love life pick up, but your creative drive is strong and flawless, and your love life finds just the right balance.

APRIL 2010

Thursday, April 1 (Moon in Scorpio) Your research and investigative skills are heightened today. Whether you're searching for a specific piece of information or insight into an issue or concern, let your intuition guide you. You have the resolute determination to do whatever needs to be done for you to achieve your goal.

Friday, April 2 (Moon in Scorpio to Sagittarius 1:54 p.m.) Mercury enters your sign today, joining Venus in your first house. Not only is this one of the most romantic and creative times for you, but your conscious mind is in complete agreement with your heart. Your thoughts are grounded, and you're seeking what is practical.

Saturday, April 3 (Moon in Sagittarius) The planets are lined up in your favor. So be sure to get involved in something you enjoy, rather than doing something out of a sense of obligation. The more joyful you feel, the likelier it is that you attract more events, people, and experiences that make you feel good.

Sunday, April 4 (Moon in Sagittarius to Capricorn 10:08 p.m.) Have you noticed that your inner world is expanding? Thank Jupiter in Aries for that. You may even be developing greater intuitive abilities. Right now, it's possible to nurture these abilities in yourself in a way so that down the road, you're as strong as you need to be.

Monday, April 5 (Moon in Capricorn) With the Capricorn moon, there's no better time than right now to practice focused intention. What is it that you desire? Define that, and then get busy manifesting your desires!

Tuesday, April 6 (Moon in Capricorn) Pluto turns retrograde in Capricorn, your ninth house, and doesn't turn direct again until September 13. During this period, you'll be scrutinizing your personal philosophy and beliefs, and you'll be able to determine which beliefs are really your own and which ones are adapted from family and friends. Once you know this, you'll be in a much stronger position to reach for and achieve your dreams.

Wednesday, April 7 (Moon in Capricorn to Aquarius 9:51 a.m.) You've got a window of opportunity related to your career. You'll have to follow the signs and synchronicities, so don't be in a rush. Sometimes, the best things in life unfold at their own pace, and we simply have to match our stride to that of the universe.

Thursday, April 8 (Moon in Aquarius) Your compassion and idealism come into play today. You may be looking for ways to integrate these qualities more effectively into your life so that you can make a big difference in the world. Your work begins within.

Friday, April 9 (Moon in Aquarius to Pisces 10:48 p.m.) Friends and groups are featured today. You may be working with a group that shares your passion or commitment to a particular idea or mission. Or this group is one with which you meet regularly, a kind of support system. Take home the ideas you discuss, and see if any of them suit your purposes.

Saturday, April 10 (Moon in Pisces) Whatever you can imagine can be manifested. And thanks to the Pisces moon, your imagination is as vast as an ocean. Your intuition is right on target as well, and when you use both in a focused way, the results will surprise you.

Sunday, April 11 (Moon in Pisces) If you haven't prepared your taxes yet, you may want to get started, since tax day is only a few days away. If you're looking for a tax break at this point, the only thing you can do is contribute to your 401(k) or a similar account for last year's income.

Monday, April 12 (Moon in Pisces to Aries 10:31 a.m.) The moon slides into your twelfth house. Feelings and issues from the past may surface today. Just deal with them and get on with it. It's not like you're some deep repository of grudges and hostilities. In fact, these feelings may originate in a past life.

Tuesday, April 13 (Moon in Aries) You're certain you're on the cutting edge of an idea, product, or marketing device—something that hasn't been done before. Don't hesitate to follow your gut on this one. You won't regret it.

Wednesday, April 14 (Moon in Aries to Taurus 7:55 p.m.) If yesterday was a precursor to today's new moon in Aries, then today is the real deal. This new moon ushers in many opportunities to work behind the scenes in some capacity. You'll have a chance to really delve into your own unconscious—through meditation, a past-life regression, writing ... well, any number of venues. Saturn forms a wide conjunction to this moon, indicating that you'll have to meet your obligations.

Thursday, April 15 (Moon in Taurus) Tax day! Just write your check and be grateful you have the money to pay. Your mood is too upbeat to let a little thing like a tax payment bring you down. With both Venus and Mercury still in your sign as well, life in general is humming along at an even pace, and you've got no complaints. Mercury turns retrograde in your sign on April 17, so be sure to back up computer files.

Friday, April 16 (Moon in Taurus) Confirm travel plans and buy tickets today if you haven't purchased them already. Mercury turns retrograde tomorrow. If you're submitting a manuscript or portfolio, send it off today or wait until after May 11, when Mercury turns direct again. If you've got contracts pending, waiting for your signature, sign today or wait until after May 11.

Saturday, April 17 (Moon in Taurus to Gemini 3:09 a.m.) Okay, here it is. Mercury turns retrograde in your sign. You know the drill on this one. The moon enters your second house too, and suddenly, you're flooded with invitations. Emotionally, your mood fits networking and touching base with friends and allies. Your biggest challenge will be deciding which invitations to accept!

Sunday, April 18 (Moon in Gemini) This moon may not be your favorite, unless you have a natal moon or rising in Gemini. Even so, its purpose is to urge you to think outside the box, to bring you out of yourself, and to communicate with people around you. You may want to consider starting a blog. That would satisfy your communication needs for today.

Monday, April 19 (Moon in Gemini to Cancer 8:40 a.m.) Your focus is on communication, particularly with family, neighbors, and members of your community. If you're a writer, this moon certainly favors hunkering down and pushing forward to beat your deadline. Even if you're not a professional writer, this moon sharpens your communication skills and adds an intuitive flavor to whatever you write.

Tuesday, April 20 (Moon in Cancer) The moon and Jupiter form a harmonious angle to each other, expanding your inner, intuitive world. It's also possible that the combination exaggerates feelings you have concerning your home and family. So if you catch yourself overreacting to something, step back, detach emotionally from the situation, and take a few deep breaths.

Wednesday, April 21 (Moon in Cancer to Leo 12:43 p.m.) Don't hesitate to show off your talents today. Other people are receptive to your ideas. Your family could need your emotional support today, so you may have to balance various obligations and responsibilities. But this shouldn't be a problem for you. Usually, you're pretty organized.

Thursday, April 22 (Moon in Leo) You may tackle a home-improvement project on which you've procrastinated. Be sure you have the time to commit to it this time so you can finish it. Few things bug you more than half-finished projects, especially where you live.

Friday, April 23 (Moon in Leo to Virgo 3:25 p.m.) Okay, so today love and romance may distract you, but that's as it should be. After all, what is life without romance? Love can take many forms, and your focus could be your creativity.

Saturday, April 24 (Moon in Virgo) Time to pay close attention to details. Whether it's in a relationship, a creative project, or an issue connected to your kids, the information you need lies in the details. One of your kids may need additional emotional support right now.

Sunday, April 25 (Moon in Virgo to Libra 5:18 p.m.) Venus enters Gemini, your second house, where it remains until May 19. During this period, your finances should run smoothly. You may be spending more money, but you'll be earning more too. The checks aren't just in the mail; they're in your mailbox.

Monday, April 26 (Moon in Libra) A perfect moon for a Monday. Teamwork and cooperation are called for. It's important that you listen with an open mind to the opinions of coworkers and employees and try to integrate what they say into what you're doing. You're usually a very good listener, and today is no exception.

Tuesday, April 27 (Moon in Libra to Scorpio 7:30 p.m.) When the moon moves into your opposite sign, there can be underlying tensions. But if you're aware of the possibility, you can deal with the tensions before they get blown out of proportion. Today's absolute bottom line is about research and investigation.

Wednesday, April 28 (Moon in Scorpio) Today's full moon in Scorpio may bring news or insights concerning a partnership. Whether business or romantic, you're in the power seat. Thanks to a beneficial angle to this moon from Pluto, you understand exactly what's involved and how to deal with it.

Thursday, April 29 (Moon in Scorpio to Sagittarius 11:36 p.m.) Your joint resources come into play today—any financial arrangements with others. If you've applied for a mortgage or loan recently, back up until Mercury turns direct on May 11. Don't sign any contracts yet!

Friday, April 30 (Moon in Sagittarius) Itching to travel? Then hit the road. If it's spring where you are, the seduction of the open road is going to be difficult to resist. And it's Friday. Treat yourself to a long weekend. Embrace it as an adventure.

MAY 2010

Saturday, May 1 (Moon in Sagittarius) Your focus shifts to the mundane—taxes, insurance, or wills. But if you're headed out of town for an adventure you started yesterday, wait till Monday to iron out the details.

Sunday, May 2 (Moon in Sagittarius to Capricorn 7:00 a.m.) Whatever you're doing today is approached with a determination and resoluteness that may take the people around you by surprise. You're tired of waiting for things to happen. You're going to *make* them happen. So focus on what you want, and then get out of the way and let the universe do its work!

Monday, May 3 (Moon in Capricorn) In another eight days, Mercury turns direct again. So put off travel plans until then. Also, don't sign contracts; keep backing up your computer files. You may want to consider buying an external hard drive for your computer so that everything you need is stored safely in a place separate from your computer's hard drive.

Tuesday, May 4 (Moon in Capricorn to Aquarius 5:52 p.m.) Your friends and acquaintances are among your most valued resources and connections. Today, you honor those friends in some way. This could be anything from an informal gathering at your place to something much fancier. You've got the visionary edge here. Use it.

Wednesday, May 5 (Moon in Aquarius) Your mind zips along, gathering and testing ideas and hunches and discarding those that don't seem to suit your needs. What you are left with is a panoply of opportunities that require some work on your part. But you've never shirked work or responsibilities, so you dive in with your enthusiasm and your resolve.

Thursday, May 6 (Moon in Aquarius) Professional demands may cause some tension at home. But you're good at balancing, and you shouldn't have any trouble smoothing things over. You're in demand right now. Bosses and peers are watching to see how you perform and meet the challenge. You don't disappoint them.

Friday, May 7 (Moon in Aquarius to Pisces 8:34 a.m.) This moon is friendly. It softens your innate stubbornness and deepens your imagination and intuition. Try to focus on your own wishes and dreams today, and allow your intuition to guide you in the best way to achieve what you want.

Saturday, May 8 (Moon in Pisces) Right now, Uranus is still in Pisces, so that planet and the moon combine to create emotional excitement and unexpected events. But on May 27, Uranus will move into Aries, your twelfth house, and suddenly, buried stuff begins to surface. This stuff can be memories from past lives or events from childhood that you've forgotten. By reclaiming these memories, you are reclaiming your personal power.

Sunday, May 9 (Moon in Pisces to Aries 6:30 p.m.) You don't hesitate to take risks today—not external risks, but internal, emotional risks. It may involve committing to a relationship, an idea, a project, a creative hobby, or a trek across the Andes. No telling. But one way or another, this is an activity you probably do alone or with a couple of other people at the most.

Monday, May 10 (Moon in Aries) Your passions are stoked today by a confrontation with someone connected to a nursing home, hospital, or some similar facility. Or through confronting something in your own life that you pushed way underground. Resolve the situation as quickly as possible.

Tuesday, May 11 (Moon in Aries) Mercury finally turns direct today. It may have been a long haul for you, and now you have the opportunity to unravel the tangled ball of thread the Mercury retrograde caused. But you can start planning for a trip in earnest now; be sure you don't travel between August 20 and September 12, the next retrograde period.

Wednesday, May 12 (Moon in Aries to Taurus 3:49 a.m.) The moon joins Mercury in your sign. Your conscious mind is very much in agreement with your emotions. So if you're dealing with what might be prickly issues, don't obsess. You come out on top, and it doesn't require too much effort.

Thursday, May 13 (Moon in Taurus) You'll love today. The new moon in Taurus happens just once a year and sets the tone for the rest of the year. New opportunities surface in your personal life and with Jupiter forming such a beneficial angle to this moon, expansion and luck are the key words.

Saturn forms a slightly wider but also beneficial angle to this moon, indicating that the opportunities are well-grounded and serious.

Friday, May 14 (Moon in Taurus to Gemini 10:19 a.m.)
So how can you make use of the new-moon-phase energy? Start new projects, meet new people, generate new ideas, pitch new ideas, or make new sales contacts. It's all about *new*. And you.

Saturday, May 15 (Moon in Gemini) Your nickname is the bull, and today the people around you understand why. Bulls charge when they rage, they refuse to move when others want them to, and like Ferdinand, some of them refuse to fight or allow their buttons to be pushed. Today you sink into yourself and find your own way. But really try to be flexible.

Sunday, May 16 (Moon in Gemini to Cancer 2:47 p.m.) The moon forms a harmonious angle to Jupiter, so your emotions are expansive. This is a good thing if your heart is filled with love, enthusiasm, and optimism. But it can be a challenge if you're overprotective or jealous. Jupiter expands whatever it touches. Remember that.

Monday, May 17 (Moon in Cancer) This moon can trigger your nurturing qualities and can make you overprotective of the people you love. But today, it also increases your intuition and imagination. You're able to nurture the people around you more effectively and genuinely.

Tuesday, May 18 (Moon in Cancer to Leo 6:07 p.m.) Your home or family is in the public view today for some reason. It doesn't mean you're on exhibit, but perhaps one of your children is in a school play or perhaps your house is on the market. At any rate, add some fresh flowers to your dining room table, and light a scented candle.

Wednesday, May 19 (Moon in Leo) Aren't you in for a treat? Venus enters Cancer today, where it remains until June 14. During this period, romance may be as close as your neighbor's house, or within your immediate community. If you're active online, you could meet someone in an online community. If you're involved already, this transit helps soothe any misunderstandings you and a partner may have had while Venus was moving through Gemini. If you're a writer, your skills will now have a distinctively intuitive flavor to them.

Thursday, May 20 (Moon in Leo to Virgo 8:59 p.m.) Romance and creativity may go hand in hand today. You could be writing a romance novel—or simply approaching your romantic relationship in a more creative way. Do only what you enjoy.

Friday, May 21 (Moon in Virgo) Check and recheck whatever you write, and be sure that in all your communications, you're saying exactly what you want to say. The Virgo moon asks that you pay close attention to details in all areas, but particularly about what you feel. If something feels slightly off, figure out why and correct it. Or do something that makes you feel better and more positive.

Saturday, May 22 (Moon in Virgo to Libra 11:50 p.m.) Relationships and social connections take center stage today. You may get together with employees or coworkers for some sort of gathering: an office party, an office excursion, or even a seminar or workshop that everyone attends.

Sunday, May 23 (Moon in Libra) Cooperation goes a long way today. You may be planning a get-together this week with coworkers or employees and enlist the aid of trusted friends or family members to arrange your agenda. Your artistic sensibilities are heightened with the Libra moon, and your approach to life generally is softened.

Monday, May 24 (Moon in Libra) In several days, Uranus enters Aries, your twelfth house. You may be feeling the approach of this transit already, through surprising and unexpected insights into your own psyche. Be gentle with yourself. The insights you gain aren't supposed to make you more self-critical.

Tuesday, May 25 (Moon in Libra to Scorpio 3:18 a.m.) With the moon entering your opposite sign, your mood is more intense, secretive, and passionate. This moon favors research and investigation into the odd, the anomalous, or the downright strange. If you're searching for a particular kind of information, go online first.

Wednesday, May 26 (Moon in Scorpio) You're able to pick up on other people's moods and feelings with uncanny accuracy. In fact, you're a kind of psychic sponge. So it's important to be around positive, upbeat people today and to maintain your emotional integrity.

Thursday, May 27 (Moon in Scorpio to Sagittarius 8:16 a.m.) Two things are on the zodiac agenda today. The full moon in Sagittarius, your eighth house, may bring sudden, unexpected news from abroad, about resources you share with another or about taxes or insurance matters. Also, Uranus enters Aries and forms a wide but harmonious angle to this moon, bringing an element of excitement and surprise.

Friday, May 28 (Moon in Sagittarius) Itching to travel? You know you are, so why not indulge yourself? Book a trip to some exotic spot you've never visited before. The trip could turn into a spiritual quest.

Saturday, May 29 (Moon in Sagittarius to Capricorn 3:44 p.m.) The Capricorn moon is a friendly one for you. Today, it helps you to ground an idea and to push ahead in some area. You're willing to work longer hours, you don't hesitate to delegate if you feel pressed for time, and you're able to plan ahead effectively.

Sunday, May 30 (Moon in Capricorn) Saturn turns direct in Libra, your sixth house. Finally, you can put what you've learned these past few months to work for you. Take the lead and gather your group—friends, employees, and coworkers—and get down to the business at hand. You'll find the right structure for what you're working on.

Monday, May 31 (Moon in Capricorn) Neptune turns retrograde in Aquarius and doesn't turn direct again until November 6. Since this planet moves so slowly, the retrograde gives you a chance to examine your ideals and compassion, and to figure out a way to integrate these qualities into your career. Once Neptune turns direct again in November, you'll be in an excellent position to put what you've learned to work for you.

JUNE 2010

Tuesday, June 1 (Moon in Capricorn to Aquarius 2:08 a.m.) If you live north of the equator, summer is almost here. And today, that upbeat feeling you have is poured into your professional life. You're beginning to understand how you can integrate your idealism and ideals more readily into your career.

Wednesday, June 2 (Moon in Aquarius) Visionary? That's you today. And you've grounded your visions in reality, backed them with facts, and can certainly garner the support you need. You come out way ahead of the pack by the end of the day.

Thursday, June 3 (Moon in Aquarius to Pisces 2:34 p.m.) The moon stands alone today in Pisces; Uranus has moved on into Aries. It forms a nice angle to your sun, increasing your intuition, imagination, and compassion. But be careful that you don't become a sucker for a sob story. Quite often, this moon has your head moving in one direction—and your heart in another. Wait until the moon enters your sign to make major decisions.

Friday, June 4 (Moon in Pisces) Can you imagine the unimagined? If so, then you can have it. That's how strong your resolve can be, and with the aid of the Pisces moon, you can make it happen.

Saturday, June 5 (Moon in Pisces) Feeling the suddenness of events yet? Feeling the underlying excitement? If so, it's Uranus in Aries. You may have conflicting feelings from time to time over this transit, particularly when the surprises knock you down. But remember that Uranus's task is to shake up the status quo.

Sunday, June 6 (Moon in Pisces to Aries 2:51 a.m.) Jupiter now joins Uranus in Aries, your third house. This combination will expand the surprises and suddenness inherent in the nature of Uranus, but will also increase your insight, cause you to take risks you might not have taken, and force you to think outside the box. These actions will have repercussions in various areas of your life, and for a time, you will have to be much more flexible.

Monday, June 7 (Moon in Aries) Mars enters Virgo, where it will be until July 29. This transit should heat up your sex life and put romance at the top of your agenda. It should also stimulate your creative life, which you'll approach with great diligence to detail and a critical eye. But don't be too critical. Nothing kills creativity faster than criticism.

Tuesday, June 8 (Moon in Aries to Taurus 12:42 p.m.) The moon is in your sign, and any decisions that you have delayed making can now be made with certainty that it is in your best interest. Your love life should be moving along quite nicely, with just the right dash of surprise and excitement. This translates as satisfaction in other areas of your life too. When your personal life runs smoothly, so does everything else in your life.

Wednesday, June 9 (Moon in Taurus) With Venus in Leo and your fourth house, it's possible that a flirtation is now starting to heat up. Also, Mars is in Virgo and your fifth house now, which stimulates your sexuality, your capacity for enjoyment and pleasure, and your creativity. This all sounds like a wonderful recipe for a romantic relationship that is fun, exciting, and sensual.

Thursday, June 10 (Moon in Taurus to Gemini 7:12 p.m.) Mercury enters Gemini and your second house today and remains there until June 25. During this period, there's a lot of discussion about finances. You may have some unforeseen expenses, but you've got the money to pay for them.

Friday, June 11 (Moon in Gemini) This moon favors communication, travel, networking, and the realm of ideas. It forms a harmonious angle to Uranus and Jupiter in Aries, which helps to expand your ideas and bolsters your communication skills. You gain unusual insights into the working of your own emotions.

Saturday, June 12 (Moon in Gemini to Cancer 10:51 p.m.) Today's new moon in Gemini should usher in financial opportunities and opportunities for communication and networking. If you're a professional writer, this moon could attract writing projects and the chance to work with others of like mind.

Sunday, June 13 (Moon in Cancer) This water sign moon is certainly more in alignment with your earth-sign sun. It adds an intuitive and nurturing element to all your communications and makes you more aware of the details of your daily life. You're on a definite roll. Don't blow it.

Monday, June 14 (Moon in Cancer) Venus enters Leo, your fourth house, and remains there until July 10. During this period, your family life should be unfolding smoothly, but there's activity at home that could be distracting. You may refurbish your home office or the entire house in some way. You may decide to put your house on the market, but can't figure out where you would like to move. It's best to wait on these kinds of decisions until Venus enters fellow earth sign Virgo.

Tuesday, June 15 (Moon in Cancer to Leo 12:55 a.m.) The moon hooks up with Venus in your fourth house. The combination of these two planets brings an intuitive understanding of your partner's needs and desires. If you aren't involved, then the combination leads you to the right person at the right time. It's also a nice combo for any creative projects in which you're involved.

Wednesday, June 16 (Moon in Leo) The moon forms a harmonious angle with Mercury in Gemini. This combination boosts your sense of adventure and your need to try something different. So go for it, and don't look back!

Thursday, June 17 (Moon in Leo to Virgo 2:42 a.m.) With Saturn in Libra all year, and currently moving in direct motion, you're solidifying your support base at work. You may also be more diligent about your physical routines. You flourish in a routine that benefits you in some way, but otherwise chafe at restrictions that others may seek to impose on you.

Friday, June 18 (Moon in Leo to Virgo 12:41) Dot the Is, cross the Ts, and read the fine print. These qualities are part and parcel of the Virgo moon. But this moon also helps you to make the esoteric practical and comprehensible to people who don't have your knowledge.

Saturday, June 19 (Moon in Virgo to Libra 5:13 a.m.) The moon joins Saturn in your sixth house. Intuitively, you grasp the situation you're facing today. But it could take you a while to realize that the key to success today is teamwork and cooperation. Listen to what others have to say.

Sunday, June 20 (Moon in Libra) If you're competing with a coworker for a raise or promotion, it's important to listen to your heart. Do you really want what is being offered? Or are you competing merely to compete? There's nothing wrong with competition for the sake of competition, but be prepared to commit extra time and energy if you land the promotion or raise.

Monday, June 21 (Moon in Libra to Scorpio 9:14 a.m.) The moon enters passionate, secretive Scorpio and places emphasis on your partnerships—both romantic and business. Play your cards close today. Continue to work as you are, but don't advertise what you're doing or why. If the partnership involved is a romantic one, be honest and explain why you would rather keep certain information to yourself for now.

Tuesday, June 22 (Moon in Scorpio) On June 26, there's going to be a lunar eclipse in Capricorn, your ninth house. Read about it in the big-picture section and start preparing for it now by honoring your power as an individual to bring about change in the world.

Wednesday, June 23 (Moon in Scorpio to Sagittarius 3:11 p.m.) The moon enters your eighth house, highlighting resources you share with others. If you're in the midst of a divorce, for instance, then this moon helps you to grasp the big picture. If you're involved in business with someone else, then that person may need your support today. This moon also favors travel and delving into the esoteric and strange.

Thursday, June 24 (Moon in Sagittarius) You've got your sights set on an exotic destination, but you may think you don't have the money or time to take the trip. You're wrong on both counts. Create the time, crank up your desire, and somehow it will all come together. That's the kind of magical universe in which we live.

Friday, June 25 (Moon in Sagittarius to Capricorn 11:22 p.m.) Mercury enters Cancer, your third house, where it remains until July 9. This transit is terrific for all communication. In fact, if you're a writer or if you do any kind of regular writing in your work, the words simply flow now. You become more consciously intuitive during this transit.

Saturday, June 26 (Moon in Capricorn) Today's lunar eclipse in Capricorn triggers emotions related to publishing, higher education, your worldview, and foreign travel and individuals. Pluto is exactly conjunct to the degree of this moon, so you're in a powerful position to make decisions and bring about change.

Sunday, June 27 (Moon in Capricorn) Your planning is beginning to pay off. You can see the long-range repercussions of whatever you're working on, and you like what you see. You've grounded your ideas and dreams in the real world, but without losing sight of how magically things can occur.

Monday, June 28 (Moon in Capricorn to Aquarius 9:53 a.m.) Even though air and earth don't mix well, this moon has benefits for you. It allows you to detach emotionally from the world around you and to focus on what you would like for yourself and your loved ones in the future. Figure it out. Then get out of the way and let it happen.

Tuesday, June 29 (Moon in Aquarius) Pretty soon, you'll be entering the last month of the summer. A part of you feels nostalgic about the passage of time, but another part of you welcomes it. However, the only thing that we can be sure of is this second. Your point of power always lies in the present.

Wednesday, June 30 (Moon in Aquarius to Pisces 10:11 p.m.) Imagine, intuit, and let your heart lead the way. The Pisces moon softens up the part of you that may have grown hard. Let your compassion speak.

JULY 2010

Thursday, July 1 (Moon in Pisces) Friends are your focus today—making them, taking stock of your relationship with them, and hanging out with them. Your intuitive connection with one close friend is what you use as a measurement of other friendships.

Friday, July 2 (Moon in Pisces) Publicity and promotion for your company's product or your own creative works are ideal for today. People will be receptive to you and to whatever you're publicizing. Some travel could be involved. Even if the travel takes you to a place you've been before, you find it all very enjoyable.

Saturday, July 3 (Moon in Pisces to Aries 10:45 a.m.) The moon joins Uranus in Aries in your twelfth house. This combination can be volatile if you're not careful. People come along who seem to push all the right buttons. Don't get angry. Use your energy in meditation or in some type of physical activity.

Sunday, July 4 (Moon in Aries) Happy July Fourth! If you're one of millions of people traveling over this holiday weekend, then yesterday's forecast applies for today too. Patience will take you much further than hostility. If you're celebrating the holiday at home, surrounded by family and friends, you're less likely to feel restless.

Monday, July 5 (Moon in Aries to Taurus 9:30 p.m.) Uranus turns retrograde in Aries, your twelfth house, and begins to move back toward Pisces. Over the next few months, you may be experiencing some of the same stuff you did during the past seven years. If you learned whatever Uranus was supposed to teach you, the transit back through Pisces will pass you by practically unnoticed.

Tuesday, July 6 (Moon in Taurus) The moon is in your sign, and you're ready to take on everything. Mercury in intuitive Cancer is in a beneficial angle to this moon, so you're able to follow your intuition and your emotions to make the right choices.

Wednesday, July 7 (Moon in Taurus) Your emotions and your head are in perfect sync today. This makes it easier to achieve what you want by the end of the day: no angst. And if anyone demands that you do something differently, you have the strength to say no.

Thursday, July 8 (Moon in Taurus to Gemini 4:51 a.m.) Money and finances, friends and networks of acquaintances—what are the relationships between them? Sometimes financial opportunities come through people who are in your life already. It's who you know today that counts.

Friday, July 9 (Moon in Gemini) Mercury enters Leo and remains there until July 27. During this time, you can expect a lot of discussion centered on your home and a lot of family activity in general. Short trips are certainly likely. You may be offering your opinion more than you usually do.

Saturday, July 10 (Moon in Gemini to Cancer 8:38 a.m.) Venus enters Virgo and your fifth house, marking the start of one of the most romantic periods for you all year. If you're not involved, you may be before this transit ends on August 6. This transit also increases your creative drive. You may want to post a do-not-disturb sign on your door.

Sunday, July 11 (Moon in Cancer) Today's solar eclipse in Cancer triggers events involving your relatives, your neighbors, or your community. Mars forms a harmonious angle with this moon, indicating a lot of activity and forward movement as a result of the events that unfold.

Monday, July 12 (Moon in Cancer to Leo 9:54 a.m.) With the moon and Mercury in the same sign and house today, you're in rare form. You don't mind being singled out for something if it gives you a chance to say your piece. In fact you may actually seek the spotlight—and find that you enjoy it!

Tuesday, July 13 (Moon in Leo) If events from the eclipse still have you reeling, take a few deep breaths. Ground yourself by doing some yoga postures, or spend a few minutes sitting quietly, letting your mind empty. You'll find that things really aren't as frantic as they may appear.

Wednesday, July 14 (Moon in Leo to Virgo 10:15 a.m.) The moon joins Venus in Virgo. This pleasant combination highlights your love life and creativity. Emotionally and intuitively, you reach out for what you need, and Venus helps to reel it in. Details in all things make the difference today.

Thursday, July 15 (Moon in Virgo) Aren't you lucky! Today, in romance and love, your life reads like a fortune cookie. Your creative drive is also strong, so it's possible to work on or even complete creative projects that you may have postponed. You do something for someone else because the other person is in need.

Friday, July 16 (Moon in Virgo to Libra 11:25 a.m.) You're in the sort of mood that often baffles you. Instead of going on about your own business, you feel compelled to enter into a cooperative agreement with other people. Can teamwork really accomplish what the group hopes? You have to give it a try.

Saturday, July 17 (Moon in Libra) This air-sign moon can trigger a need for lovelier surroundings. So today you could be beautifying your home or office in some way. Fresh paint, fresh flowers, or perhaps a new piece of art or furniture would do the trick. If you're fixing up someone else's room, make sure that person approves of what you're doing.

Sunday, July 18 (Moon in Libra to Scorpio 2:43 p.m.) As the moon enters your opposite sign, there's a certain amount of inner angst that occurs. It's easy to mitigate, if you follow the dictates of the Scorpio moon: investigate, research, meditate, and nurture your intuition. This moon also stirs your passions, and with Venus still in Virgo and your fifth house, your romantic partnership may be taken to a whole new level.

Monday, July 19 (Moon in Scorpio) In another six days, there's a full moon in Aquarius that may bring news concerning professional matters. You could be experiencing it at any time leading up to this full moon. Your partner—business or romantic—may not want to discuss some issues with you today. If possible, wait until the moon enters Capricorn on July 23.

Tuesday, July 20 (Moon in Scorpio to Sagittarius 8:49 p.m.) If you have a copy of your birth chart, find out where Sagittarius falls. Do you have planets in that sign? If so, this moon blends with that particular planet. For instance, if you have Jupiter in Sagittarius, then you can expect your intuition to expand and to feel magnanimous. You may also have to watch your spending!

Wednesday, July 21 (Moon in Sagittarius) Your mood is gregarious and upbeat today, due in part to Venus and Mars in your fifth house of romance, love, and creativity. A new romantic interest may have deeper designs than you do, so be honest about your intentions and desires. Saturn turns direct in Libra, your sixth house. It's now easier to integrate your responsibilities and obligations into your daily work life.

Thursday, July 22 (Moon in Sagittarius) Uranus is up to its old tricks today, shaking up the status quo and forcing you to think outside the box. Once you do this, you'll have the big picture, and that will help you bring together a plan for success. Never hesitate to reach for the unknown. It's one of the ways that you grow and evolve as a spiritual being living in a physical universe.

Friday, July 23 (Moon in Sagittarius to Capricorn 5:40 a.m.) The moon joins Pluto in Capricorn. This combination often puts you in the seat of power. Whether the power is exerted in a relationship, your personal life, a job, be careful not to abuse your authority.

Saturday, July 24 (Moon in Capricorn) You're setting the stage today for the full moon in Aquarius tomorrow. Even though it's the weekend, it won't hurt to plan the week's work agenda ahead of time. On other fronts, education or foreign travel or both are highlighted today.

Sunday, July 25 (Moon in Capricorn to Aquarius 4:39 p.m.) Today's full moon occurs in the career sector of your chart. Uranus forms a close and harmonious angle to this moon, suggesting that the news—whatever it is—happens unexpectedly. Also, Saturn forms a harmonious angle to the moon, so whatever structures evolve from the news or related to your career are solid and dependable. A raise or promotion, perhaps?

Monday, July 26 (Moon in Aquarius) Your boss and peers enjoy your forward-thinking ideas. And today, your ability to express these ideas, either verbally or in writing, is exceptional. In fact, you may want to write it all out first so nothing slips your mind.

Tuesday, July 27 (Moon in Aquarius) Mercury joins Venus and Mars in Virgo. This trio of planets makes you very precise, detail-oriented, and critical. Just try not to be critical of a partner or yourself. In fact, be as critical as you like in your own head, but don't express any of it to others.

If you're involved in a creative project, use your criticism on that.

Wednesday, July 28 (Moon in Aquarius to Pisces 5:00 a.m.) Your mind zips along at a lightning pace, and your partner or whomever you're spending the day with may have a hard time keeping up. That's fine. If it's a workday, you somehow manage to make things fun not only for yourself, but for the people around you as well.

Thursday, July 29 (Moon in Pisces) Mars enters Libra and your sixth house, where it will remain until September 14. During this period, teamwork and cooperation will be highlighted, particularly when the moon is also in Libra. Networking with employees and coworkers will be important. Lots of discussions ensue in which everyone's opinions and thoughts are heard and taken into consideration.

Friday, July 30 (Moon in Pisces to Aries 5:42 p.m.) For a relationship that begins now, it's important that you don't bend over backward to please the other person. You may be spending more time exercising regularly too. But choose a form of exercise and a routine that won't bore you so that you'll keep it up.

Saturday, July 31 (Moon in Aries) With the moon now in your twelfth house, you're cleaning your inner house. You get some help here from Uranus in this house, with sudden insights and ideas that take you even deeper into your own unconscious.

AUGUST 2010

Sunday, August 1 (Moon in Aries) The moon joins Uranus in your twelfth house, a sure recipe for surprising insights into the workings of your own unconscious. Jupiter is also in this sign and house, so whatever insights you gain will expand your understanding of the hidden forces in your own life. Everything you learn in this regard can be used as fodder for a creative project.

Monday, August 2 (Moon in Aries to Taurus 5:13 a.m.) The moon enters your sign again. You've made it through another cycle of moons, and you're still intact, right? This should be proof that you're a survivor of the first order, able to endure and flourish regardless of what's going on around you.

Tuesday, August 3 (Moon in Taurus) Venus continues its transit of Virgo and your fifth house for another few days. This moon forms a nice angle to Venus, so your love life and your creativity should be humming along at a pleasant pitch. You can, of course, keeps things moving along like this even after August 6, when Venus enters Libra. Just be open and receptive to your partner and communicate honestly.

Wednesday, August 4 (Moon in Taurus to Gemini 1:54 p.m.) Checks really are in the mail. Your finances are more solid than you believe today. You may be looking for additional sources of income, perhaps through a part-time job or some sort of home-based business.

Thursday, August 5 (Moon in Gemini) Communication, both verbal and written, is highlighted. You may be saying your piece to someone in your immediate circle of family and friends. Be gentle but direct. Let the other person know you're serious about what you feel. That will have better results than a direct confrontation.

Friday, August 6 (Moon in Gemini to Cancer 6:50 p.m.) Venus enters Libra and your sixth house. Between now and September 8, your daily work life unfolds more smoothly, with a greater emphasis on teamwork and cooperation. If you're not involved right now, an office flirtation may take on greater significance and a whole new meaning.

Saturday, August 7 (Moon in Cancer) This moon is a friendly one for you. It awakens a kind of nostalgia in you for the good old days. It also makes you much more aware of the value of community, neighborhood, and relatives. One or both of your parents may figure into the day's events.

Sunday, August 8 (Moon in Cancer to Leo 8:23 p.m.) Let's take stock. With both Venus and Mars in Libra, it's quite possible that you and someone you have met through work are now spending more time together outside of work. Today you need to balance your desires and those of your partner, and reach some sort of understanding that suits you both.

Monday, August 9 (Moon in Leo) Today's new moon in Leo should usher in opportunities related to your home and family. If you've been hoping to move, this moon could bring the opportunity to do it. If your house is on the market, this new moon could bring the buyer. If you want to start a family, this new moon could start the process!

Tuesday, August 10 (Moon in Leo to Virgo 8:02 p.m.) The moon joins Mercury in Virgo. You and your partner may be deep into intimate conversations about the nature of your relationship and what you both are looking for. This kind of honest communication may deepen your commitment to each other.

Wednesday, August 11 (Moon in Virgo) Your mind and your heart are in close agreement today. It means that you don't take guff from anyone about anything. If you enjoy physical activity, then today you may not only hit the gym, but take a yoga class or a long bike ride as well.

Thursday, August 12 (Moon in Virgo to Libra 7:44 p.m.) Aesthetics and fairness are your focal points. They could involve any area of your life, but most certainly center on a relationship that may be equitable in some way. You may not be able to fix the world's problems in a single day, but you can surely fix this problem.

Friday, August 13 (Moon in Libra) You're trying to wrap things up in anticipation of the weekend. You may have to delegate some responsibilities and duties to other employees. Your reluctance to do so could keep you at work later than anticipated. So grit your teeth, and ask others to help out.

Saturday, August 14 (Moon in Libra to Scorpio 9:27 p.m.) Intense emotions and deep passions rule the day. You're at the center of a storm of your own creation, and even if you feel you can't call the shots, you do. Do it without regret or apology.

Sunday, August 15 (Moon in Scorpio) You're on a search for something, and whatever it is may be intangible. It could be a quality or a state of mind. Your investigative skills are remarkable, and by the end of the day, you're well on your way to finding what you're looking for.

Monday, August 16 (Moon in Scorpio) A week into the new moon in Leo and you may be feeling the impact of opportunities. You may have so many opportunities from which to choose that your dilemma is picking the opportunity that seems the best for you. This isn't a left-brain issue. What do you feel intuitively?

Tuesday, August 17 (Moon in Scorpio to Sagittarius 2:35 a.m.) If you're applying for a loan or mortgage, you shouldn't have any trouble getting one. In fact, today your emotional shift focuses on shared finances, including stuff like taxes and insurance. Be careful about big-ticket items you buy in the hopes of a tax write-off. Check first with your accountant.

Wednesday, August 18 (Moon in Sagittarius) With the big picture at your fingertips, there are places to go and people to see who will help you connect the dots in a more meaningful way. So don't push away information that comes to you in unconventional ways. Be open and receptive.

Thursday, August 19 (Moon in Sagittarius to Capricorn 11:18 a.m.) The moon joins Pluto in your ninth house. The combination emphasizes the strength of your beliefs and philosophy about how the universe works and your place in it. Don't allow someone else to try to talk you out of something you really want to do. If it feels good, then do it. Back up computer files today. Mercury turns retrograde tomorrow.

Friday, August 20 (Moon in Capricorn) Mercury turns retrograde in Virgo until September 12. By now, you know the drill. And since this retrograde occurs in your fifth house, romantic relationships and creative projects may experience sudden, unexpected detours. Try to communicate concisely and clearly.

Saturday, August 21 (Moon in Capricorn to Aquarius 10:38 p.m.) The moon enters your tenth house, shifting your emotional focus to your career. You're exploring how your foresight into trends might be used professionally. You're looking for gaps in the market that your product or services could fill. Isn't that how entrepreneurs get started?

Sunday, August 22 (Moon in Aquarius) The moon forms a beneficial angle with your ruler, Venus. The combination of influences should add intuitive insight and deeper feelings to a romantic relationship. It also bolsters your creative adrenaline so that any ideas you have seem to take on lives of their own, and you simply channel the results.

Monday, August 23 (Moon in Aquarius) With Mars still transiting Scorpio and your seventh house, partnerships have plenty of force and power behind them. Be sure that you read the fine print on any contracts, particularly now that Mercury is retrograde. Delay signing until after September 12.

Tuesday, August 24 (Moon in Aquarius to Pisces 11:11 a.m.) Today's full moon in Pisces brings plenty of social invitations and also news concerning some wish or dream that you have. Pluto forms a positive angle to this full moon, so you're the one calling the shots today.

Wednesday, August 25 (Moon in Pisces) Imagination can take you anywhere, open any doors, and make anything possible. If you can imagine it, it can happen. So don't worry about how it will happen—simply believe that it will, and allow your imagination to run as wild and fast as it can.

Thursday, August 26 (Moon in Pisces to Aries 11:49 p.m.) The moon is now alone in your twelfth house, stirring up old memories, some of which may be rooted in past lives. These memories can come to you through dreams, periods of relaxation or meditation, or even during periods of physical activity where your mind and body are focused on a particular task.

Friday, August 27 (Moon in Aries) A week into the Mercury retrograde and you may be experiencing more than your share of snafus. Just hang in there. Pretty soon it will be September, and you have a new moon in Virgo to look forward to on September 8. By then, Mercury will nearly be out of its retrograde, and you can anticipate new opportunities for romantic partnerships and creative projects.

Saturday, August 28 (Moon in Aries) You've gone deep underground, way down into yourself, looking for answers. The answer may be simple: Clean house. Get rid of beliefs that no longer serve your best interests and that may be holding you back. Focus on what is positive and upbeat in your life.

Sunday, August 29 (Moon in Aries to Taurus 11:36 a.m.) The moon is in your sign. This certainly helps mitigate some of the effects of Mercury's retrograde, especially where romantic relationships and your creativity are concerned. The firmer you are about what you're doing and what you feel, the more readily the universe responds.

Monday, August 30 (Moon in Taurus) You've got your agenda set, and nothing will stop you from implementing it. You're clear on where you're going and clear on where you've been. You're a force of nature today, and no one will mess with you!

Tuesday, August 31 (Moon in Taurus to Gemini 9:20 p.m.) There's a palpable shift in the air this evening. Emotionally, you may become more detached and restless. You're ready for change, but you aren't sure what that means. By Friday, you'll know.

SEPTEMBER 2010

Wednesday, September 1 (Moon in Gemini) Mercury won't turn direct for another twelve days, so any money you're owed may not arrive until after that date. It's a good day to set up a budget, if only to get some idea of what you're earning and what's going out and where it goes.

Thursday, September 2 (Moon in Gemini) Bills from a vacation or some other summer expense may be coming due. Try not to panic. You're in good shape financially, but to settle your own mind, you may want to take on several more hours of work a week. A part-time job, perhaps?

Friday, September 3 (Moon in Gemini to Cancer 3:51 a.m.) This is a friendlier moon for you. It highlights your nurturing qualities—both how you nurture others and how you are nurtured. This nurturing extends not only to your family, but to people who are like family: employees, coworkers, and neighbors. In a sense, this communal family is how you learn about cooperation and teamwork.

Saturday, September 4 (Moon in Cancer) Over the long Labor Day weekend, you'll have ups and downs, thanks to the change in the sign of the moon. But for today, the world seems to be just about perfect, with plenty of time to kick back with friends and family and enjoy yourself. Discussions may ensue with a close family member or friend whose views differ from yours.

Sunday, September 5 (Moon in Cancer to Leo 6:46 a.m.) Your mood fluctuates from yesterday. You may have less patience with family members today, so try to keep your criticism to yourself. If you don't like something, try to turn your attention toward what you do appreciate.

Monday, September 6 (Moon in Leo) Your home and your family are more in the public eye today. It could be that you've updated your family blog with photos about your latest project or trip. Or perhaps your home is on the market, and you're getting a lot of showings. Whatever is going on, it may feel like an invasion of privacy to you.

Tuesday, September 7 (Moon in Leo to Virgo 6:54 a.m.) The moon enters your fifth house of romance, creativity, and children, so all of these areas are highlighted. The Virgo moon asks that you pay close attention to details today and not just in the areas mentioned above. You're able to ground your projects and ideas in a way that makes them understandable to others.

Wednesday, September 8 (Moon in Virgo) Two stellar events today influence not only your moods but every facet of your life. First, the new moon in Virgo, your fifth house, ushers in opportunities for romance and love, as well as creative opportunities. If you're not involved now, you may well be before the full moon on September 23. There may be lots of discussions and perhaps even some travel with your partner. Venus enters Scorpio, your opposite sign, where it will be through the end of the year. This transit stimulates activity with all partnerships—personal and professional. It could take a personal partnership to a deeper level of commitment.

Thursday, September 9 (Moon in Virgo to Libra 6:02 a.m.) Between October 8 and November 18, Venus's transit will be moving retrograde, so that's the time when partnerships are most likely to experience bumps and bruises. If the partnership in question involves business, be careful about signing contracts during that period.

Friday, September 10 (Moon in Libra) The moon joins Saturn in Libra, bringing a kind of heaviness in terms of responsibilities. But when it comes to friends and social networking, the contacts you make now will endure and help you to build solid structures in your daily work life.

Saturday, September 11 (Moon in Libra to Scorpio 6:22 a.m.) The moon joins Venus in Scorpio, heightening your emotions about a partnership. You're after the bottom line in this relationship, but the bottom line proves to be too slippery to pin down all at once. This discovery will be gradual.

Sunday, September 12 (Moon in Scorpio) Mercury turns direct in Virgo, a relief for your creative endeavors. Now things in the creative area will begin to move forward again, so any delays you may have experienced are history. Your love life should begin to straighten out as well, especially with Venus in your seventh house.

Monday, September 13 (Moon in Scorpio to Sagittarius 9:52 a.m.) Pluto turns direct today in Capricorn—welcome news if you're in education, the travel business, or publishing. This movement should bolster the natural tendencies of your sun, helping to ground everything you do. The moon also enters Sagittarius, making it likely that you share your time and energy with others.

Tuesday, September 14 (Moon in Sagittarius) Mars enters Scorpio, joining Venus in your seventh house. This combination is a sure recipe for an intensely sexual and passionate relationship. If the relationship is a business partnership, then things should be backed by plenty of high energy and even some emotional drama. These two planets travel together until October 28.

Wednesday, September 15 (Moon in Sagittarius to Capricorn 5:30 p.m.) The moon joins Pluto in Capricorn, your ninth house. This combination adds power and drive to your emotions. It's the kind of power that can move mountains, crash through obstacles, and bring about the manifestation of what you desire. Use it wisely. It will occur at least once a month until 2024, so note the patterns of events that unfold today.

Thursday, September 16 (Moon in Capricorn) You're in a prime spot to strategize and plan and implement your agenda, whatever it may be. The longer range the plans, the better you'll do. You've got the vision, foresight, and physical stamina to see the plans through to completion.

Friday, September 17 (Moon in Capricorn) Prepare your professional stuff for Monday. You'll have to get a jump on things once the weekend is over. Until then, start planning your next trip and be sure that it fits your needs and desires—rather than just those of the people around you. The next Mercury retrograde occurs between December 10 and December 30.

Saturday, September 18 (Moon in Capricorn to Aquarius 4:35 a.m.) Even though it's Saturday, your emotional shift toward professional matters is practically inevitable. No need to obsess. Just do whatever you feel you need to do to prepare for Monday and the week ahead, and then get on with your weekend.

Sunday, September 19 (Moon in Aquarius) Your visionary qualities today are terrific. Use them to peek into your own future. What do you see yourself doing six months from now? A year from now? What are your professional and personal objectives? What do you want most in your life?

Monday, September 20 (Moon in Aquarius to Pisces 5:15 p.m.) With the moon in imaginative Pisces, you and friends gather today to brainstorm, imagine, and pretend. Sounds like theater, doesn't it? Perhaps it is a form of theater, but one in which your audience is a group of people whom you trust and who share your passions and interests.

Tuesday, September 21 (Moon in Pisces) Since Uranus is now retrograding and has returned to Pisces, expect the unexpected today. Events, both internal and external, may occur suddenly, without any warning. The excitement keeps you on your toes, but also maintains an adrenaline rush that you enjoy. A change in routine is just what the universe ordered.

Wednesday, September 22 (Moon in Pisces) Your will is as strong as your imagination and your determination. These qualities translate as a magnetism that draws other people to you. They figure you've got the answers.

Thursday, September 23 (Moon in Pisces to Aries 5:47 a.m.) Today's full moon in Aries lights up your twelfth house. This moon is at zero degrees and fifteen minutes, in a cardinal sign. That means it will stimulate all four cardinal points in your chart—the twelfth house, what is hidden; the sixth house of daily work; the third house of communication and your conscious mind; and the ninth house of your worldview. This should trigger activity in all of these areas.

Friday, September 24 (Moon in Aries) Turning inward, you're discovering you have more knowledge and insight than you thought. In fact, most if not all the answers you seek are at your fingertips. Believing in yourself may be all that it takes to turn things around.

Saturday, September 25 (Moon in Aries to Taurus 5:17 p.m.) The moon is in your sign, and you're in rare form! You may be thinking quite deeply about a relationship and would like the commitment to deepen even more. Don't push things or back off out of fear. You're in a powerful place today. Make good use of it.

Sunday, September 26 (Moon in Taurus) With both Venus and Mars opposite the moon and your natal sun sign, there could be some pressure on you to be a part of something that goes against your grain. Or maybe it simply goes against your grain today. If it doesn't feel right or boost your spirits, run in the opposite direction.

Monday, September 27 (Moon in Taurus) As September begins to wind down, you could feel a kind of urgency about achieving what you set out to do this year. You've actually done better than you thought you would in many areas of your life. Give yourself a pat on the back. You've earned it.

Tuesday, September 28 (Moon in Taurus to Gemini 3:12 a.m.) You may be going through your e-mail and client lists, looking for new contacts and business. As long as you're acting from a foundation of enthusiasm rather than fear or desperate need, you're on the right track. The idea is networking.

Wednesday, September 29 (Moon in Gemini) With Mercury now in direct motion, you're doing very well in terms of expressing how you feel. Keep up the good work, and apply it to your finances. If you think someone is taking advantage of you financially, don't hold this stuff in. It'll just eat away at you.

Thursday, September 30 (Moon in Gemini to Cancer 10:47 a.m.) A nice moon for the end of the month. You stick to what you know. Your parents could need a helping hand today, so do whatever you can to facilitate their lives. Tomorrow, it's October and a whole new chapter begins.

OCTOBER 2010

Friday, October 1 (Moon in Cancer) What makes you feel most secure? You may not find the whole answer today, but you'll be dealing with security issues. Whether it's a certain amount of money in the bank that makes you feel most secure or your family and friends, the issues that surface cause you to mull over the areas of your life that you value most.

Saturday, October 2 (Moon in Cancer to Leo 3:22 p.m.) With the moon entering your fourth house, you're in rare form today. You may be feeling some angst about a situation or relationship within your immediate family or connected to your parents. Just deal with it the best way you can, and wait until the moon enters Virgo to make any major decisions.

Sunday, October 3 (Moon in Leo) Mercury enters Libra, your sixth house, where it will remain until October 20. This should activate all kinds of discussions and activities with coworkers as well as friends. Social invitations flow in over the next few weeks. Pick and choose carefully; your time matters.

Monday, October 4 (Moon in Leo to Virgo 5:00 p.m.) Decisions you've delayed making can now be made with a clear heart and mind. If a romantic relationship is at the core of the decision, there's no time like the present to decide what you want and where things are going—or where you would like them to go. The same goes for all creative endeavors.

Tuesday, October 5 (Moon in Virgo) The moon is entering its darkest phase now, right before the new moon on Thursday. This period sometimes brings up issues that have been buried, much like planets transiting the twelfth house. Some possibilities: anything that involves details, health, romance, creativity, and children.

Wednesday, October 6 (Moon in Virgo to Libra 4:52 p.m.) The moon enters your sixth house today, preparing you for the new moon tomorrow. Your daily work routine and your daily health maintenance come under scrutiny today—either your own scrutiny or that of people around you. Perhaps your partner has been bugging you to get more exercise. Well, today is the day to do it.

Thursday, October 7 (Moon in Libra) Today's new moon in Libra should usher in new opportunities in your daily work routine. This could mean projects, responsibilities, or employees. Both Saturn and Mercury form wide but significant conjunctions to this moon, indicating that the opportunities that come to you are serious ones, and that discussions will ensue.

Friday, October 8 (Moon in Libra to Scorpio 4:52 p.m.) Venus turns retrograde in Scorpio, your opposite sign, and won't turn direct again until November 18. During this period, relationships can experience bumps and bruises and so can creative projects. Resist buying things like paintings, sculpture, or other artistic objects. There can sometimes be physical discomforts or inconveniences associated with Venus retrograde—the air conditioner in your office dies, for instance, or you buy a car and discover something wrong with it.

Saturday, October 9 (Moon in Scorpio) Passions run high today, particularly because the moon and Mars are traveling together. You're able to keep your head together, because you understand these feelings will be different tomorrow. You're in a strong position to conduct research.

Sunday, October 10 (Moon in Scorpio to Sagittarius 7:09 p.m.) Other people's resources come into play today—a mortgage company, a bank, an insurance company, or even a partner's income. If you've applied for a loan or mortgage, you may want to check on the status. Tend to the details, but seek the bigger picture.

Monday, October 11 (Moon in Sagittarius) Today you really do have the big picture. In some area of your life where you are puzzled or mystified by events, relationships, or experiences, you'll be able to grasp what's actually going on and will be able to make adjustments accordingly. By tomorrow, you'll have a firm idea about what those adjustments should be.

Tuesday, October 12 (Moon in Sagittarius) With the moon in fun-loving Sagittarius, your buoyant mood keeps your life on an even keel today. You may be searching for answers to a puzzling enigma, a personal issue, or even a spiritual question. If you don't find everything you're looking for today, don't get discouraged.

Wednesday, October 13 (Moon in Sagittarius to Capricorn 1:17 a.m.) You awaken feeling as if you can build an empire. You may not be able to build it all today, but it's possible to lay the cornerstones. You're an excellent strategist even on a bad day, but with the Capricorn moon to ground you, your skills are extraordinary.

Thursday, October 14 (Moon in Capricorn) Other cultures and people from other countries play a significant role in the day's activities. If you're self-employed, you may be expanding your business or product to overseas markets, or a person who knows these markets is helping to make it possible. The moon is conjunct to Pluto now, always a powerful combination. Use your personal power judiciously.

Friday, October 15 (Moon in Capricorn to Aquarius 11:24 a.m.) With the moon joining Neptune in your tenth house, your compassion and idealism are forces to be reckoned with. How can you integrate these two components more effectively into your career? Or is there some way these characteristics can find more expression in another facet of your life?

Saturday, October 16 (Moon in Aquarius) It's easy to apply your visionary qualities to your career today. Ideas abound for how the status quo can be changed, and you aren't afraid to start implementing those changes. You may encounter some resistance from coworkers and peers. Once you convince them of how sound your ideas are, your support multiplies.

Sunday, October 17 (Moon in Aquarius to Pisces 11:52 p.m.) This water-sign moon triggers your imagination and helps to bring about the manifestation of something you want. Friends and groups of like-minded individuals prove helpful, so don't turn down any social invitations. The individuals you meet today will prove helpful down the line.

Monday, October 18 (Moon in Pisces) Whatever you can imagine can become true. This is really the Pisces moon litany. For today, try to manifest one thing through the power of your imagination, and you will. Keep it simple. Instead of trying to manifest a million bucks in one fell swoop, manifest a penny at your feet on the sidewalk.

Tuesday, October 19 (Moon in Pisces) Now that you feel more confident about manifestation, make a list of the experiences, events, and relationships you would like to have in your life. Then get out of the way, and allow the universe to practice its magic.

Wednesday, October 20 (Moon in Pisces to Aries 12:24 p.m.) Mercury enters your seventh house. You and a business or romantic partner will be in deep discussions about the relationship or details of the business partnership between now and November 8. Mercury in Scorpio always seeks the absolute bottom line, the ultimate truth. Investigation and research are highlighted.

Thursday, October 21 (Moon in Aries) The moon enters your twelfth house. Time to clean your inner house! Clear out beliefs and thoughts that no longer serve your highest and best purpose. Become more aware of the moments when negative or limiting thoughts enters your mind. Acknowledge them; then change the thoughts to something more positive and upbeat.

Friday, October 22 (Moon in Aries to Taurus 11:31 p.m.) Today's full moon in Aries receives a beneficial angle from Neptune, so you're able to draw on your intuitive abilities to gain the most from any insights you gain today about the nature of your own unconscious. Motives—your own or those of people around you—are easily discernible. By tomorrow, when the moon enters your sign, you'll know exactly how this information can be used to your benefit.

Saturday, October 23 (Moon in Taurus) The moon is in your sign once again. Mars, Venus, and Mercury are opposite the moon and your natal sun. The positions of the planets put a lot of pressure on you to get your partnerships in order. In fact, a relationship may be so intense right now that you think of little else. If it's a personal relationship, the bottom-line question is whether it's about lust or love. If it's a business partnership, you may be questioning whether the partner is actually right for you and your business.

Sunday, October 24 (Moon in Taurus) You're at your peak today. Not too much is an obstacle when you're feeling like this. The trick is to remember the feelings of being on top when you're at a low point. Then try to lift yourself up to the way you feel today. If you can do that at will, it's a step toward mastering greater control over your own destiny.

Monday, October 25 (Moon in Taurus to Gemini 8:48 a.m.) You may be feeling as frisky, but the energy is primarily mental. There are no limits to your ability to cull information and disseminate it to wherever you feel it needs to go. If you have a blog or your own Web site, then today is the best time to update it—or even to revamp the format and look.

Tuesday, October 26 (Moon in Gemini)   Time to balance your checkbook and figure out how your budget is faring. As you take stock of your finances, you discover you're in better shape than you thought. If you're in college or the parent of a child in college, you've got the details figured out. There may be some additional expenses, but nothing huge.

Wednesday, October 27 (Moon in Gemini to Cancer 4:15 p.m.)   Your relatives, as well as neighbors and members of your community, may be involved in the day's activities. You may be tapped for some sort of neighborhood or community project, and if it interests you, you're glad to volunteer your time and energy. Just don't volunteer out of a sense of guilt.

Thursday, October 28 (Moon in Cancer)   Mars enters Sagittarius and your eighth house and remains there until December 7. This transit makes it likely that you travel overseas or have more contact than usual with people who live overseas. You may be thinking about taking college or graduate-level classes. Taxes and insurance could creep into the picture too.

Friday, October 29 (Moon in Cancer to Leo 9:39 p.m.)   Home and family are the day's highlights. You may be helping out a relative who needs emotional or physical support. Or someone at home is out in front of the public more than usual. Is your home on the market? If not, it could be soon.

Saturday, October 30 (Moon in Leo)   The foundation of your life is your focal point today. That could be family, home, career, partner, or just about anything. Take deep breaths if you're stressed, and then get off by yourself for vigorous physical activity. That's sure to burn off most of the angst you may be feeling.

Sunday, October 31 (Moon in Leo) Happy Halloween! With the moon entering your fifth house of fun and pleasure, do whatever makes you feel good. If you have kids, then get out and trick-or-treat with them tonight. Create memories for yourself and your family.

NOVEMBER 2010

Monday, November 1 (Moon in Leo to Virgo 12:51 a.m.) As the year begins to wind down, you start November by taking stock of where you have been and what you have achieved, and look forward to the future. What would you like to achieve or do or experience before 2010 ends? How can you make these things happen? A business or personal partner shows you the way.

Tuesday, November 2 (Moon in Virgo) Details lie at the crux of a matter that tags your heels. Connect the dots, and other pieces immediately fall into place. Once you've got the details nailed down, the bigger picture begins to assume clarity that you haven't had in a while. If you can hold both pictures in your mind simultaneously—the details and the bigger picture—then you'll be well ahead of the competition.

Wednesday, November 3 (Moon in Virgo to Libra 2:19 a.m.) Teamwork and cooperation are usually a component of the Libra moon. But today, there's also an artistic component—an aesthetic characteristic that translates into your approach to your daily work. You may do something as small as add a potted plant to your windowsill or something as large as repainting your office a color that suits your present state of mind.

Thursday, November 4 (Moon in Libra) Your strength lies in numbers. How many people support your ideas and goals? Have you explained your vision clearly enough for others to understand? You may have to return to basics initially, but once you get things in order, you race full speed ahead.

Friday, November 5 (Moon in Libra to Scorpio 3:16 a.m.) Intense passions could get the best of you today if you're not careful. Think about what you say before you say it, and be aware that your emotions may cloud what you think. Wait until after the new moon to make decisions.

Saturday, November 6 (Moon in Scorpio) Today's new moon in Scorpio ushers in opportunities in partnerships of all kinds. Mercury forms a wide conjunction with this moon, indicating there's a lot of discussion and perhaps some travel as well concerning these new partnerships. Neptune turns direct in Aquarius, your eleventh house, allowing you to now integrate your idealism more effectively into your career.

Sunday, November 7—Daylight Saving Time Ends (Moon in Scorpio to Sagittarius 4:28 a.m.) With both Jupiter and Uranus back in Pisces, your network of friends should be expanding by quantum leaps once again. Your vision of what you would like for yourself—your wishes and dreams—is also undergoing revisions. You may be joining a group of like-minded individuals who support your dreams.

Monday, November 8 (Moon in Sagittarius) Mercury enters Sagittarius, where it will be until November 30. This transit energizes your mind in refreshing ways. You're suddenly on fire with ideas, new kinds of wishes and dreams, and you may feel sudden, inexplicable urges to hit the road. It's important to follow your impulses during this transit. They will lead you into new areas for exploration.

Tuesday, November 9 (Moon in Sagittarius to Capricorn 9:37 a.m.) Once again, the moon joins Pluto in Capricorn. The duo won't always play out by putting you in the driver's seat. It depends on what the other planets are doing as well. But if you aren't in the power seat today, you're sure thinking a lot about what it means to be powerful. Perhaps the secret here is intense desire backed with vivid visualizations, then stepping aside so the universe can do its job and make things sharpen.

Wednesday, November 10 (Moon in Capricorn) If you think you've got the answers, then you probably do. You just have to dig deeply enough to find them. Or uncover the right information at the right time. And that information may come to you from an unexpected source—buried in some piece of foreign news, perhaps, or through someone in another country who has the expertise that you do not. Trust the process, whatever it is.

Thursday, November 11 (Moon in Capricorn to Aquarius 6:33 p.m.) The moon joins Neptune in your tenth house. Now that Neptune is moving direct, this moon has a softness and emotional detachment that it may have lacked earlier in the year. You can use this detachment to push forward with your agenda or project without having to worry about whether it's the right thing to do. You know what's right and what isn't.

Friday, November 12 (Moon in Aquarius) Today may feel like an old song—about love or idealism gone awry, about ending wars and hunger and poverty. Let your emotions galvanize you toward positive action.

Saturday, November 13 (Moon in Aquarius) Whether you work from home or from an office, your preference is definitely home. You could spot a gap in the market that enables you to create a product or service and to move your office permanently to your home.

Sunday, November 14 (Moon in Aquarius to Pisces 6:25 a.m.) The moon joins Uranus and Jupiter in Pisces, your eleventh house. This combination of planets makes it likely that you're on an intuitive roll, able to glean information in nontraditional ways. Follow your hunches, particularly as they relate to a dream or wish that you hold for yourself. Emotionally, things may get overblown, but the situation isn't as serious as it may look.

Monday, November 15 (Moon in Pisces) You and friends may travel together today. Whether it's for business or pleasure, the journey brings unexpected rewards: insights, connections, or new possibilities. You realize you're the creator of your own reality. This knowledge changes your approach to, well, just about everything. It's empowering to realize that what you experience is a result of your deepest beliefs. Change the beliefs, and your experience reflects it.

Tuesday, November 16 (Moon in Pisces to Aries 7:00 p.m.) The moon enters your twelfth house. Old memories and issues are stirred up. The roots of these issues may lie in past lives or in your early childhood. Perhaps it's time to treat yourself to a past-life regression. Once you deal with these memories and issues, something in your current life should clear up.

Wednesday, November 17 (Moon in Aries) Tomorrow two planets turn direct, and the effect for you should be quite tangible. So in terms of relationships and creative projects, delay making any big decisions until tomorrow or the day after, when the planets have stabilized in direct motion. You're cleaning your inner house today, getting ready for the moon entering your sign on November 19. You already know what means—clear up old projects and obligations. Prepare yourself for new opportunities.

Thursday, November 18 (Moon in Aries) This should be a near-perfect day. Both Venus and Jupiter turn direct. Since Venus rules your sign, you can expect pleasant improvement in love, romance, creativity, and all your partnerships. Jupiter is turning direct in Pisces, which should put you on a fast track toward the realization of your hopes and dreams.

Friday, November 19 (Moon in Aries to Taurus 6:05 a.m.) With the moon in your sign and Venus and Jupiter both moving direct again, today should be even better than yesterday! With the Thanksgiving holidays approaching, you're busy with preparations. Whether the festivities are at your place or you're leaving town, you're able to sweep your desk clean of everything that needs to be done. Your plans for the holiday weekend are set and ready to be implemented.

Saturday, November 20 (Moon in Taurus) With tomorrow's full moon in Taurus coming up, you may be feeling the effects already. Sudden, unexpected news or events could be headed your way. Both should be positive and in some way will expand and broaden your personal life. Quite often, events triggered by a full moon are felt several days on either side of the exact date.

Sunday, November 21 (Moon in Taurus to Gemini 2:46 p.m.) The full moon in Taurus happens just once a year. This one is in the final degrees of Taurus, so those of you born between May 18 and May 20 should feel it most strongly. Venus squares the degree of this moon, so there could be some tension in a romantic relationship. But it's remedied easily through honest discussion and an expression of appreciation for your partner.

Monday, November 22 (Moon in Gemini) Lots of communication ensues today—through e-mail, phone, and faxes. It may involve finances or issues like mortgages and insurance. But you have a good grasp of finances and probably know where your money is spent and how much of it is going out and coming in. Minor adjustments may have to be made in your budget.

Tuesday, November 23 (Moon in Gemini to Cancer 9:14 p.m.) There's a palpable shift in your mood tonight, when the moon enters Cancer, your third house. Now your emotions truly are preparing for Thanksgiving, with this most nurturing of moons. Test yourself. Over the course of the next two days, observe how you nurture others and vice versa. This will tell you a great deal about yourself and the people you care about.

Wednesday, November 24 (Moon in Cancer) You spend more time with relatives today. Whether these people are arriving in your town or you are arriving in theirs, a sense of jubilation and celebration is in the air. Your communication skills are heightened and heavily influenced by your intuition.

Thursday, November 25 (Moon in Cancer) Happy Thanksgiving! If nothing else, it's the perfect day to express gratitude for what you have and how you live. Be sure that gratitude extends to the people around you—family, friends, coworkers, and whoever is near and dear to you.

Friday, November 26 (Moon in Cancer to Leo 2:01 a.m.) Feel a bit out of sorts today? It could just be because it's the day after Thanksgiving. But it's also possible that you are seeking more recognition for yourself or for someone in your family and may not know how to get it. Instead of feeding your frustration, detach emotionally from the situation and don't consider it again until the moon enters Virgo on Sunday.

Saturday, November 27 (Moon in Leo) In several days, Mercury enters fellow earth sign Capricorn, and your mind will be much clearer and more directed. Any decisions that require forethought, grounding, and focused intention should be postponed until November 30, if possible. For today, stay focused on the task at hand.

Sunday, November 28 (Moon in Leo to Virgo 5:34 a.m.) Details and perfectionism come into play. You may turn a critical eye on a partner or one of your children. Or, another possibility, you may be unduly critical of yourself. Toss out the criticism. Today should be about enjoyment and having fun—something we all need to experience more frequently.

Monday, November 29 (Moon in Virgo) Love and romance certainly top your list today. It's also likely that your creative adrenaline is pumping hard and fast. If you've got a creative project stuck away in a drawer somewhere, get it out, dust it off, and start going through it. What do you need to do to it to make it viable?

Tuesday, November 30 (Moon in Virgo to Libra 8:16 a.m.) Mercury enters Capricorn, where it will remain for the rest of the year. It will be retrograde from December 10 to December 30, so if at all possible avoid traveling during that time. As you're about to enter the last month of 2010, take some time to evaluate how you have used this year. Have your time and energy been well spent?

DECEMBER 2010

Wednesday, December 1 (Moon in Libra)   The moon joins Saturn in your sixth house, increasing the likelihood that you may feel burdened today with obligations. Even if your actual obligations aren't that great, they will feel huge. Your best way to navigate the quagmire of emotions? Cooperation, teamwork, and networking. Cultivate the art of listening.

Thursday, December 2 (Moon in Libra to Scorpio 10:44 a.m.)   Your bottom line today involves a close partnership. You may be asking yourself who this person really is, why he or she seems so enigmatic, and how you can penetrate what seems to be their barrier. You'll figure it all out in due time.

Friday, December 3 (Moon in Scorpio)   With both the moon and Venus in intense, passionate Scorpio, your love life should be humming along at a pleasing pace. In fact, you and a partner may be going into business together or embarking on a joint project of some kind, so it's important that you understand each other's needs and expectations.

Saturday, December 4 (Moon in Scorpio to Sagittarius 2:00 p.m.)   In some area of your life, you're after the broader picture, and today you stumble upon clues that help you piece things together. The information could come through something you read on the Internet or hear on the radio. Information, of course, is useless unless you know what to do with it. So get busy and figure that out.

Sunday, December 5 (Moon in Sagittarius)   Today's new moon in Sagittarius should usher in opportunities in education, publishing, foreign travel, investment, and in terms of shared resources. With Saturn forming such a strong, beneficial angle to this moon, any opportunity that surfaces around this time is apt to be serious and long-lived. Uranus also turns direct today in Pisces, and will begin to move toward its conjunction with Aries. While it's still in Pisces, use its energy to gain insights into friendships and your own wishes and dreams.

Monday, December 6 (Moon in Sagittarius to Capricorn 7:17 p.m.) The moon joins Pluto in your ninth house, with both planets forming nice angles to Uranus and Jupiter. Talk about a terrific recipe for personal empowerment. In fact, it's to your advantage to keep track of your nighttime dreams now, because they may yield important information about the future.

Tuesday, December 7 (Moon in Capricorn) Mars joins Pluto and the moon in Capricorn and remains in this sign through the end of the year. The combination of these three planets is certain to propel you forward in terms of your long-term goals. You could be heading overseas now, too, or off to college or graduate school early next year. If you're a writer in search of a publisher, Mars could bring the right person into your life.

Wednesday, December 8 (Moon in Capricorn) If you're planning a trip overseas, be sure to keep in mind that Mercury will be retrograde between December 10 and December 30. Perhaps your trip should be delayed unless, of course, you don't mind sudden changes in your schedule and can go with the flow. Office parties and holiday festivities are on your social calendar now, and your challenge is deciding which ones to attend. Your schedule is jammed, so use your time wisely.

Thursday, December 9 (Moon in Capricorn to Aquarius 3:32 a.m.) Mortgages and loans are easier to obtain now, thanks to the new moon in Sagittarius several days back. You may also want to take advantage of this new moon by looking for end-of-the-year tax breaks. Don't buy just to buy, but if you've been considering a big-ticket item like a computer or some other work-related device, now is the time to purchase. Back up your files. Mercury turns retrograde tomorrow.

Friday, December 10 (Moon in Aquarius) Mercury turns retrograde today in Capricorn. You know the drill for this. But in addition to exercising the usual precautions, pay close attention to everything connected to education, publishing, and your worldview. In other words, you may be shifting and shuffling things around in these areas. Don't make any final decisions until New Year's Eve.

Saturday, December 11 (Moon in Aquarius to Pisces 2:41 p.m.) The moon joins up with Uranus and Jupiter in Pisces, always an intriguing and exciting combination. You may not know what to expect today, so just go with the flow and be open to the unexpected. If there's an area of your life where you're especially rigid, this combination is guaranteed to break the rigidity.

Sunday, December 12 (Moon in Pisces) On a search for the perfect holiday gift for a special person in your life, let your intuition guide you. If you feel prompted to enter a store that seems way off the beaten track of your usual buying habits, do so. That's where you'll find the special gift you're seeking.

Monday, December 13 (Moon in Pisces) Your imagination grasps what your left brain cannot. As long as you don't doubt the information you receive, you'll have the inside scoop on a relationship, situation, or event. You or a group to which you belong could be volunteering your time and energy for some sort of charity event. Or perhaps your group is taking up a collection for a particular worldwide cause.

Tuesday, December 14 (Moon in Pisces to Aries 3:15 a.m.) With Christmas just around the corner, you may be doing some last-minute shopping. A lot of people supposedly stress out around this time of year, but you take it all in stride, relishing the moment, enjoying the lights, decorations, compassion, and kindness that seem to permeate the air.

Wednesday, December 15 (Moon in Aries) You're preparing, once again, for the moon's entrance into your sign tomorrow. That means you may want to spend some time alone today, perhaps preparing for out-of-town guests or for your trip out of town. If you're the outdoors type, and the weather is good, you may want to burn off some energy through physical exercise. The point with this moon is to turn your eyes within and look for new ways of doing things.

Thursday, December 16 (Moon in Aries to Taurus 2:49 p.m.) This afternoon, the moon in your sign forms a terrific angle to Mars, Mercury, Uranus, Jupiter, and Pluto. With the odds so stacked in your favor, it's likely that you can do whatever you set out to do and then some. Your personal charisma and magnetism draw people to you and help you to garner the support you need.

Friday, December 17 (Moon in Taurus) Onward! That's your mantra for today. Whether you're clearing off your desk for the holidays, finishing your shopping, or preparing for guests, or all of the above, you do it well. By the end of the day, you're more than satisfied with how you have used your time and energy.

Saturday, December 18 (Moon in Taurus to Gemini 11:38 p.m.) The full moon is coming up in a few days, and you may be feeling the effects already. There could be news concerning finances, siblings, or even someone in your neighborhood or community. Social invitations are rolling in already too, and they include options for celebrating the incoming New Year.

Sunday, December 19 (Moon in Gemini) Your budget for the holidays may be strained right now. Resist using your credit cards; that will only cause a lot of angst in January, when the bills come due. Instead, focus your will and intentions on attracting the money you need.

Monday, December 20 (Moon in Gemini) You and your partner may be involved in a joint creative project that has a tight deadline. Pace yourselves. You don't have to work on this 24-7. Just be sure that when you do get together to work, your time counts, and you're able to meet the deadline you've set.

Tuesday, December 21 (Moon in Gemini to Cancer 5:22 a.m.) Today's full moon in Gemini receives a challenging angle from both Uranus and Jupiter in Pisces. Uranus, as the planet of sudden and unexpected change, may hurl some surprises your way around this date. Jupiter, which represents expansion, may make these surprises seem worse than they actually are.

Wednesday, December 22 (Moon in Cancer) The people you love are those who count right now. Nostalgia runs fast and furiously through your memories. Now you can create new memories for yourself and your loved ones.

Thursday, December 23 (Moon in Cancer to Leo 8:51 a.m.) The sun and Pluto are both in Capricorn today, making it likely that authority or people who represent authority for you are figuring into the day's events. Whether this is good or negative depends on the circumstances and your perception of these people. However, some possible areas of contention include: in-laws, foreign-born individuals, religion, and politics.

Friday, December 24 (Moon in Leo) How fitting that on Christmas Eve, the moon is in your fourth house—home, hearth, and family. Be sure to express your gratitude today to the people who are supportive of your dreams and goals and who are always there for you. And in one way or another, you're recognized by others for your talents and uniqueness.

Saturday, December 25 (Moon in Leo to Virgo 11:15 a.m.) Merry Christmas! How appropriate that the moon is in your fifth house of romance, love, enjoyment, and children. Regardless of how you celebrate or with whom, the Virgo moon is friendly with your natal sun, so you're loved and supported!

Sunday, December 26 (Moon in Virgo) What better time than today to draw up your New Year's resolutions? What would you like to experience and achieve in the New Year? How many of your resolutions for this year did you accomplish? Brainstorm with a friend. Discuss all this with family members. You'll come away with a set of resolutions that are realistic enough to achieve.

Monday, December 27 (Moon in Virgo to Libra 1:39 p.m.) There could be a certain burdened feeling about today. It may have to do with tackling crowds at the mall for your holiday returns. Or perhaps more guests are arriving now for New Year's, and you would like to retreat into your own world for a bit to recharge your batteries.

Tuesday, December 28 (Moon in Libra) Socialize, network, get out, and be seen. You and friends or family may take in a new art exhibit, an art film, or something comparable. Your own artistic sensibilities are heightened. Perhaps art or some facet of the arts should be integrated into your New Year's resolutions.

Wednesday, December 29 (Moon in Libra to Scorpio 4:50 p.m.) The moon and Venus are joined in Scorpio, your opposite sign. This combination certainly makes for a romantic day, great talks, or a candlelight dinner. Tomorrow Mercury turns direct. Perhaps you and your partner should get out of town for New Year's.

Thursday, December 30 (Moon in Scorpio) Mercury turns direct today. Your plans for New Year's should be pretty solid now and probably won't change much before tomorrow night. You could be feeling a little frantic, though, which tends to happen just as Mercury changes directions. Breathe.

Friday, December 31 (Moon in Scorpio) Another romantic day and night. If there's any tension at all between you and your partner, it's probably due to a misunderstanding left over from when Mercury was retrograde. Put it all behind you. You're on your way into the New Year—and a whole new decade!

HAPPY NEW YEAR!

SYDNEY OMARR

Born on August 5, 1926, in Philadelphia, Pennsylvania, Sydney Omarr was the only person ever given full-time duty in the U.S. Army as an astrologer. He is regarded as the most erudite astrologer of our time and the best known, through his syndicated column and his radio and television programs (he was Merv Griffin's "resident astrologer"). Omarr has been called the most "knowledgeable astrologer since Evangeline Adams." His forecasts of Nixon's downfall, the end of World War II in mid-August of 1945, the assassination of John F. Kennedy, Roosevelt's election to a fourth term and his death in office ... these and many others are on the record and quoted enough to be considered "legendary."

ABOUT THE SERIES

This is one of a series of twelve *Sydney Omarr® Day-by-Day Astrological Guides* for the signs of 2010. For questions and comments about the book, go to www.tjmacgregor.com.

○ SIGNET

COMING SOON

SYDNEY OMARR'S® ASTROLOGICAL GUIDE FOR YOU IN 2010

Brimming with tantalizing projections, this amazing single-volume guide contains advice on romantic matters, career moves, travel, even finance, trends and world events. Find year overviews and detailed month-by-month predictions for every sign. Omarr reveals everything new under the stars, including:

- Attraction and romance
- New career opportunities for success in the future
- Global shifts and world forecasts

...and much more! Don't face the future blindly—let the Zodiac be your guide.

Available wherever books are sold or at
penguin.com